Travels with Boogie

Mark Wallington was born in Swanage in Dorset in 1953. He worked for a while as a gardener in London before becoming a scriptwriter and a journalist. In 1982 he walked the South West Coastal Path and his subsequent book, *500-Mile Walkies*, became a bestseller. In 1992 Mark Wallington published his novel *The Missing Postman* and then wrote the script for the award-winning television play starring James Bolam. *The Day Job*, Mark Wallington's account of his early career as a jobbing gardener, was published by Hutchinson in 2005 and is now available in Arrow paperback. He is much sought-after as a film and television writer, working from his home in the High Peak in Derbyshire. He is married with two children.

Travels with Boogie

MARK WALLINGTON

Illustrated by Douglas Hall

arrow books

Reissued by Arrow Books in 2006

19

500 Mile Walkies © Mark Wallington 1986
Boogie up the River © Mark Wallington 1989

This edition first published by Arrow Books in 1996

Arrow Books
The Random House Group Limited
20 Vauxhall Bridge Road, London SW1V 2SA

www.randomhouse.co.uk

Addresses for companies within The Random House Group Limited
can be found at: www.randomhouse.co.uk/offices.htm

The Random House Group Limited Reg. No. 954009

A CIP catalogue record for this book
is available from the British Library

ISBN 9780099503125

Penguin Random House is committed to a sustainable future for
our business, our readers and our planet. This book is made from
Forest Stewardship Council® certified paper.

Printed and bound in Great Britain by Clays Ltd, Elcograf S.p.A.

500 Mile Walkies

For my mother and father

500 Mile Walkies

Mark Wallington

Illustrated by Douglas Hall

Acknowledgements

Many thanks are due to the following, without whose help I might still have gone on this trip but would never have returned: to Sean Neylon for the loan of his dog and a spare T-shirt; to Sue Fields for the stove and rucksack; to Pat Allen for the sleeping bag; to Steven Danos for the tent; to my grandmother for the spending money; to Mrs Donaldson for buying me the boots; and to Dick Fiddy for lending me his spoon.

Thanks also to Steve 'Backhand' Smith, to Jes Hulme and Gwen, and thanks and lots of other things to Toni.

Contents

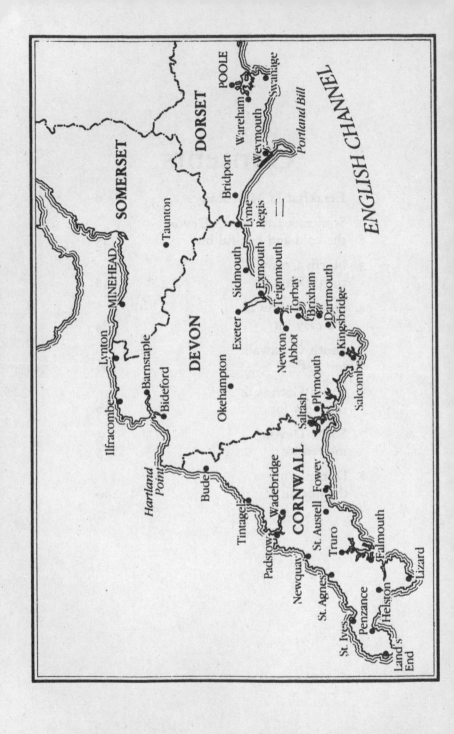

1. Breakfast in Minehead

Some towns inspire. They have an air of adventure and a sense of urgency. They are mysterious and just a little frightening. You know as soon as you walk into them they are special places.

Minehead isn't one of them. Vladivostok is, but Minehead isn't. I was in Minehead.

I was sitting in a beach shelter at the end of the promenade. According to the felt-tipped graffiti, Michael and Donna had had a good time there in June 1980; further along the bench Pete and Sarah had got it together in July 1981; then in September of the same year Gary had done something on his own halfway up the wall.

A beach shelter of experience then. Unfortunately, my business there involved nothing more promiscuous than breakfast: Weetabix and bananas, and I ate in silence,

largely because I was on my own, also because I was
contemplating my sanity and if you do that out loud the
chances are you're mad.

A milkfloat passed with a rattle and a hum. At the other
end of the promenade the machine gun nests of Butlin's
loomed out of the mist and were gone. I stared into my
bowl. In two mouthfuls' time, I intended to cross the road
in front of me and follow the footpath that led off up an
alleyway to the top of North Hill. There, I planned to
turn sharp left and continue walking, ever faithful to the
coast, until I'd trekked around the entire South-west
peninsula and come to rest on the sheltered shores of Poole
Harbour in Dorset, five hundred miles away.

Simple enough, and four months previously on a
January evening as I sat before maps and books in the
warmth of the Swiss Cottage Reference Library, it had all
seemed like an exceptionally good idea. Now, at seven
o'clock on a grey morning in early May at the bottom of
North Hill, it seemed like a stupid one.

An eye of blue peeped through the mist and closed
again. Minehead yawned, stretched, scratched, rolled over
and went back to sleep. I'd arrived there the previous
evening and had hoped the place might fire my
enthusiasm. I'd imagined it might have the feel of a border
town, the embrace of a seething port full of bars with low
ceilings and characters with eye patches and wooden legs.
But no. Minehead was a collection of red-bricked guest
houses and white soundless bungalows and Somerset
County Council signposts telling you not to do things.
Quite simply, it lacked the basic ingredients of an embarkation point – think of Vladivostok and the imagination is
immediately gripped by the intrigue of the Trans-Siberian
Railway. Minehead has a similar sort of relationship with
Butlin's.

I scraped my bowl clean, licked the spoon and packed

up. I took a deep breath, rose to my feet, swung my rucksack over my shoulders, surveyed the sheer face of North Hill, took another deep breath and then slumped back onto the bench.

Five hundred miles. I tried to translate the distance but it was impossible. It was a hundred thousand double-decker buses laid end to end. It was like walking from 20 Inglewood Road, London NW6 to the intercontinental all-night Paki deli on West End Lane and back, two thousand times. If you stood the path upright it would be a hundred times higher than Everest. It was, more to the point, fifty times further than I'd ever walked before. I decided to have another Weetabix.

Immediately, there was a black flash and there at my feet sat a strange dog-like creature auditioning for the title role in *Oliver Twist*: head cocked at an angle of forty-five degrees, one paw hanging limply, eyes big and wet as puddles, an empty plastic bowl clenched in teeth, an expression that says: 'If you don't give me half of what you're eating this very minute, I shall surely slash my wrists'.

It was Boogie, my intensely unattractive travelling companion. A moment or two earlier he'd been a black dot in the distance, zig-zagging down the promenade, his ever probing nose propelling an empty bowl of Winalot before him. Now, thanks to the bizarre audio equipment lodged inside his skull – incapable of hearing a dog whistle blown in his ear, yet sensitive to the sound of a cereal packet being opened at a range of two miles – he was at my side, subjecting me to this outrageous display of overacting.

When the pool of saliva around my feet was ankle deep I could stand it no longer. With tears in my eyes I poured him another bowl of Winalot and flooded it with milk. His head dived in with a splash and for a moment I think

I may have felt a twinge of pity for this little Cockney doggie with the rodent features. A walk to him meant once round the block and even that ran the risk of a fifty-pound fine; any greater distance he faredodged on the Underground. The only clue he'd had to the expedition ahead of him was a cry of 'Walkies!' as I'd led him out of the house the day before.

Then, slowly, his face emerged from the pasteurised depths, dripping, a look of suspicion dawning. You could see the mental recorder inside his minute brain rewind until it arrived at the last occasion he'd been treated to two breakfasts. Of course! It was the time he'd been lured to the vet. There a very nice young man had greeted him with a pat on the head, stroked him and called him a good boy and then rammed a polythene-gloved hand right up his rectum. Boogie's eyes had inflated, his ears steamed and since then he's been reluctant to accept anything other than cold tea for breakfast unless he's got his back to the wall, and I can't say I blame him.

Now he stared at the bowl, confused. He stared at me. He stared back at the bowl. He glanced over his shoulder. He picked up the bowl in his teeth and backed nonchalently away. There was a scamper of toe-nail on concrete and once more he was a black dot in the distance.

The best journeys have no motives. They are capricious affairs, made for no other reason than they exist, for no other goal than fun.

But try telling people that. They'll say, 'Yes, but why are you doing it?' They want a declaration, an objective that gives the trip a plot; something of the 'To prove Vikings could have done it in open boats', ilk.

I'd thought long and hard to try and give this walk some sort of purpose, but had found it difficult. To begin with I'd considered its geographical implications, but as a journey it just wasn't original enough. Devon had no lost tribes, Cornwall no rivers with sources undiscovered. I was going on a hike round the peninsular coastal path and I was unlikely to prove anything about the earth that couldn't already be looked up in the *Shell Guide to the West Country*. I wasn't even going to be the first person to walk the path in its entirety; my test was purely one of stamina; if I wanted to get myself in the record books I'd have to walk it backwards or blindfold.

So I turned to its personal significance: was I escaping from something? Was I turning my back on the nine-to-five monotony of the working week? Unlikely, I didn't have a job. Was I then perhaps setting out as a protest? Or was I searching for the Man Within, the Real Me, was spiritual development my goal? Nah, I couldn't convince myself, and in the end the best reason I could come up with was that I thought I might impress this girl I'd met at a party before Christmas.

Now, as motives go this may sound one of the less edifying, but at this point I think it's worthwhile looking back through history at the various voyages of discovery and making note of just how many pioneers set out not to chart the unknown and extend the limits of human endurance but to impress girls they'd met at parties. You'll find none of them did, which I think is a shame. If only one of the great adventurers could have stepped off his mountain or boat and instead of delivering some glib speech concerning Man and Destiny, have announced that he did it to impress Debbie whom he met round Doug's place a fortnight before, then the world would be a better place – we'd probably still think it was flat, but it would be better.

I was doing it to impress Jennifer, but before she appears on the scene we must have one of those neat cinematic effects where the screen mists over and the voices fade to be replaced by children's screams and funny haircuts as we are magically transported back in time. In this case to the jelly-fish fights, wasp stings and sandy Mivvis of Swanage beach in the late fifties, early sixties.

I was born and brought up in this south-east corner of Dorset and, like every local child, I treated the beach as my back garden. In every memory I have sand between my toes and in every photo I'm in shallow water trying to drown or being drowned by John Widdowson, the butcher's son.

As John and I grew older we both went to work for his father who'd sold his butcher's and opened a chicken-and-pie shop. With meat in his blood John graduated to a delicatessen, while I came over all sensitive and abandoned the populous sands of Swanage for the wild cliffs that stretched away to the west. I'd wander dreamily over them, at an age when I knew I could change the world if only I could get up earlier in the morning. But it was when I discovered that these coastal paths stretched for another five hundred miles that I realised here, maybe, was a chance to transcend sensitivity and become enigmatic. I began to compile mental pictures of every stretch. When I moved to London I put a map of the South-west on my wall and stuck pins in it. At parties, like any other heterosexual young male, I'd try and corner girls, but after a couple of drinks, instead of trying to put my hand up their jumpers, I'd wax lyrical about the rugged contours of Cornwall, the creamy headlands of Devon and the chalk stacks of Dorset. At first they'd think it was all some weird form of foreplay, then they'd get bored and walk off.

At one of these parties I met Jennifer. She had long hair, big eyes and a boyfriend called Ralph and I fell for her immediately. She treated me differently from other women: she didn't walk off when I spoke to her. At first

I thought she might be some sort of coast-path groupie,
but slowly I realised she was interested. She knew her
Great Hangman from her Little Hangman. She knew
where Bolt Head was. She'd even walked the stretch
around The Lizard. Our relationship grew. At a New
Year's Eve do she intimated she could fall in a big way
for a man who walked the whole path. Despite a mouthful
of mushroom quiche I managed to answer immediately
and with great chivalry, 'I'm going to do it this spring.'

She stood there in her neat black dress, wiping bits of
egg and pastry off her front. She was impressed I could
tell.

'I don't believe you,' she said, and then Ralph appeared
and asked her if she wanted to dance to 'I'm Turning
Japanese' by The Vapours. She said she did and I was left
to contemplate the road to Minehead.

Not that this was an unusual position for me. Each
January for years I'd told friends I was going to do the
walk that summer, but then that summer I'd always ended
up in Rimini or somewhere. This year felt different
though. A combination of forces seemed to be at work
pushing me out of London. The strongest one was my
landlady who threw me out of my flat. But then I began
to open cupboards and maps of Cornwall would fall out.
All things were suddenly portentous and in desperation I
scurried towards my usual escape hatches:

'I haven't got any money.' But it looked as though I'd
be spending the summer in a tent anyway and it was
cheaper to camp on the coast path than in the West End.

'It's the wrong time of year.' But May was just around
the corner, precisely the right time of year.

'I haven't got the equipment.' But friends lent me everything I needed with an alacrity I found disturbing.

One final effort: "I haven't got a dog. You've got to
take a dog with you on a walk like this . . .'

Boogie isn't my dog. When I said I borrowed everything for the journey I meant everything.

Boogie lives with Sean who used to live with my sister. They had a squat in South London. Walking home from the fish and chip shop one evening, Sean noticed two shiny black eyes peering from beneath a kerbed taxi cab. There, huddled against a wheel, lay the abandoned baby Boogie.

Even then he was a strange-looking creature. According to a local shopkeeper he was an only child, and yet he'd still been discarded as the runt of the litter. Sean picked him up and immediately Boogie zapped him with one of those lambent looks that would in later life earn him extra helpings of breakfast. Sean was helpless. He cradled the pitiful mite in his dufflecoat pocket next to a warm piece of rock and carried him home.

A dog's upbringing on the council estates of Stockwell and Brixton is a tough one. Boogie would get beaten up daily, usually by cats, but like everything that survives down there he soon grew streetwise and by his first birthday he was a jet black spiv strutting about the streets of London like a barrow boy.

As Sean's lifestyle improved so did Boogie's; come to think of it, so did my sister's. They crossed the river and moved to West Hampstead. They paid rent and even acquired a spare room – a dangerous move when there are people like me about. I came to stay a weekend and left a year later. It was during this time I came to understand, as well as is possible, what a freak of nature Boogie is.

To call him a mongrel is an insult to mongrels. When I first met him I wasn't even sure he was a dog. He has a thinly wrapped frame, two-feet high and arched like a hyena. Perched on top is the face of an imp and a pair of highly original ears. He looks like a cross between a fox and a Morris 1000.

In defence of his looks, Sean claims Boogie is a dog with character, which is true, a horrible one. His calamitous infancy has left him devious and insecure, a fickle animal who'll go home with anyone carrying a takeaway curry. He spends his time hanging around the bookies and watching television in shop windows. He can operate pelican crossings. He jumps on buses and goes up the West End. He has a taxi driver's Knowledge and can understand rhyming slang. He thinks the Kennel Club is a night spot. He prefers pavements to grass. He cocks his leg on lampposts rather than trees. His only experience of the countryside is the time he got run over by a Luton-bound Green-line bus. In short, Boogie and nature have nothing in common.

Yet when I needed a dog to take on this walk, he was the only candidate. The idea of letting this product of concrete and carbon monoxide loose on the natural high drama of the South-west coast was irresistible. It was introducing the beast to beauty and it immediately gave the journey a whole new dimension. .

They were traumatic times when Sean and my sister parted. Four years of possessions had somehow to be divided. Boogie was fought over like a child.

'You have him!'

'No! You have him!'

'You found him, you have him!'

'He prefers you, you have him!'

In the end Sean got custody in a deal that included the Kenwood mixer. So it was him I telephoned one evening late in April.

'I'm going to walk the South-west coastal path.'

'Sure, sure.'

'No, really, I mean it this time.'

'Are you trying to impress some woman?'

'Listen, I'm leaving next week and I want to take Boogie with me.'

A pause, then,

'You'll never guess what I thought you just said.'

'I said I want to take Boogie with me.'

A longer pause.

'Is this something to do with the Kenwood mixer?'

'No. I just want him as a . . . as a . . . as a sort of travelling companion. I'll need him for about five weeks.'

The telephone went dead, followed by a knocking on my front door.

Sean has been blessed with a face uncannily similar to Dennis the Menace, a feature he's quite proud of. Whenever he gets invited to fancy dress parties he puts on his red and black hooped jersey and manages to look more like Dennis the Menace than Dennis the Menace does. He runs around firing sausage rolls from his catapult and wins a prize every time. He's a bit of a prat really.

Subscribers to the *Beano* will need no reminding that Dennis has an evil pet dog named Gnasher. As I opened the door Sean and Boogie stood there looking as if they'd stepped right out of the strip.

Sean was on edge, unsettled by the prospect of five Boogie-free weeks. He wouldn't come in, he just stood on the doorstep fidgeting. He handed me a cheque for Boogie's spending money, told me not to worry about him going too near to cliff edges and then he hurried off, whistling. I was left with that familiar smug face looking up at me, black and mischievous, with an expression that said: I've only been here a minute and I've already done something really unpleasant.

I decided to leave the day after the Spring Bank Holiday.

I packed just the bare essentials but somehow the bare essentials weighed twenty-five pounds and seemed to consist largely of Winalot, Kennomeat and assorted canine accessories.

Not that I could begrudge Boogie his baggage allowance. His role in this venture was crucial. He was my conversation piece. At the very sight of him even the most standoffish passers-by would stop in their tracks, do a double-take and stare like those actors in B horror movies when they first see The Thing.

'What on earth is that?'

'It's a dog.'

'Never!'

'It's true, says so on his licence.'

'That's the strangest looking varmint I've ever seen. Want me to shoot it?'

'No! He comes from London, that's all.'

'Dorothy! Come here and have a look at what happens to dogs when they go to London.'

Soon you've been introduced to the whole family, then to the village, been given a cream tea, treated down the local pub, offered a bed for the night, served a fried breakfast and then it's on to the next village to repeat the whole process. Well, that was the idea anyway.

And it was then I began to realise that the distance I was hoping to cover was unimportant. The path had far more potential than an extended hike and I shouldn't regard it in terms of mph. It was, above all, a journey from place to place. I'd be passing through four different counties, and the parochialities would change with the landscape. And then, of course, there was the wildlife. The coastal paths had to be a naturalist's cornucopia. I'd forgotten everything I'd ever learnt about flowers and fields and animals and insects; here perhaps was a chance to re-educate myself.

In this respect I was in much the same sort of position as Boogie. I too had been seduced by the urban environment. Living in London for ten years had cramped my instincts. Despite a Dorset upbringing I had no understanding of how the countryside worked. I'd use this trip to sharpen my senses, harden my hands. I'd eat dandelions and berries. I'd buy some herbal tea bags. I'd take a hook and line with me and catch fish. I would, I decided, grow a moustache.

'One dog and one human being to Minehead, please,' I said to the ticket officer at Victoria Coach Station, and Boogie and I boarded the express service to Bristol. The battle for the Falklands had just begun. As we manoeuvred through the West End traffic every street corner bore the news of the ill-fated H.M.S. *Sheffield.* Then the coach accelerated up onto the M4, the city was left behind and I opened *Seven Years in Tibet* and lost myself in the adventures of the intrepid Heinrich Harrer, an Austrian mountaineer who, in 1939, whilst making preparations for an assault on the 25,000 ft Himalayan peak of Nanga Parbat, became interned in India on the outbreak of the Second World War. Undaunted, he maintained his fitness and plotted a daring escape over the Himalayas into the neutrality of Tibet. As the coach sped past Reading he was fighting off leopards in the Indian jungle. At Swindon he had his first confrontation with a grizzly. As Bristol appeared in the distance he met his first yak. I think it was at Taunton, after we'd changed buses, and Herr Harrer was climbing 10,000 ft peaks before breakfast, that I remembered I was totally unfit. I closed the book. Big deal! Surely the best way to train for a long distance walk was to do a long distance walk. Leopards and things were bridges I'd cross when I came to them.

Off the motorway and past vivid yellow fields of rape,

the coach wound along country roads to Minehead. Boogie hadn't enjoyed the trip. He's normally quite happy in vehicles as long as he can whine, jump about and make a general nuisance of himself. His real delight is to stick his nose out of the window so that the slipstream blows little globules of snot all over the other passengers. Of course this doesn't go down too well on a National coach though, and so for the first two hours he sat on the floor and whined. This was followed by two hours of lying on the seat and whining, which was followed by two hours of whining with two paws on the floor and two on the seat. Then for the final leg of the journey, he whined with his nose pressed up against the window, leaving a slippery film on the glass when we disembarked.

It was dark by that time. We walked through and out of Minehead, under a full moon and a starry crisp sky, until we reached some sort of park where I decided to make my first camp.

I'd collected my tent the previous evening and hadn't had time to familiarise myself with it. I just assumed it would be simple enough for a man of my camping experience to erect. It was only when I stood staring at the heap of what appeared to be totally unrelated bits of canvas, wood, plastic, metal and string that it occurred to me my camping experience was zero. Sure, I'd spent holidays under canvas before but I'd always been given jobs like pricking the sausages and there was usually an Akela to run to in times of crisis such as this.

Boogie sat on the grass in the moonlight, watching nonplussed as I rummaged through the components like a child with a jigsaw. Half an hour and many obscenities later I crawled into this seven-cornered affair with a door in the floor and an outrageous list to port. Boogie followed me, still baffled, so baffled in fact, his next move was to try and seduce me. Maybe he was just trying to enter into

the spirit of things – you know, camping holidays and all
that – whatever, he wasn't my idea of a holiday romance
and I banished him to the bottom of the tent where he
dutifully guarded my socks.

I slept little that night as the temperature dropped to
freezing. The friend who'd lent me the sleeping bag had
boasted of its thermal qualities. An ice age, he'd told me,
could arrive during the night and I wouldn't know about
it until I got up in the morning. What he didn't tell me
was that he'd just washed the bag and dried it in a tumble
dryer and that all its insulation now lay shrunken into a
one-inch-square patch. It was, mind you, a very warm
one-inch-square patch, but the rest of the bag was like
sleeping in a packet of crisps. I put on every article of
clothing I had; I stuffed newspaper down my trousers; I
thought about taking Boogie up on his offer; anything to
get warm and to sleep. But it was futile and as soon as
dawn broke I decided to get moving.

I crawled out of the tent feeling like death which was
a coincidence since the park turned out to be a graveyard.
I'd slept next to Mrs Enid Rutherford 1887–1951 who,
I'm pleased to say, spent a far more restful night than I
did. I quickly packed up and headed off towards the front.
Boogie, who isn't at his best in the morning anyway,
slouched behind me looking as though he could use a
cigarette.

Since then I'd sat in this, Minehead's most permissive
beach shelter, growing increasingly more despondent and
seeking solace in Weetabix and bananas. Beside me sat a
brown paper bag containing my lunch. I peeked inside; a
walnut yoghurt, some salami and a bar of Aero looked
back. With a 'the more I eat the less I have to carry' shrug
– I'm a good shrugger – I took out the yoghurt.

I forget what brand it was but God obviously eats it.
As I tore the lid off, the sun burnt a hole in the mist and

like a spotlight flooded the promenade with spring light, making clearly visible the coast of Wales across the Bristol Channel.

And then the sounds of the morning were suddenly everywhere: radios, cars and smokers coughed into life. A Post Office van stopped by the beach shelter and parped. What! A letter for me? Nope. Boogie was playing dead in the middle of the road. Stuffed with breakfast he lay there, his belly a hairy box of Winalot. I dragged him out of the way; the mail must go through.

With a bucket of sunshine over its head, Minehead picked up a little: windows sparkled, the sea became blue and the flags of Butlin's flew in all colours. The mist rose and tugged at my spirits and I clutched at a flicker of enthusiasm. Five hundred miles. It was just a number. Eating two Weetabix a day it would take about sixty bix or two and a half family packs. It didn't seem so far in those terms.

And what a journey lay ahead of me. To begin with a two-day trek over the wild hills of Exmoor. Then on along the battered coast of North Cornwall, round the granite blocks of Land's End, past the smuggling coves of the south and finally the familiar trails of Dorset. It was a walk back home. The thought so moved me I started on the salami.

I consulted the map. Porlock Weir, nine miles away, was my first port of call and a good spot to stop for lunch, which I now noticed had dwindled down to the Aero bar. No matter, the sun had inspired me. I swung the rucksack over my shoulders and set off across the road with determination renewed.

Halfway to the other side my rucksack broke. A rivet flew through the air never to be seen again, a pin dropped to the ground, a strap slipped loose and the whole thing swung from my shoulder like a sack. I retraced my steps to the shelter and with a piece of engineering wizardry, fixed it with a matchstick.

Having encountered and overcome my first obstacle, I reached the other side of the road with a sense of achievement. A quick mental calculation told me I had already travelled fifty yards and that I had only four hundred and ninety-nine miles, one thousand seven hundred and ten yards left. Things were going well, and as I started up the hill even Boogie became enlivened. He darted ahead of me, hell-bent for Land's End. I followed in marching time. After a hundred yards I took off my pullover. Halfway up I ate the Aero.

2. Somerset and North Devon: the cold and painful bit

Exmoor is a wave-like series of steep hogsbacks and valleys that rolls inexorably to the sea. There's no room even for a coastal plain; the last hill simply plummets hundreds of feet into the Bristol Channel, resurfacing again in Wales. It's like a rollercoaster with a particularly nasty water-chute.

The moor's reputation is, of course, legendary, thanks originally to R. D. Blackmore's novel of fogs and bogs and rogues, *Lorna Doone*; and more recently to local folk who, knowing when they're on to a good thing, have published the novel in a tea-towel edition and jazzed the location up with a few tax-deductable legends of their own – it's Ford Cortinas that get swallowed in the myres these days rather than the more customary lone horsemen.

This notoriety tends to lose a lot of its credibility during the season when you creep cautiously into such traditionally perilous places as the Doone Valley to discover an unfearing bunch of day trippers playing French cricket; but it's an image that should never be underestimated. Legends are invariably rooted in truth and moors such as these are prone to devastating displays of strength. The Lynmouth disaster of 1952 was a terrifying example. The three million gallons of flood water that washed away the little port that night came from the land not the sea.

This, the ominous side of Exmoor's character, was the one that greeted Boogie and me as we climbed over the stile that marked the boundary of the National Park. There, pressed up against a wall, lay a dead sheep, its eyes pecked out by birds, its belly ripped open. What animal had done the original damage I didn't like to guess, but it had the effect of a shrunken head on the edge of Indian territory, and if drums had started up in the distance I'd have turned back there and then.

Boogie, on the other hand, took it all in his stride. He sniffed at the corpse and then sidestepped it as if it was a wino lying in the street. His only problem that morning was stiles. He clearly couldn't see the point of the things; he clambered over them, legs apart, like an old woman climbing onto a bus. Otherwise, though, he seemed perfectly happy, gambolling across the moorland, intoxicated on the fresh sea air, and chasing a blue plastic bag caught on the wind – rabbits criss-crossed the hillsides, pheasants rose out of the scrub like helicopters, but Boogie was chasing the plastic bag. This attempt to turn him into a proper dog was going to be harder than I first imagined.

A few steps behind him, however, my rehabilitation programme was progressing no better. I spent most of that first morning flicking frantically through my wildlife book trying to identify birds that wouldn't stay still or else were too boring to deserve a mention. The only real excitement came when I'd climbed to the top of Selworthy Beacon and looked out over a breathtaking panorama of moorland and water to see a giant wingspan taxi down the hill towards the sea and take off. It had great white wings with red markings; it also had a crash helmet and an undercarriage and I didn't need to consult my book to realise I'd spotted not so much a bird as a hang-glider. This was a disappointment at first, but I consoled myself in the knowledge that there are only about four thousand members of the British Hang-Gliding Association, which made one as rare to see, apparently, as an arctic tern.

Other embarrassing mistakes followed – the shrill chink which had followed me all morning and belonged, I was convinced, to a kittiwake, turned out to be the sound of the dog lead slapping against my water bottle. And after a while I decided all this identification business was rather too much like train-spotting. I thought about compiling my own classification table – the gull with the bald head, red beak and short thin legs, I could, for example, call Brian because it reminded me of my father – but it was all unnecessary. I didn't need to know the names of flowers and birds to enjoy them.

During a fit of cultural resolve in the drawing-board stages of this trip, I'd promised myself I'd take an interest in the various literary locations en route. Thus Porlock, for all the talk of its notoriously steep hill and picturesque harbour, was of note as far as I was concerned as the home of the Person from Porlock, that unfortunate figure in literary history held responsible for the premature ending to Coleridge's 'Kubla Khan'. As the great poet sat furiously scribbling down the epic he'd only just composed in an anodyne-induced dream, the Person from Porlock arrived and detained him on some trivial business matter. By the time Coleridge was allowed to return to his pen and paper, the remaining two or three hundred lines had escaped him.

I stood on the weir thinking: so this is where the Person from Porlock came from. Then I bought some eggs and Kennomeat and pressed on, wondering how long this literary thing would last.

The path climbed steadily and then ducked under the canopy of Culbone Woods. The trees hid the sea, only the rhythm of the waves filtered through. Eventually we reached a clearing and the miniature Culbone Church. A leaflet inside claimed this was the smallest church in England and seemed as proud of its mention in the *Guinness Book of Records* as in the Domesday Book. It was a beautiful, tranquil setting, everything scaled down: the narrow valley, the stone seats, the graveyard. It conjured up elves and dwarfs; branches strained in the wind, tinder snapped underfoot; I became aware of my surroundings I failed to notice a distinct absence of Boogie. I just tiptoed on through the woods, looking for the light at the end of the tunnel until the tension was broken by a primal scream, and I spun round to see an hysterical sheep burst through the trees and motor down the path, its back legs overtaking its front. I stood to one side and let it pass. A few lengths behind came Boogie, that mint sauce look in his eyes. As he tore by I stuck out a firm stick. Before he'd hit the ground the sheep was chewing grass.

My fault, of course. I should have had Boogie on a lead in sheep country. The problem was he and his lead had never got on. As soon as you hooked him to it, one of two things happened: a) you dislocated your arm, or b) he asphyxiated himself. In London this was never any problem, he just followed pavements everywhere as if he was on rails. Only when a cat pulled a face at him would he be tempted to change course and then he'd let out a scream like a police siren and give chase. He rarely caught one though, and on the few occasions he did he hadn't a clue what to do next. The cornered cat would turn and hiss madly and Boogie would stand there looking puzzled as if he was on a correspondence course and the next lesson was still in the post. If he'd have caught the sheep he'd probably have treated it in similar fashion, given it a head-butt perhaps and then walked off. But in places like Exmoor where every year some sort of rumour goes round of a monstrous beast with two heads on the prowl murdering all the livestock, farmers tend to get trigger happy. The notices on gateposts warning against dogs worrying sheep weren't joking; for what he'd just done Boogie could have been shot on sight, no trial or anything.

We'd entered Culbone Woods on a bright Somerset afternoon and emerged in a chilly Devon dusk. After the shroud of trees I suddenly found myself all alone on a bare, windswept cliff – alone? What was I talking about? I had Boogie. My faithful companion, my chum, man's best friend and all that. I looked down at the trusty little fella: a steaming pink and grey tongue hung from the corner of his mouth and trailed along the ground. Froth clung in a film around his chops and a ribbon of snot had wrapped itself around his snout. I patted him on his back and got a handful of sheep dung. The thought of spending a night in a tent with him was repulsive – but then Foreland Point lighthouse came into view, and round the headland, Lynmouth. There were boats in the harbour, houses full of electricity and car headlights sweeping through the streets. It was like coming home after a day's work.

The path met the road at the hamlet of Countisbury. Before me stood the church of St John the Baptist and the Blue Ball Inn. Both doors were open. I thought maybe I should thank the Lord for seeing me safely through this first day, and what better place to do it in than the pub.

Inside were a landlord and an exceedingly bald man, playing the fruit machine violently. He thumped it, swore at it and threatened the fruits individually. Boogie and I limped to the bar. We'd walked twenty miles, too much for the first day and we were already beginning to pay for it. I slumped on a stool. Boogie collapsed on the floor by the door, conveniently positioned to break the neck of the next person to walk in. The bald man stopped playing the fruit machine the way the piano player stops when the outlaw strides into the saloon. He wandered over to us, made some reference to Rin Tin Tin, and asked me where I'd come from.

'Minehead,' I told him, proudly.

He smirked, unimpressed, then put his pint pot down, leaned against the bar on one elbow, closed one eye and gazed at the ceiling with the other. It was local legend time.

'In 1899, on a dark and stormy night . . .' A classic opening if ever there was one, and he continued in similar style to relate the story of a two-masted brigantine caught off the coast of Porlock in atrocious seas. Fifteen people were on board and the Lynmouth lifeboat was called, but: 'the waves were crashing over the lifeboat house . . .' Here he did a passable impression of waves crashing over a lifeboat house . . . 'and they couldn't launch. So, the coxswain says to his men, he says, "Men, let's tow the lifeboat to Porlock and launch it there", and that's just what they did, towed the boat over them hills all the way to Porlock, 'bout as far as you walked today.'

He swigged from his beer and waited for a response. I couldn't think of anything to say so I said, 'Cor!' which seemed to do the trick, because he licked his lips and returned to the fruit machine. He thumped it, called it a bastard and grunted at it when a coin fell out. He called this a bastard as well and then shoved it back in.

The landlord told me I could pitch my tent in the field behind his pub, but with the clear starry sky forewarning another frosty night, I really wanted to be amongst some trees or tucked up against a wall. I found both near the churchyard, just the other side of the graveyard. It was like staying in a chain hotel.

This time I managed to create an octagonal shape to the tent and have a pole left over besides. But once again I was too cold to care; all that concerned me was eating and then collapsing. The same applied to Boogie. It had been a hard day for him and was about to get harder: I'd lost his can-opener. I looked into his weary little face which, although pitiful, had that 'dinner or else' look about it. Envisaging headlines of the 'Headless Camper Found in Bizarre Mad Dog of Exmoor Horror', style, I hurried back to the pub clutching his can of Kennomeat.

This time the landlady appeared from the back room. Behind her the sound of gunshots came from the TV.

'Hello,' I said politely, 'I'm camping and I was wondering if you could open this can for me.'

She looked at me sympathetically; 'I've got some nice chicken and mushroom pies if you'd prefer.'

I laughed and explained it was for my dog. She laughed and I knew she didn't believe me. But she opened the can and I ran back to the tent leaving a fresh trail of dog food lingering on the air.

I woke Boogie up and fed him, then put some eggs inside myself and myself inside my sleeping bag. At our respective ends of the tent we curled up as tightly as possible: Boogie stuffed his nose up his bum; I hugged my knees and tried to dream of heat.

Instead, I dreamt of a storm. The sea was washing the path away. I was marching ever onward but something was holding me back. I looked round and saw I was towing a lifeboat. The crew were threatening me, demanding to know what I'd done with their can-opener. I dropped the rope and ran, only to be obstructed by the Person From Porlock. He delayed me on some trivial business matter, before metamorphosing into a monstrous two-headed beast, grinding its teeth in my face. I woke to find Boogie trying to get into my sleeping bag, his nose next to mine, his teeth chattering uncontrollably. It was 5.30 a.m. and I knew I'd sleep no more. I felt cold and rigid; my whole body ached and the thought of abandoning what little warmth I'd managed to generate and motivating myself all over again was utterly depressing. I thought of home – anybody's home. I thought of my electric kettle and my toaster. I thought of my duvet. I thought of Jennifer. I was just about to combine the last two thoughts when Boogie farted softly but dangerously, and I dived out of the tent, the romance of the moment gone for ever.

My feet and I have always got on. I've never worn winkle pickers or painted my toe-nails and in return they've steered well clear of verrucae and have even scored one or two memorable goals from the left wing.

Now, however, they were unimpressed.

My boots were the one piece of equipment bought new for the walk, and, of course, they were the one piece that shouldn't have been. The shop assistant had managed to convince me they were special – 'revolutionary' was the word I think she used. She said they were just in from Italy, the leather had been specially treated and they didn't need to be worn in, and this was my lucky day because they just so happened to be on offer.

It was a cruel piece of salesmanship. When I reached Lynmouth on that second morning, I sat on the harbour wall and pulled off my socks then hurriedly put them back on again lest the council complain. For there, where my feet normally were, were two bulbous extremities, gnarled and ruddy, with a colourful display of blisters and now about four sizes larger than when I'd left Victoria Coach Station. What strange disease is this, I thought, which makes feet grow alarmingly overnight? From their curious discoloration I could only diagnose trench foot. I needed a chemist badly. Amongst the row of shops selling Lorna Doone memorabilia I found one.

It's truly amazing the effect cotton wool, plasters and a splash or two of witch hazel can have on sore feet: absolutely none, except to act as extra padding and make it difficult to get your revolutionary boots back on. To make matters worse, my rucksack now began to dig into my shoulders. I walked with a limp and a stoop, as I stumbled out of town Lynmouth geriatrics offered me their arms.

Following a metalled path that hugged the cliff, we reached the much photographed Valley of The Rocks, a neat piece of glacial landscape gardening, which has left a series of spectacular rocky pinnacles rising out of the valley like crumbling fortresses. On their tops herds of wild goats sit and stare at the herds of wild tourists who spend their holidays sitting and staring at the goats.

It was Saturday morning. The car parks were filling, the Kodachrome was being loaded and as Boogie passed through the picnic sites, a hundred sticky hands landed on his head, each one followed by, 'You're a funny looking chap, arncha?'. By the time we'd reached the seclusion of Woody Bay he was nursing an identity crisis not to mention a migraine.

We sat on a jetty by the beautiful cove soaking our paws in the sea and looking glum. I felt drained and began to look around for a place to pitch the tent for the night. Since it was only 10 a.m. this was all rather demoralising.

'My feet hurt right up to my head,' I said to Boogie.

'Try some of this,' he replied.

'Try some of wha . . . ?' Oh my God! One day out and already hallucinating!

'You'll find it helps,' said the same voice and I turned round to see a grey-haired lady with a striking rosy complexion. She had a knapsack on her back and in her hand she proffered a bottle of baby oil.

'I always rub it into my feet after a day's hiking,' she said.

I thanked her and massaged some of the oil into my sores. Then I offered her a piece of nougat and asked where she was walking to.

'Nowhere in particular,' she said, 'just heading west.' And she sat down and explained how she and her husband had taken walking holidays in North Devon each spring for twenty years. He had died four winters before, but she still came on these annual rambles. They were like anniversaries, although she confessed to feeling lonely occasionally, walking on her own. I suggested she should walk with a dog and she turned to Boogie who cowered, expecting the usual clout and insult. But she gave him a long, deep stroke the length of his body and in return he gave her the sheep dung treatment. She studied her hand awhile then looked at Boogie. He responded with a sickly grin and she snatched back her baby oil and said goodbye.

We continued through woods choked with bluebells and riddled with streams that crossed the path and poured over moss-covered grottoes, which sounds pretty idyllic and peaceful whereas in fact the scene was one of devastation. Fierce storms the previous winter had broken and uprooted countless trees and sent them crashing down the cliffs. They in turn had crushed lesser trees and the result was an open wound that would take years to heal. The breeze carried the buzz of chain saws as foresters cut up the debris.

The trail to Heddons Mouth was green, soft and high, adjectives which by this time accurately described the state of my feet. Having threatened industrial action all morning, my left leg finally enforced a go-slow soon after lunch. My right quickly came out in sympathy and as we reached the river gorge at Hunters Inn every other limb united to bring about a general strike.

I turned inland and decided to quit for the day. I couldn't find a graveyard so I had to pitch the tent on a rather lush site by a stream and under some trees, which, after studying my nature book for a lengthy period I was able to identify, beyond any shadow of a doubt as sycamore . . . or maple . . . Actually, they might have been plane.

But food was going to be the problem. There was a pub nearby, but its menu stopped at crisps; the only shop was a local crafts and pottery outlet and the nearest village was a mile or two inland up a hill which made me lose my appetite every time I contemplated it. There was only one thing for it, the fishing line!

I limped back to the beach, stuck a worm on my hook and spent the rest of the afternoon laid out on a rock watching my red float bob on the blue sea. The sun lowered, the rocks cast contorted shadows on the eastern cliff, my hunger grew. This is more like it, I thought. A man, his dog, a fishing line and the setting sun. The scene reminded me of menthol cigarettes.

Suddenly I felt a tug on the line. I yanked it in only to find the bait had gone along with the hook and a line of weights. Round one in the battle between me and the fish had gone unanimously to the fish. And predictably, the only seafood I tasted that night came in the form of three bags of prawn cocktail crisps, which I followed with as many bags of salt and vinegar. Boogie opted for cheese and onion.

We sat in this big empty pub; each crisp reverberated round the room, rattling the horse brasses. I read some more of *Seven Years in Tibet*. Heinrich Harrer talked about meals cooked for him by half-naked native girls. If he ever got really hungry he just slaughtered a wild animal. I was at the part where he describes how he kept warm by burning yak dung when the landlord of the pub appeared and said, 'Since you're camping, you might like to know it's going to freeze tonight.'

They were the only words I heard all evening.

Mind you, they were words of painful precision. Whatever 'it' was it certainly did freeze that night and so did everything else. I crawled out of the tent the following morning in my now familiar arthritic state to find the fly sheet as frosted as an ice lolly; Boogie had to break the ice on his water bowl to get a drink. It was all becoming too much for him. First his can-opener and now this. His nose prodded the ice with despair and I could sense capitulation. I tried to enthuse:

'C'mon, there's a good boy. Who's a good boy, eh? Who'sa good boy, eh? Eh? Who's coming for walkies, eh? Who's coming for five hundred mile walkies? Eh? Who'sa goo . . .' I stopped, feeling suddenly embarrassed. His sulk hadn't improved. He looked at me wondering why I was talking like an idiot. His expression said, 'Don't anthropomorphise me, mate!' I packed up in silence, splashed myself in the icy stream and swung my rucksack over my shoulder. Another rivet catapulted off. I replaced it with a matchstick and set off into Nature's rush hour.

This was the best time of the day to walk. As we climbed the hill up to Trentishoe Common, rabbits sprinted in all directions, foxes trotted home after the night shift, gulls circled overhead like stacked airliners and insects hovered from stamen to stamen, engines idling. It was a display that touched even Boogie's blunted instincts. As a rabbit darted across the path and disappeared into a briar patch, he let out his war cry and gave chase. At last, I thought, he's going to be blooded. There followed a commotion: screams, grunts, the odd gnaw, perhaps the sound of flesh being torn, bones broken. The undergrowth shook and Boogie emerged, thorns in his nose, brambles in his tail, a plastic bag in his mouth; yellow this time.

The morning warmed and the mist cleared to reveal the mighty bulk of the Great Hangman, a thousand feet high and the unofficial peak of the Somerset and North Devon stretch.

My feet felt rather better this morning and I strode up the gradual gradient, pleased to be enjoying myself at last. And as we neared the summit, the sun, having had a Sunday morning lie-in, made a bleary-eyed appearance from beneath an eiderdown of cloud. I began to chase my shadow and my pace quickened with a hundred yards to go to the top, then twenty, then ten, five, another step and we were there and it was absolute exhilaration. The view stretched back to Foreland Point where we'd spent the first night and on to Ilfracombe where we'd probably spend the next, and we were above it all with the whole day to do as we liked.

Doing what we liked at that particular moment involved eating and little else, and we descended over Little Hangman and into Combe Martin for breakfast.

Combe Martin's claim to fame is as the second longest village in Britain, which as claims to fame go has to be one of the most stupid and does nothing but make you wonder what the longest is.

If it is Britain's second longest village then it's probably because the combe it sits in is Britain's second narrowest. The one and only street winds inland for about two miles. We walked a hundred yards of it until I found a grocery store where I bought our supplies for the day. These I promptly dropped all over the pavement sending rivulets of milk rushing to the nearest drain. Back I went for a replacement pint, while Boogie, inspired by this accident, decided to give the second longest village in Britain a special performance of his very own milk bottle trick.

This, predictably, involves drinking the milk rather than spilling it and requires a sleight of paw taught him by Black Jack Jake the one-eyed whippet of SW9. Black Jack ran a protection racket on the Stockwell Park Estate and struck terror in every resident, man and beast. He was wanted for three separate pavement violations and rumour had it that he once caught rabies but had 'shrugged it off'. He lost his eye the night he and three of the Lambeth Labradors went to break his brother out of Battersea.

Anyway, the milk bottle trick: the paws cradle the bottle and the tongue pierces the foil top and slurps out the cream. The paws then deftly tilt the bottle and the tongue does some more slurping. Just before the bottle over-balances, the paws let go and the bottle totters back to its original position, half a pint diminished. The dog then scarpers as the lady of the house, short of something to put on her cereal, emerges in her dressing gown and discovers the crime. The first thing she'll do is look up and chances are she'll see a sparrow: 'Bleedin' birds!' she'll mutter and then shake her fist and shuffle back inside. Incredible, half a pint missing and still the birds get the blame. Birds with straws perhaps.

Away from his home patch Boogie wasn't so discreet. As I came out of the store for the second time, I saw a group of Combe Martin's finest housewives watching in silence as Boogie worked his way from bottle to bottle, doorstep to doorstep, up the street. It wasn't anger the ladies displayed so much as disbelief. I apologised profusely, placed my new pint down on the first step, ran back into the shop and bought the appropriate number of replacements from a shopkeeper who was by now convinced I was up to something but couldn't work out what, other than that it involved milk. Then I grabbed the white moustachio'd Boogie and together we bowed out of the second longest village in Britain and adjourned to the beach where we ate large quantities of bread and Winalot.

After breakfast I bought Boogie another can-opener, which cheered him up no end, but then I poured a bucket of water over his dung-infested coat which immediately depressed him again. The real activity of the morning, however, was called Finding the Path to Ilfracombe and proved to be a complete puzzle. Signposts tried to direct walkers through farmers' living rooms or else over vertiginous cliffs. At one point I stood in the middle of a field, dwarfed by crops, and lost my temper, which I'm ashamed to say I took out on a slug.

Eventually I found a road and marched through the traffic into the resort. This was the first sunny weekend of the year and the day-trippers decanted from their coaches, squinting in the unaccustomed sunlight, baring pale fore-arms and faces.

The town, however, looked as if it had been caught unprepared. Everyone was painting or cleaning. The café owners along the quay were all up ladders, swinging hammers, or else they'd dragged tables and chairs out onto the pavement and were attacking them with Vim. I bought a twin-flavoured ice cream I couldn't tell either of the flavours of, and laid myself out on a bench by the harbour.

Within minutes I was asleep. The sunshine on top of three restless nights just knocked me out. Boogie was in the same condition. He lay supine on the pavement while I sat with my head in an ice-cream cone. Someone woke me up and asked where we were walking to; I told them the awesome truth and you could still hear them guffawing as they climbed back onto their coach. Apparently we didn't look the sort.

Clearly the situation needed to be reviewed. I contemplated sleeping during the day and walking at night; then I contemplated buying a decent sleeping bag; finally, I contemplated spending the night in a bed and breakfast which, despite prods of derision from within, won the game easily. It wasn't, I managed to convince myself, so much surrender as tactical withdrawal.

But I wouldn't, I decided, withdraw into Ilfracombe. If we remained stationary for long in this place the chances were we'd be given a coat of gloss and nailed to the pavement. Instead I set off to cover the four miles to Lee Bay, along a crooked path that snaked beguilingly away into the distance over a wild cliff, with views of the Isle of Lundy for the first time on the horizon. The light that evening had a weird electric quality, accentuating the greys and greens, as six-o'clock sunbeams pierced the clouds in sharp shafts and played on the water as if in portend of some biblical drama – the parting of the Bristol Channel, perhaps.

Lee Bay turned out to be the prettiest place we'd come across: a cluster of cottages, with a village pub, a village stream, a village teashop and, down the road towards the bay, a village eyesore – an enormous blank hotel staring out to sea with all the charm of a prison.

Outside the pub sat an old man in an even older jacket. He was leaning on a stick, presumably waiting for opening time. I asked him if he knew of anywhere in the village offering accommodation. He nodded his head and said no; it was too early in the year. I was about to resign myself to another night in my sleepless bag, when he added,

'Mind you . . .' he hesitated and glanced over his shoulder, 'there's always Duff Farm.'

As he spoke the sun went behind a cloud and somewhere in the hills a dog howled.

Duff Farm lay some distance up a hill that led inland. A roughly painted piece of wood bearing the name had been stuck in the verge pointing down a track banked with bluebells. We followed it and there, in a shallow valley, sat the most delightful old farmhouse, whitewashed and with a thin trail of smoke rising from its slate roof.

I walked up to the stabled front door but before I could knock it was tugged open and there stood a giant of a woman, Her great frame filling the doorway and casting me and half the yard in shadow. My open-mouthed gaze slowly rose up her physique, taking in her bare, red arms that hung from her side like hams and her mountainous unsupported bosom that swung low from milkmaid's shoulders. Balanced on top of all this was a big round face, flushed and pretty, and she beamed as she stepped forward to greet me like a long lost son. Instantly an horrific black thing, all teeth and saliva, leapt out of the shadows behind her and landed heavily on Boogie. It was Rubens, the family pet monster and he was in a bad mood.

With jaws locked the two tumbled across the yard in mortal combat. I tried to disengage them and in the process felt one of Rubens' myriad teeth embed itself in my finger. This attack on a potential guest clearly struck

Mrs Duff as bad for business and she waded into the fray, picking up her hundredweight dog and despatching him over the garden wall in the manner of a shot-putter. There was a yelp, then a thud and finally a silence. She turned to examine my finger.

'Just a scratch,' I said.

'Scratch? Looks more like a hideous gash to me,' she diagnosed, and pushed me into the house. Boogie dusted himself down and followed.

I was never asked if I wanted to stay, just led into a big room full of books and crockery and gum boots and sat down by a smouldering log fire. Boogie was laid luxuriously in Rubens' chair and fed milk and gravy, and I had my finger bandaged, while a great steaming and dented black kettle poured forth a continuous lava-like flow of thick dark stuff called tea, and Mrs Duff put her feet up and told me her life story.

She and her family had come to Devon from the South-east a few years previously when her husband took early retirement from the post office. He'd turned his hand to farming, she to bed and breakfast. The first few years had been a struggle, then a friend told her about advertising, and with one of the least conventional strokes of marketing strategy ever conceived, she placed ads ir *The Rambler* and in *Stage*. Since then the summers at Duff Farm have been a bizarre marriage of pop groups playing guitars until the early hours in one room, and ornithologists rising at the crack of dawn in the next. Geologists would stay there on holiday and leave having learnt how to juggle. The kids would come home from school and find their rooms let to a family of trapeze artists.

I was the only guest that night, although the house wasn't empty for long as, one by one, the Duffs trooped in. Mr Duff and his youngest boy had been down to a party at the vicar's and came home laden with buns. Two more boys tumbled in, grubby and hungry from an afternoon's fishing and two teenage daughters completed the family.

The house was suddenly full of noise and the smell of cooking and Mrs Duff the matriarch emerged, struggling to restore order. Boogie was the centre of attention. He was fed biscuits and treated like a corgi; I was placed in the hands of a daughter and taken down to the local pub for the evening.

Jenny Duff was a bright eighteen-year-old with a deep love of Lee Bay and an even deeper desire to leave it. We sat in the Grampus, while a local group played and sang songs concerning the things farmers got up to at night, and Jenny talked about how difficult it was to find anything but seasonal work around Ilfracombe. Friday, when the giros were doled out, was a social event as much as anything, a weekly get-together for old school friends. We stayed until closing time and then strolled back up the hill. The night was clear, the moon framed the trees with silver, the lights of the farm glowed in the valley and, as we walked towards them, Jenny warned me about breakfast.

For breakfast at Duff Farm is a meal for champions, an Everest of food few men have ever been able to conquer. There's the story of a Welsh miner who came to stay and who fancied himself as a bit of an eater. Each morning he'd work his way through the plateful placed before him and so each morning Mrs Duff piled it higher. He conceded defeat on the last breakfast of the holiday when he found two pork chops on top of the usual blowout.

I slept wonderfully well that night in a low-beamed room at the top of the house. In the morning I had a bath and spent ten fruitless minutes searching my face for signs of a moustache; then I put on a clean shirt and went downstairs to do battle.

Mrs Duff met me in the hall. 'Hungry?' she said.
'You bet.'

'Good,' she said, 'good,' a tactical grin flashing across
her face, and then she flung open the breakfast-room door
and propelled me inside. There, confronting me, was a
table groaning under the weight of a couple of million
calories; nothing effeminate like orange juice or muesli,
just piles of protein.

I thought I did quite well really. In fact, by surrep-
titiously slipping Boogie a couple of beefburgers and sausages, I managed to make quite an impression on the fried
mound. But then, just when I thought I was on the home
stretch, Mrs Duff wheeled in her trump card: a steaming
plate of scones and jam. I surrendered unconditionally and
the remains were wrapped for my journey.

By now the Duffs were descending en masse. Both
daughters were rushing round in dressing gowns, the boys
were making sandwiches so thick they wouldn't fit into
their satchels. One squashed his in and salad cream
squirted all over his exercise books. The cats were
drinking milk out of the jugs on the table, a duck waddled
in from the kitchen, a man whom I'd never seen before
strode in in gum boots, sat down, introduced himself as
Victor and poured himself a basinful of Shreddies. Finally
Rubens charged in, bent on revenge. Boogie and I were
just in the way. I paid Mrs Duff £3.50 and kissed her
goodbye. As I left a ventriloquist phoned to book three
nights in August.

I walked slowly back to the coast. The *Michelin Guide*
would probably have awarded Duff Farm minus ten stars
but it's one of the few bed and breakfast establishments
where a chicken is liable to lay an egg on your plate, and
the only one I ever stayed in where I spent longer at
breakfast then I did in bed.

At Saunton the path disintegrated into sand. I wandered over dunes for a while but the Taw estuary was ahead and I knew sooner or later I'd have to take a lengthy diversion inland.

In a beach café a map hung on a wall. If I walked along the B3231 a few miles I'd reach the A361 which I could follow to the A39. This would take me over the Taw and eventually into Bideford. There I could cross the bridge over the Torridge and walk along the A386 to Northam and finally the B3236 back to the coast.

I strode off, but after a mile it seemed daft and I caught a bus.

We changed at Barnstaple for the connection to Westward Ho! The bus filled with school kids; Boogie lay under the seat, yelping occasionally as the pupils from Barnstaple Comprehensive took it in turns to tread on him. An eleven-year-old with more facial hair than I had, sat down next to me, but immediately vacated the seat as an elderly man stumbled past. This could have been the result of good upbringing but was more likely due to the elderly man pulling him out by his blazer collar.

The man squashed up to me; we sat with arms tightly folded.

'So, what's Dubrovnik like?' he said, giving me a flash of his senior citizens' bus pass.

I smiled, weakly, and said, 'Pardon?'

'Dubrovnik? What's it like?'

Just a looney on a bus, best ignore him.

Then I realised: he was referring to my rucksack. I'd borrowed it from a girl who'd been to Greece the previous year and the front was peppered with little holes where she'd spilt Retsina, and decorated with badges from the places she'd passed en route. They bore slogans like: Mt Olympus Youth Hostel Forever, and I Love Dubrovnik. I could have explained all this, admitting I'd never even been to Yugoslavia, nor indeed to any country beginning with the letter Y. Instead, I chose to quote a guide to the Adriatic I'd once browsed through at the dentist: 'Dubrovnik?' I said, 'Oh! it's magical.'

'I'd like to get on a bus one day,' the fellow went on, 'and instead of asking for a return to Westward Ho! ask for a return to Dubrovnik.'

This surprised me. I'd just been thinking what an exciting town Westward Ho! sounded. I mean there aren't many place names that have exclamation marks after them. It's not Rio de Janeiro, exclamation mark, or Istanbul, exclamation mark, is it? They just have plain old boring full stops. 'Westward Ho!! please,' I'd said to the conductor in a spirited voice (adding a further exclamation mark for full effect) and felt a thrill of excitement as he looked up from his *Daily Mail* crossword and tore me off a little pink ticket.

However, as we passed the Welcome To Westward Ho! sign and the bus picked its way through the guest houses to the front, I began to see my neighbour's point. Charles Kingsley, from whose novel the town took its name, visited here once and said he didn't like it. Over the years, a number of locals have probably said the same thing about his book, but that doesn't alter the fact that Westward Ho! despite its punctuation, is little more than a line of holiday accommodation.

On the promenade a lone ice-cream van stood buffeted by the fresh breeze. Inside, a man surveyed the long grey beach through binoculars, but it was far too early in the season for topless bathers. The few people on the sands were dressed in woollens and only a child or two paddled along the shore. We walked past an impressive number of litter bins and a shanty town of peeling beach huts and after Boogie had had a couple of limp fights with local dogs we followed an old railway line out of town.

Each night so far I'd managed to camp near a pub or within reach of some sort of facilities. But tonight, I'd decided, would be my first in the wild. It was eight miles from Westward Ho! to the next coastal habitation and I'd camp somewhere in between.

The path clung to the rim of the cliffs for an hour or two, then, as the light began to fade, it ducked into woods. Since the first day I'd come to enjoy these shrouded stretches – they made all the senses keener. I liked the smell of nettles and damp wood, and the rustles in the undergrowth. At one point I heard some little footsteps behind me and turned to see a trail of broken foliage and, at its end, a fox as red as the sunset.

The fox stared at me. I stared at the fox. The fox stared at Boogie. Boogie stared at the fox. I stared at Boogie. Boogie stared at me. We both stared back at the fox, but it had gone leaving a faint aroma of garlic.

I camped in a tiny clearing and made some tea and soup. Boogie began to shiver again so I gathered him a bed of ferns, but there was a warm covering of cloud that night which would keep out the frost, and I felt confident we'd sleep. Although not for a while. I lay there listening to the noises outside: the bending of the trees, the distant waves, the night birds and the general nocturnal traffic trotting past the tent.

I kept a diary as I travelled, a dog-eared document containing copious notes on the socioeconomic effect of rampant tourism on the South-west, interspersed with regular bulletins of the condition of my feet.

The weather also featured, although in that department I'd clearly reached a creative impasse as early as day five: '13 May: woken by birdsong. The sky was . . .' Here I remember unzipping the tent and checking the sky. It was a sort of blue; the trouble was it had been a sort of blue since Minehead and I was fast running out of adjectives. I'd used azure, turquoise, sapphire, electric, aquamarine, pale blue, dark blue, royal blue, bluish. There were no blues left. I studied the heavens and let my imagination rip. They were the colour of my next-door neighbour's Austin Allegro, no doubt about it.

The sky was the colour of Mr Pearson's blue Austin Allegro as we walked out of the woods and into the precipitous village of Buck's Mills. I hadn't a clue what time it was; my watch had said 3.30 for three days now and I was having to tell the time by the sun. It was easy to differentiate between day and night by this method but the bits in between were tricky.

My stomach told me it was breakfast time, although the hushed state of Buck's Mills told me my stomach was fast. In the few cottages the curtains were drawn and down on the beach the water lapped the shore in an early morning calm.

I had a guide book which gave all the relevant information about places en route, such as blow-by-blow accounts of local naval battles fought against the Danes, and what village life was like during the Carboniferous period. Apparently, after the dinosaurs left Buck's Mills, its history was dominated by the Braunds, a family of Spanish stock who probably arrived via a shipwreck and within a few generations had come to inhabit most of the village. The book said the men were all very strong and the girls very beautiful, but it didn't say what time they got up in the morning and sold milk, so I left the village sleeping. I'd take breakfast in Clovelly, I decided. I could see it along the curve of the coast, about an hour's walk away.

But it was three hours before I got there; there were two reasons for this: the first, an interruption for a lecture on the import and export of minerals in the West Country during the nineteenth century; the second, my incompetence at judging distances.

The lecture was given to me by an enthusiastic man in shorts whom I met sitting on a bench overlooking the first view of Clovelly Harbour. He was eating a chocolate biscuit and reading a book. The biscuit was a Wagon Wheel, the book, a study in industrial archeology.

'Come from Buck's Mills, have you?' he said.

I told him I had indeed.

'Fantastic lime kilns in Buck's Mills, eh! Fantastic!'

Lime kilns? Ah! Those derelict jobs on the beach; I'd wondered what they were.

I sat down and he poured me a cup of tea from his flask and began to explain how before the railway reached the West Country, essential imports such as solid fuel and limestone for fertiliser could only be brought in by sea, usually freighted over from South Wales. Each port then owned its own lime kiln or kilns and when the stone arrived it was processed on the spot and distributed to local farmers in powder form. The remains of these kilns stood all along this coast.

This little man had travelled by foot and bus all the way from St Ives and he talked excitedly of the copper and tin mining areas of North Cornwall where the coast was stained red and the cliffs were lined with old stone pumping houses that stood crumbling into the sea. He spoke in pictures and waved his Wagon Wheel about expressively, and he stressed that in the two weeks he'd been touring the West Country he'd had only one cream tea.

Like Buck's Mills, the interesting thing about Clovelly is the way it's discovered the knack of defying gravity. The village clings to the cliffside by its fingernails; cantilevers desperately support the slim buildings and from the beach one is easily convinced the whole thing is a skilfully built back-drop.

We walked down the steep, cobbled main street towards the harbour. It dripped charm and whitewash as the redecoration of North Devon continued, but it was an undeniably beautiful place and despite its obvious dependence on the visitor still managed to look lived in. It was full of cats and washing lines and smoking chimneys. In a garden a man sat chopping wood and in another a woman planted rows of brilliantly coloured flowers in miniature beds. She had a sign on her wall asking visitors to treat the village with respect.

'What sort of flowers are those?' I asked.

'Don't know,' she said, in an effortless Midlands accent, 'Poly something; I got them in Bideford.'

Boogie and I sat on the harbour wall and had breakfast. A few fishing boats bobbed on the water and, just outside the harbour, the lifeboat lay at anchor, asleep with one eye open.

A fisherman stood on the bows of his boat mending lobster pots. Boogie wandered over and smelt him.

'Mending your lobster pots?' I said and immediately considered it as my entry for the Most Obvious Statement of the Year Award 1982.

The fisherman lifted his head slowly. He had a face like a Shredded Wheat and hands that looked as though they were gloves. I waited eagerly for his reply, a piece of fisherman's wisdom: 'Always mend your lobster pots on a Tuesday when there's an east wind and an "M" in the month' or some equally indispensable gem.

He screwed up his absurdly blue eyes. 'If your dog pisses on my ropes I'll have him for shark bait.'

'Right!' I said.

I sent a postcard to Sean – although with Boogie gone

he'd probably have moved house by now – then we sat on the beach in the sun. After five days of the dry, salty wind blasting my face, my skin had quickly become tanned. Equally as quickly, however, it was now disintegrating.

My nose in particular was suffering. Everywhere I went I left bits of it behind. My original one had shed itself in a couple of days. A new model had burst through, red and throbbing, but now that too had dropped off and a third one was blooming like one of those poly somethings. I lay resting my open guide book over my face, wondering how many noses I had left.

Words look funny upside down and close up. I worked them out one by one. There were the usual bits about Clovelly's role in the Ice Age, then the word Cute dominated, closely followed by Cobbled and Charming, with Cannibal getting a number of mentions.

Cannibal?

I lifted the book. Yep, it definitely said cannibal. It seems that in days gone by, Clovelly was the home of the infamous Gregg family, a xenophobic bunch prone to kidnapping lone travellers, then robbing, murdering and eating them and not necessarily in that order. That's something they don't put in the brochures, I thought, then sat up, suddenly alive with goose flesh. The harbour was deserted. The sun had sneaked behind a bank of cloud and there was a chill in the air: cannibal weather without a doubt. I washed out our respective bowls and we set off at a pace for Hartland Point.

After the assuagement of Duff Farm, my general condition had improved considerably. My revolutionary boots were beginning to mould themselves to my feet, and, apart from stiff shoulders and the odd occasion when I'd remove a sock and take a lump of dead toe off with it, I was in reasonable shape. I was even beginning to understand my metabolism and how it responded to different fuels. Chocolate, for example, was ideal for striding up hills. A cheese sandwich was the fodder best suited for trudging across sand. A fig roll before each stile and I'd leap over it like a hurdler.

Boogie, however, was having problems. His pads were sore and since Westward Ho! he'd developed some sort of limp. The suspicious thing was that it alternated from leg to leg. I wondered if there was a strain of limp which was contagious and, if so, could I catch it? Risking infection I examined his paws, but there were no thorns, no abrasions or swellings. He was, like me, just stiff, and there was no remedy for that other than exercise.

His biggest handicap, though, was mental rather than physical. The shortage of tarmac had disorientated him and at times he clung to me like an agoraphobic. Also, the peculiar habits of the other animals he was meeting, some for the first time, had left him in a state of deep culture shock.

Sheep we'd managed to sort out. Since that first confrontation, he'd come to associate them with large helpings of pain and now he left them alone. Seagulls, however, were a different matter. Something inbred in him told him he ought to chase them. Fortunately, something else inbred in him told him, frequently just in the nick of time, that he couldn't fly.

Rabbits presented a similar problem. At the first sign of Boogie they'd raise their heads above the grass and sprint for home. Boogie's limp would suddenly disappear and he'd be all legs as he gave chase. But coastal rabbits tend to build their burrows neatly tucked under the cliff face, which is all very convenient if you're a purpose-built ball of fur, but a bit dicey if you're a charging mongrel from Brixton who has yet to grasp fully the concept of cliffs.

At the edge, the pursued rabbit would duck under and disappear and it was then I could see the panic in Boogie's eyes. His neck would stretch back, his body weight would be thrown one hundred per cent inland and four very rigid legs would embed themselves in the turf, leaving burns on the grass as they ran out of Mother Earth and momentum carried him on into thin air. He'd hang there for a moment, cartoon-style, then dash back to the land and sit, wiping his brow and panting.

It was cows, however, that posed the biggest threat: they chased him.

As we left Clovelly the path continued through more woods, then opened out and we crossed a stile into an expanse of pasture. To the right, the cliff edge; to the left, large numbers of cattle. One by one they lifted their large, unconcerned faces, then they saw Boogie and immediately this herd of placid milchers grew horns and were suddenly transformed into a charging army of beef.

Boogie surveyed the situation, then realising he was the target of the stampede, did the sensible thing and looked round for the nearest barrier to put between himself and his assailants. I fitted his requirements nicely.

Someone once said "as an ally to speed, fear has it over rage." That's bollocks! I hurtled through the grass towards the other end of the field but in seconds I could feel the cow's breath on my neck. Boogie clung to my heel, eyes closed waiting for impact; in desperation I dived for the stile and missed by about thirty yards. Turning round I could see a black, brown and white blur steaming towards me.

'I'm just an innocent bystander!' I shouted. 'It's him you want!'

I looked round for Boogie just in time to see his little black bum wriggle through the stile and to safety.

'You bastard! You little bastard!' I shouted and, like the fallen matador, turned to face certain death. It was then I thought to say, 'Shoo!'

To a cow, they stopped, utter surprise registering on their dumb faces. They looked at each other: 'Hey, you never said he was going to get tough.'

'Shoo!' I shouted again, and this time waved my arms about a bit.

'All right, all right; we're going. Look we're walking away, okay? Just lay off with the shooing.'

They backed off. I snorted, the dominant species, then picked the dung out of my hair and sprang over the stile, and that's when I trod on the pig.

Fortunately Devon pigs aren't as aggressive as Devon cows, as Boogie had discovered. He was strolling around the animal inspecting it as if it was a second-hand car; not once did it even bother to lift its nose out of the dirt.

Now, the sea grew agitated, the wind began to gust and the landscape lost all its finesse. You could feel Hartland Point long before you could see it.

On the map the promontory is a right angle, a corner where all the elements meet. In reality they collide, and the friction is frightening. The currents writhe in a vortex of grey water; the monstrous cliffs appear contorted under their own pressure and the waves hit them like trains. It's not a particularly attractive place, there's nothing subtle about it, it just looks mean.

We stood on the Point, above the lighthouse, as the cliffs groaned and Boogie's ears filled with the wind as though he might take off. And as we turned the corner and headed south you could see the coastline had changed. The round shoulders of Exmoor had gone; ahead lay jagged, weather-beaten cliffs of sandstone and shale. Even the plants were different; the woodlands had been replaced by a sparse table-top, and the vegetation was low and salt-encrusted. A squat, pink flower seemed to survive best and clumps of it grew in every crack in the rock. Otherwise only the gulls were at home here. They rose and fell on thermal elevators, harnessing the force of the wind rather than battling against it.

For the next three hours we hiked over this wild terrain, as banks of clouds mustered offshore and rode in on the Atlantic swell, and even the grass turned grey. The path was tough and steep, but the effort subconscious. I'd never seen cliffs like these before. The bedding planes were folded over each other, twisted and squashed, some were sliced clean and square as a cake, others were sharp as a broken bottle.

We climbed combe after combe, past Hartland Quay where a small hotel gazed nervously out to sea, past Speke's Mouth Mill, with its spectacular waterfall that tumbled over steps to the beach; and as the light began to fail we finally climbed the last hill in Devon and saw Cornwall stretching away into the clouds. It was just headland after headland and we were going to have to climb every one of them.

At the prospect my legs threatened unofficial stoppages again, and I decided to make camp in the next valley. But first an unforgettable scene: a fox appeared on the brow of the hill and ran inland along a ridge. Two cubs then appeared and followed at a sprint. Finally, Boogie leapt out of the bushes and ran after them for all he was worth. The foxes soon outpaced him and he slowed and started limping again, but for a moment they were all running in line along the hilltop, silhouetted in the twilight.

The stream in the valley bottom marked the county line. I stood in Devon debating whether to cross or not.

No point in tiring myself out, I thought, I could deal with Cornwall in the morning, and I pitched the tent where I was.

As I brewed up, a man in a crash helmet appeared. I looked around but could see nothing resembling a motorbike anywhere. Under his arm he carried a Hoover which on closer inspection turned out to be a metal detector. He was, he informed me, looking for sunken treasure; Spanish gold and doubloons were what he was particularly after but anything of immense value would do.

'You camping?' he asked. It was a 'Mending your lobster pots?' sort of question, or it should have been. I was after all sitting right outside my tent, but looking at the abstract shape I'd managed to coax out of it that night, I suppose I could have been there for all sorts of reasons.

I told him, yes, I was camping, and although I was dying to know why he was wearing a crash helmet, I contained myself and asked him what he thought the weather would do.

Like all West Country men when you ask them this question, his hand reached impulsively for his chin and he adopted the legs apart stance of a weather guru. He studied the sky, smelt it, felt the texture of the air in his hands, breathed it in, rolled it about in his lungs, then blew it out. He nodded, and said 'Storm brewing.'

'How can you tell that?'

'Michael Fish said so on the six o'clock news. See yer.' And he turned and walked off, giving me a fine view of the Castrol sticker on the back of his anorak.

But I wasn't that bothered about the weather. I felt good that night. Outside the tent I could hear the sea crash against the rocks and inside I snuggled down into the warmth of my narrow valley and felt, for the first time, that I could manage the five hundred miles. I could feel myself growing fit; that first morning when I woke up with no inclination whatsoever to continue seemed a very long time ago. Now I was keen and confident; the journey had really begun and tomorrow was Cornwall and a whole new stretch.

3. North Cornwall: the difficult bit

'What strength of character, what a friend!' writes John Steinbeck in *Travels With Charley* as he and the eponymous Blue French Poodle set off in search of America. He mightn't have been so eulogistic had he been travelling with Boogie. A week into our journey and already the traditional relationship between man and dog was beginning to wear thin.

Team spirit was the first problem. I'd stride purposefully ahead only to look round and see Boogie had chained himself to a bus stop. If I threw a stick for him he'd look at me in bewilderment, so much as to say: 'You threw it, you fetch it.'

The second problem was farting.

The storm that had been forecast for that last night in Devon never did materialise, at least not outside the tent.

I stuck my head out at one point to see a starry sky with the moon on the wane although still strong enough to cast shadows. At sea the lights from one or two fishing boats glimmered and the waves had lost their swell.

Inside the tent, however, conditions were atrocious, gale force in fact, as Boogie lay in the corner threatening to explode. At regular intervals his little body would lift itself up, a trump would escape from its recesses and the sweet smell of the spring night would be flattened by the pong of Kennomeat mixed with ditches. I'd plead with him to stop; I couldn't believe any animal could produce anything so horrible; but he'd just look up with a 'Wasn't me!' expression, then turn over and do it again. I lay by the tent flap, expecting a complaint from the local rabbit population.

But it's an ill wind, and it did mean that I got up early. The following morning I'd crossed the bridge and climbed the first hill in Cornwall before the sun had cleared the headlands to the east. Ahead the sculptured coast continued; after the calm of the night the waves had picked up again and the cliffs muscled together in preparation for another day's pounding.

And now the combes were taking on a pattern. We'd climb to the top of one and look ahead to the next; it wouldn't seem far; what would seem far was the bottom of the valley and unfortunately to reach the former, one had to cross the latter. The path would wind down to a thin green line of vegetation that followed a stream to the beach, often via a waterfall. We'd cross over stepping stones or a wooden bridge, then climb the next hillside to the top where we'd look ahead to the next combe; it wouldn't seem far; what would seem far was the bottom of the valley and unfortunately . . . etc. etc.

It could have grown monotonous, but the great thing about nature is, just when you're beginning to get tired of one aspect, it conjures up another equally as attractive. Take bluebells, for example: very pretty flowers and the first billion I really enjoyed looking at. Just as I was starting to get bored with them, though, they were taken off and replaced by those tough little pink flowers I mentioned earlier. They smothered every hillside on these open cliffs; I tried to tip-toe around them at first, but they were becoming as prolific as grass.

To avoid a particularly mean-looking combe we turned inland and walked a semi-circle through the hamlet of Morwenstow where the graveyard bore sad witness to the days of sail when this coast claimed untold numbers of mariners. A white figurehead marked the graves of the captain and entire crew of the good ship *Caledonia* lost in 1843. They were buried by the most notable figure in Morwenstow's history, the rather eccentric Rev. Hawker, an unconventional vicar given to walking round with a pig on a lead, or dressing up as a mermaid and sitting on the beach. But then he was shepherd to an unconventional flock of parishioners, the sort who thought nothing unchristian about guiding ships onto rocks and pillaging the wrecks.

Back on the path we found a hut made from driftwood where the reverend would sit and write poetry. I sat there and had elevenses and read with interest the Graffiti Through The Ages exhibition on display. The earliest messages were carved with knives and were just initials. Then came the invention of the nib and writers celebrated by scratching their full names and those of their loved ones. The advent of the biro clearly coincided with the sexual revolution and visitors wrote their names, the names of their loved ones and the things they got up to with their loved ones. Finally the felt-tip arrived on the scene and the age of the New Romantic. Graffitists wrote their names, the names of their loved ones, the things they got up to with their loved ones, and the football team they supported.

Past Sharpnose Point and the giant saucers of the satellite-tracking station, the coast relaxed a little and the tide pulled out to reveal vast stretches of sand. Bude was just around the corner and surfers bobbed on the water straddled across their boards. But the waves that had thumped the cliffs all morning seemed somehow tame when confronted with these wide bays and the sport was no spectacle. The surfers just sat there, letting the swell pass beneath them, patiently waiting for the big one.

Bude was flat and nondescript, a collection of guest houses around a golf course. But it was my first Cornish town and I wanted to celebrate. 'Home-made Pasties On Sale Here' said a sign in a bakery window. I bought one and went and sat on a sealock at the end of the town's canal system. In fact, this was a pretty part: a few barges were tied up along the towpath and the canalside was lined with brightly coloured cottages which were unique in Bude insomuch as they didn't have signs hanging outside telling you how many rooms with hot water they had and whether they owned a colour TV or not.

I tried to find a way into my pasty. A bull-headed bird, black with tints of blue, sidled up to me and winked. I didn't know its name but was about to find out. A woman came out of her cottage, lifted up her dustbin lid and a similar bird flew out, screaming raucously. 'Bloody jackdaws,' she said, and shuffled back inside.

Meanwhile my pasty was posing problems. I tackled it with a knife and the knife came off worse. Crumbs flew in all directions and the jackdaw was pushed aside as the local gull population took an interest. They were mostly grey birds, or a mottled brown and white, and for all their grace in flight, were rather uninteresting. Only the large ones with black backs caught the eye. They had the build of Lancaster bombers and motored through the air elbowing everything else out of the way. They normally flew in pairs and now a couple came in low at nine o'clock, over the canal. The other birds scattered in alarm as the black-backs soared, banked and settled soundlessly on an ice-cream hut.

Still my pasty denied entry. Eventually I broke it over my knee and found inside a steaming mass of yellow and white stuff vaguely reminiscent of school dinners, I took a bite and the thing bit me back. Home-made Pasties On Sale Here was obviously a cleverly worded lie that should have read: Mass-produced Pasties, That Bear No Resemblance Whatsoever To The Real Thing, On Sale Here. Still, they could only get better. I had a feeling I'd be eating a lot of these during my time in Cornwall.

We continued past the beach huts and caravans that straggled along Widemouth Bay, but soon the wild cliffs resumed; wild and steep; wild and very steep; wild, very steep and after a day of them, tedious. I wanted to reach Crackington Haven that night as I knew there was a pub there – probably a fishermen's haunt, an old smugglers' dive, with nutty beer and full of garrulous Cornish characters with tales of the sea. Every hilltop I reached I imagined I was going to see the village nestling in the valley below. But the path just plunged in familiar fashion down to another combe and then climbed up another identical hill and I walked on, realising that I was beginning to hate those bloody little pink flowers.

The North Cornish coast is positive proof that the sun sets in the west. As we climbed the last hill before Crackington Haven, it was already well on its way to the horizon, a shimmering red and yellow vessel sinking into the sea, dragging its golden sail under with it. The sky turned red, making all the local shepherds really happy, and Boogie and I caught our first sight of the Coombe Barton Hotel.

In contrast to the seafarers' tavern I'd envisaged, the pub had big windows, pool tables, fizzy beer and eight flavours of crisps. I stumbled in with a dirty face, dirty trousers, dirty boots and a dirty dog and ordered a pint of the first liquid thing I saw. The barman very kindly filled up Boogie's bowl and we drank deeply, with all eyes on us.

Through the bottom of the glass I could see two ladies in cocktail dresses. I grinned at them. It was probably a dirty grin.

'I'm looking for somewhere to pitch a tent,' I said.

They huddled together. A surfboard hung from the ceiling over their heads.

'There's a campsite in Bude,' one of them said. She came from London.

'Are you from London?' I asked.

'No,' she said, 'Shrewsbury.'

A man walked in with a shirt unbuttoned to reveal liberal quantities of Splash On. He ran his eyes along the optics behind the bar, sniffed, and then ordered a schooner of lager and a packet of smoky bacon crisps. Juggling his change he walked over to the juke box and put on 'Something Stupid' by Nancy and Frank Sinatra. Then he sat down next to the ladies under the surfboard and offered them a crisp. I got the impression he did the same thing every night.

'Do you know you do the same thing every night?' said the woman from Shrewsbury, but the man was tapping his foot and singing: 'And then I go and spoil it all by saying something stupid like I love you,' through a mouthful of beer and crisps. Only when his eyes fell on the torpid form of Boogie did he stop.

'They're looking for a place to camp,' said the woman from Shrewsbury.

'Have you tried the campsite in Bude?' said the man.

I explained I'd just walked from Bude.

'Why?' he said.

And I further explained that I was walking the South-west peninsula coastal path and that, all being well, I'd reach Poole Harbour in a month or so.

'Why?' he said again, and I was going to say, because I wanted to impress this girl I'd met at a party just before Christmas, but I thought they'd all laugh, so I said:

'For fun'.

They all agreed I didn't look the sort, and then the man bought me a drink and told me he was a watch repairer, and that he'd recently come from Shrewsbury to set up a business. He'd had a lean winter, he said, but was sure he'd do well during the summer. I couldn't understand how a business like his would fluctuate with the tourist season. Surely, I was about to say, he couldn't rely on people's watches breaking down whilst they were on holiday. But then I remembered mine had.

I left the pub and waded through a stream into a field full of daisies and cowpats, and pitched the tent in some long grass. I sat inside stirring my pea and ham soup on the stove and thinking how so many people I'd spoken to in the last week had come from the Midlands or from London, how few were native West Country folk and how everything was wrapped up, directly or indirectly, with the Season.

Thinking and cooking simultaneously was obviously not my forte. One minute the soup was in the pan, the next it was all over the tent, and flames were melting the ground sheet. I jumped up in panic; what was I going to do? Then I remembered I had a Mars bar and some cheese in my rucksack. I lunged for it and in the process knocked over my cup of tea which fortunately extinguished the burning tent. I was left awash in a sea of pea green. Boogie, bless him, cleared it up.

Car doors slammed in the pub car park, as I lay on the fringes of sleep, trying to dream about walking holidays in Holland. Instead, I dreamt I was in a field being chased by cannibals and cows. The field turned into a never-ending hill; I reached a stile but before I could leap over it, the Person From Porlock appeared and detained me on some trivial business matter. I was woken by thunder, a foul smell in the air.

At the bottom of the tent Boogie looked up, trying not to appear guilty, which is a sure sign he is.

Next morning was warm and sunny. The tent grew full of light and shadows as sunbeams pierced the cotton walls. Outside I could hear a bee hum and flit and the grass rub against the fly-sheet. There was a hint of summer in the air and I decided to have a Saturday morning lie-in. Half an hour later I realised it was Friday and got up.

I hadn't really paid much attention to Crackington Haven the previous evening. As I staggered down that final hill the pub was the only building I had eyes for. Now, however, I could see it was a scattering of houses rather than a village, the valley dominated by the four-hundred-feet-high cliffs that towered over the northern approach. Like so much of the coastal geology since Hartland Point the cliffs here looked in pain. The rock face was buckled, gritty and inhospitable. It reminded me of the pasty I'd eaten the day before.

I went in search of a pint of milk. A farmhouse seemed like a good bet. I knocked on the door and a female voice from inside called: 'Is that the TV man?'

'I just want to buy a pint of milk,' I called through the

letterbox. I could hear someone stumbling towards the door, and the sound of ornaments crashing to the floor.

'Glad you could come,' she called, 'vertical hold's been playing up all week.'

'I only want a pint of milk,' I called out again. Inside, a cat squealed as it was trodden on.

'Then last night, BBC 2 went all funny.'

'Listen, I just want a pint . . .' The door was jerked open and there stood . . . no-one!

I peered into the house. It didn't look like your typical farmer's abode. Where there had once been six little rooms there was now one big one. A giant batik hung from one wall over a stack of stereo equipment. Formica was much in evidence, and on the kitchen countertop stood a packet of Smash and a microwave. Looking down I suddenly saw the four-feet-tall lady of the house.

'It's over there in the corner,' she said, indicating a huge television. 'It can't get Ceefax either.'

After much sign language and explanation, I managed to convince her it was a pint of milk I wanted. She said she hadn't got any.

I tried a few further doors. One of them swung open freely when knocked on, although the house appeared to be empty. I called out but got no answer and decided to venture no further. When this sort of thing happens in the movies, a horribly mangled body is normally lying behind the sofa.

Milkless, I soon found myself back on the coast path. A flat cap with a man underneath it appeared. He called out as he walked: 'Rolo, Rolo.' When he saw me he stopped and asked where I was headed.

'Poole Harbour.' I announced, deciding to give him all I'd got.

He nodded, and gave the familiar response. 'Why?'

'For the girls, the glamour and the night life!' I said.

He nodded again and this time winked. 'You'll enjoy Crackington Haven then,' he said and walked on, shouting: 'Rolo, Rolo.'

A hundred yards further we met Rolo. A Scottie dog, who looked as though he was travelling at speed, although a graph plotting energy output against distance covered would have shown a dog suffering severely from the law of diminishing returns. Rolo walked as though he had too many legs.

North Cornwall boasts the highest cliff in the south of England and in keeping with their flamboyant and generally hyperbolic nature, the Cornish have christened it Highcliffe. (Apparently this name was one of a shortlist, narrowly beating Bighille, Tallsummite and Loftypeake for the title.)

I warmed up on a few foothills, then began the ascent. I was in no hurry, though. I had all day. If I'd wanted to sit down and watch a snail cross the path, I could. In fact, I would. I'd sit and rusticate for a while.

The ground was still shining with morning dew and a large snail population was abroad. A fat, black one caught my eye. It had a shell ringed like a school cap and a horny little head that swung from side to side as it hurtled across the path at an inch every ten minutes. Clearly he wouldn't last at such a pace. A leaf blocked his passage and rather than take a lengthy detour around it, he elected to have a lunch break. He'd eat his way through the obstacle. Such initiative; a fascinating little creature, the snail. We had a lot in common, in fact: we both had our homes on our backs and took really long lunch breaks.

To make Highcliffe more interesting, I decided to climb it backwards; I may even have been the first to ascend it thus, although I can recommend the method to anyone for the view alone: ahead was nothing but mud and grass, whilst behind, Lundy lay shimmering in the haze and the furrowed brows of the headlands stretched back to Bude. The sky was Wedgwood blue, the sea corrugated and, as we climbed, the sound of the waves was left behind.

Like arteries, a network of paths led up the cliff. I kept to the highest, knowing it would pay dividends in the long run. At 3.30 in the morning according to my watch, we finally reached the seven-hundred-foot summit and I stood there in the middle of a rabbit warren with the wind whistling through my shorts. I was higher even than the highest gull.

I'd decided not to carry maps with me. My guide book gave an occasional direction when needed: 'turn left past the second dandelion after the rock shaped like an anvil', and that sort of thing, but even this I tried to consult as little as possible; the path had been worn by generations of coastguards long before ramblers took over and to follow it required no great feats of orienteering; I had only to keep to the curve of the coast and sooner or later I was bound to end up at Poole Harbour.

And I liked the serendipitous quality of travelling unbriefed. There was something special about rounding a headland and having no notion of what lay beyond. Discovering the hundred-feet-high waterfall at Pentargen Beach was a total surprise; likewise, rounding Penally Hill and bumping into Boscastle.

On a coast precariously short of natural harbours, Boscastle is the first place of shelter south of Hartland Point and it must have been sighted with great relief during the days of sail. Having said that, trying to navigate a sail boat into the harbour looks like the nautical equivalent of the Canal Turn at Aintree. The currents are evil and the rocky flanks at the harbour entrance form an unforgiving chicane. If the Atlantic doesn't get you, chances are Boscastle Harbour will.

But, the entrance negotiated, a natural haven presents itself: a deep, protective gorge, and a sheltered village through which the River Valency idles. I strolled past the few fishing boats and cottages, the mandatory local craft shop and a tea garden where I succumbed to a flash of temptation and ordered a cream tea for myself and a packet of ginger nuts for Boogie.

The cream tea is a West Country invention and, if taken properly, requires liberal amounts of self-indulgence. I squashed as much cream and jam as I could lift onto a scone and manoeuvred the resultant balancing act in the general direction of my mouth. All went well until the red and white mound passed the danger area of my lap. There, I must have trembled in anticipation, an amateurish and fatal mistake. Next thing all was tottering. The scone fell onto my knees, slid down my legs and headed for the lawn. Immediately a black snout appeared, a rictus of delight opened wide and most of my cream tea disappeared into the pink and black abyss that is Boogie.

On the next table two strident ladies burst into hysterics. They were dressed in the uniform of ramblers: braces, breeches, knee-length socks and extraordinarily sensible shoes. When they saw my rucksack they extended their camaraderie in Lancashire accents.

'Nice round here, isn't it? said the one wearing blue braces.

'Lovely,' I agreed.

'Not as nice as the Pennines, of course,' said the one with red braces.

'Personally, I think it's nicer than the Pennines,' said blue braces, 'mind you, it's not a patch on Pembrokeshire.'

'Pembrokeshire!' said red braces. 'Pembrokeshire's a let-down after here. I'd rather walk the Cleveland Way than the Pembrokeshire Path.'

'Cleveland Way! Don't talk to me about the Cleveland Way,' said blue braces.

Apparently, there are nine long-distance footpaths in England and Wales and these ladies had walked all of them at some time or other – or at least, bits of them all.

'We go on walking holidays together every year,' said blue braces.

'Well, not every year,' said red braces.

One of the gulls with black backs soared overhead and cried. I asked the ladies if they knew what sort of bird it was.

'Razorbill,' said blue braces, reaching for the binoculars.

'Rubbish,' retorted red braces, 'it's a great skua.' She grabbed the glasses off blue braces, knocking a plate with a scone on it precariously close to the edge of the table. For the first time during the conversation, Boogie's ears pricked.

'Of course, it might be a kittiwake,' said red braces, adjusting the focus.

'It's a razorbill, I tell you,' said blue braces, grabbing back the glasses, 'I'd recognise it anywhere.' The plate slipped nearer the table edge. Boogie edged nearer the table. 'Actually,' reconsidered blue braces, 'it could be a fulmar.'

'Much too big for a fulmar,' said red braces, tugging at the glasses. The plate tottered. Boogie began to drool heavily. The gull disappeared.

'Think it was a razorbill after all,' concluded blue braces.

'Rot,' said red braces and put the binoculars back in their case.

They asked me where I was heading. I told them and they winced.

'I don't look the sort, do I?' I said.

They both agreed I didn't and then stood to leave. At which point the plate toppled and Boogie lunged; so did blue braces. Boogie would have got there first but blue braces stood on his tail.

'Sorry,' she said and popped the scone into her mouth.

The Camelot Pottery in Boscastle was the first, rather ominous sign that we were approaching Tintagel. However, I was looking forward to my first venture into King Arthur country. At school, ancient kings of Britain, swords in lakes, damsels in distress and the days of old when knights were bold in general, were my favourite subjects; Sir Lancelot was my hero of heroes until Gene Pitney released 'Twenty-four Hours from Tulsa.' Whenever we played football the team would be: Charlton, Greaves, Best, Charlton, Best, Charlton, Charlton, Law, Charlton and on the left wing Sir Lancelot.

'Sir Lancelot? Who does he play for!' John Widdowson would protest.

'Blackburn Rovers.'

'No he doesn't. He's a knight. Knights don't even play football.'

'Knights probably invented football for all you know!'

'You've got to call yourself after a footballer or you can't play.'

'All right, I'll be Charlton.'

And walking towards the legend over acres of springy turf it was easy to believe that this stretch of coast had changed very little in thirteen hundred years: the sixth-century rambler bound for the court of King Arthur would have hiked round the impressive contours of Bossiney Haven and seen much the same mixture of wild country and battered cliffs as I did.

From then on, however, the time traveller is in for a shock. He may be able to turn a blind eye to the caravan

sites inland from Willapark Head, but the strange arrange-
ment of bricks that is the King Arthur's Castle Hotel, and
which dominates the skyline for miles around, is harder
to ignore; and no matter how keen one is to link the ruins
of Tintagel Castle with the King Arthur myth, it all rather
crumbles when you discover the remains are those of a
stronghold built six hundred years after Arthur was
alleged to have been born there. Not that so slight an
inaccuracy is likely to deter local traders who know only
too well what an endorsement from the King of the
Britons can do for business. Signs in the style of King
Arthur's Car Park and Guinevere's Filling Station abound,
and after a while you can't help but reach the opinion that
Tintagel would be a lot nicer if King Arthur, his Round
Table and the rest of his furniture had never been associ-
ated with the place.

The trick, of course, is never to let the eyes be tempted
inland, for the coastline had managed to retain its drama
and its credibility, and the footpath follows it faithfully.
As I strode over the bridge of Barras Nose there was
The Island, a thick lump of land riddled with caves and
embattled with sheer black cliffs compressed into
grotesque shapes and surrounded by white water. A thin
bridge joined the castle to the mainland and to the ruins
of a Celtic monastery, but its isolation was untampered
with. It was all a bit awesome, and while there may be
no evidence to connect Arthur with Tintagel, if I were
King of the Britons, this is certainly the sort of place I'd
choose to live.

I followed a party of school children around the ruins,
led by a master in a shiny grey suit who did a nice line in
cynicism. He talked as he walked, releasing a blazing
invective on Malory's *Le Morte d'Arthur* and Tennyson's
'The Idylls of the King'. All this to a party of nine-year-
olds. They took notes to begin with but then, when the

master wasn't looking, they'd split into the Ancient Britons and the Pagan Hordes and have sword fights with biros.

Above it all, on Dunderhole Cliff, a pretty church stood in a field of long grass and further on the ground became grey and covered in chippings as we passed through the old slate quarries that once thrived on this coast. Some old stores or offices perched on the clifftop had been converted into a youth hostel, a lonely building staring straight out to sea; but I loved the idea of staying there: to sleep in a bunk bed and to wake to that view, to have a cooked breakfast and be given my little chore by the warden – sweep out the hallway or perhaps build an extension to the kitchen – then set off again spiritually refreshed.

I knocked on the dusty door. The chances of my being allowed in were hindered on two accounts: a) I had a dog, and if there's one thing wardens hate it's people bringing their dogs to stay. (They hate it almost as much as non-members trying to stay.) And b) I wasn't a member. In the end it didn't matter though, the place was closed.

I stood on the clifftop and did my daily quota of gazing seawards. A fog bank was gathering on the horizon and rolling inexorably landwards. But it hid nothing. Throw a lolly stick off the cliffs here and its next stop would be Massachusetts.

Behind me the whine of a small motorbike approached. I turned and saw a girl park by the hostel and try the door.

'Jesus!' she said when she discovered it was closed. She was Canadian.

She asked me if there was anywhere to stay the night around here and I told her she'd find a million or so places in Tintagel. She took her helmet off and let the breeze lift her thick brown hair. She looked like the girl in the Pretty Polly tights advertisement and I tried to think of something witty, charming and imaginative to say, so she'd think: he's witty, charming and imaginative and then she'd whisk me off on her pillion, we'd eat at King Arthur's Restaurant and stay at The Holy Grail Guest House and then arrange to meet up at various intervals along the path. In fact, maybe I'd forget about the path.

'That's a nice motorbike, what sort – ' Before I could finish, she'd kicked it back into life.

'Think I'll head on down to Penzance,' she said, tucking her hair back into her helmet.

'It's a long way,' I said, having no idea where it was.

But she said she'd be there by dark and she climbed on her saddle and revved the machine to fever-pitch. As she turned to say goodbye she gave me a long deep look.

'Do you know your nose is falling off?' she said.

'Yes,' I said. 'Thanks.'

Then she was gone leaving a trail of dust behind her. At that point the mist rolled in. It was 6 p.m. and I suddenly felt lonely. I swung my rucksack over my shoulder. A rivet popped out and flew into the Atlantic. I replaced it with a matchstick and walked off. It would probably be another week before I reached Penzance.

We passed more redundant slate quarries. In some, giant pillars of stone had been left standing; they loomed out of the mist like memorials, the first reminders I'd come across of how Cornwall used to carve a living for itself.

Just past Trebarwith Strand I pitched the tent on a rather precarious plateau tucked tightly into the cliffside. As quickly as the mist had descended it dissipated and we sat on the grass, eating. A swallow or two swooped hysterically, something purple and attractive grew out of the slate by my feet, a single island of rock stood far out at sea, annoying the waves. I pulled my knees into my chest and watched the sun slip into the ocean once more. A beautiful moment, although totally lost on Boogie whose head was buried in Kennomeat. I wrote in my diary: 'If he reaches Land's End on that stuff, I'll start eating it.'

I have a stammer, have done since I was five. It began one Thursday after lunch:

'Never mind, son,' said my father, 'just don't get any ideas about being a newscaster when you grow up.'

'Think of Patrick Campbell,' was my mother's advice, although at that age I clearly didn't know my Campbells; I mixed up Patrick with Donald. What on earth has the world water-speed record holder got to do with my speech? I'd think to myself, and even now, whenever I hit a block, my eyes close and I can see *Bluebird* somersaulting over Lake Coniston in slow motion.

Over the years I've learnt to control the impediment. Only telephones prove insurmountable, telephones and conversations with other stammerers. This results in enormous bills from British Telecom and occasions such as the one in Port Isaac, the text book Cornish fishing village I strode into on a Saturday morning.

I was in a good mood. My moustache had just entered the journey; nothing outrageous, just a shadow, in fact if I wanted to grow a beard I might have to circumnavigate Britain; but it was a milestone, and I walked around the narrow streets of the village, past the tiny cottages with street-level windows, trying to catch the reflection of my newly hirsute profile.

From one house Desmond Lynham's moustache stared back as it introduced Grandstand. Now there was a fine athletic piece of facial hair; it galloped along on his upper lip like a jockey on a three-to-one favourite, and inspired me to dedicate the afternoon to sport. I'd find a good spot and stage the second round of the battle between me and fish.

Around the harbour, men stood and talked of boats. I

found what looked like a fish factory and poked my head inside. The room was littered with random bits of dead fish and by a table a young chap in a bloody apron stood chopping up all sorts of marine creatures, whistling while he worked.

'Hello,' I said, and he jumped with fright, almost putting the cleaver through his arm. 'Wonder if you know a good place round here to go fishing?'

Immediately his face began to contort. His eyes closed, the veins on his neck bulged, his foot started to tap and his face swelled and shook, his eyes opened briefly and I noticed the pupils had gone. He was one of the finest stammerers I'd ever seen.

'Ppppp . . . pppp . . . ppportq . . . uin is a ggggood sss . . . ssspot,' he said, casually.

My brain ordered my mouth to ask for directions to Port Quin, but my eyes closed for an instant, I saw *Bluebird* rise and go into a spin, and I lost control.

'W . . . wwwwhere's that?' I asked. Eventually.

'O . . . o . . . over there,' he said and pointed to a picture of a semi-clad girl on a Wadebridge engineering firm's calendar.

'How, fffffff . . .'out of the corner of my eye I could see Boogie start to get embarrassed, 'fffff..ffar?' I asked.

'Fffffffff . . .' he said – it was a bad day for 'F's' for both of us – 'fffffour miles. Lots of fffffff . . . lots of ffffff . . . lots offffffffish there,' he said, taking several runs at it. I said thanks and left, thinking: a man in his business who stammers over the word fish is in real trouble.

We followed the narrow road to Port Quin, flattening ourselves into a hedge or against a wall as cars pushed their way past. Motor traffic was a perennial problem in these parts where the roads were designed for nothing bigger than carts. Once, as I was walking along a lane with everything as rustic as could be, the peace was shattered by a pair of double yellow lines running along the verge. A mile later I came across a village and realised that cars parked thoughtlessly could quite easily have cut the community off. In Boscastle, the dominating feature after the harbour was the Pay and Display car park, and almost every other village had some similar sort of area laid aside. In Port Isaac – probably the most confined village of them all – the council had despaired and finally designated the beach a car park. The sands were now a mixture of dunnage, foraging gulls and Volvo Estates.

Port Quin turned out to be a deserted, almost derelict village. There were a few holiday homes, but they looked empty and the rest of the buildings – the older ones – were just shells. On the beach sat a man in a straw hat, throwing sticks for his beautiful collie. I asked him what happened to the village and he gesticulated and muttered something about: 'Them fish, they go away.' Like every village on this coast Port Quin had at one time had a fishing fleet. When the shoals disappeared the villagers went to work in the local antimony mine; when that went bust they went to Canada.

I threw a stick for Boogie and I think he almost considered fetching it until it plopped in the water. The collie was leaping off cliffs fetching anything thrown for him, so I left Boogie watching in the hope he might get the idea, while I clambered over rocks to a point where I could sink my line.

If the whole village packed up and left because the fishing declined it didn't say much for my chances of success. Nevertheless, I hooked a piece of salami to my line and dropped it in the water, then sat above it with grim determination: any fish that came near me was for it.

And then I could see them, three feet below the clear, sunlit surface, five or six little fishes helping themselves to my salami. I whipped the line out, the salami had gone. I hooked another piece on and returned the line to the water. The same thing happened. This wasn't fishing, this was feeding time at the aquarium. I pulled the line out again; this time the hook had disappeared as well. Round two to the fish.

I lay there awhile as the sun heated the rocks. The reason the villagers left Port Quin wasn't that the fish had gone away, it was because they had cottoned on to the game. If I couldn't beat them, I decided, I'd join them and in a fit of vigour I pulled off my clothes and leapt into the shimmering Mediterranean-blue water.

Appearances can be deceptive. What I jumped into was certainly water. It was also shimmering and blue. Mediterranean is the bit where the imagery collapses. If there's to be mention of an ocean here. Arctic is probably the most suitable.

We passed the secretive Lundy Bay, the classic North Cornish cove: black glistening rocks, steep green cliffs and a sandy beach visible only at low tide. And here an added extra, a collapsed cave leaving a natural arch, through which the sea burst.

I could see the Camel River from near here, but Pentire Point sent the path on a diversion, insisting we reach the river via its estuary and from the best viewpoint of all. It was the view I'd been waiting to see since Minehead. It consisted purely of hills, but they were the sort of hills I'd dreamed of. They were undulating hills. How long I'd waited to use that word.

But it was here also we caught our first glimpse of Bungalow country and the spirit of the landscape suddenly changed, occupied by a force far more powerful than anything Merlin and Co. had managed to conjure up the previous afternoon.

As we reached New Polzeath we cut across the fine sands of Hayle Bay into Old Polzeath, which was newer than New Polzeath and contained little else than holiday houses with square white faces staring out to sea. These were followed by a golf course, then more bungalows and I quickly wanted to get away from this side of the estuary and cross into Padstow. But the last ferry of the evening had gone and I was stranded in Rock, sailing capital of North Cornwall according to the car stickers, also noted for its secluded sand dunes, judging by the beaming young couples disappearing into them on this warm Saturday night.

Near the shore was a pub called the Mariners, a nautical sort of watering hole with bars adorned with charts, masts, seascapes and models of boats, and frequented by tanned folk with a partiality for yellow over-trousers and rope soles. Strange then that everyone should be talking about cars.

'Taking the clutch out of my Escort tomorrow,' said a man in a Guernsey pullover.

'Yeah?' said his mate, a chap with an anchor or two decorating his jacket, 'think I'll put a new head gasket on the wife's Mini.'

Don joined them, a man in a nifty naval hat. He announced he'd just bought a Marina. Surely, he's talking about yachts, I thought, but no, his Marina was a four-door, 1300 Morris and he'd traded in his Hillman for it.

I was a bit apprehensive about the place; I didn't like to admit I hadn't driven there. But I'd just made up my mind I was going to enjoy myself that night. A few minutes previously I'd remembered it was my birthday. I was going to have a party. I threaded my way to the bar and bought a drink and two packets of peanuts. One for me, one for my guest, Boogie.

A glum-looking fellow with sawn-off wellies leaned over to me as I sat at his table.

'You walking?' he said.

'No, no!' I said, thinking quickly, 'that's my Vauxhall parked outside; going to give it a decoke tomorrow.'

He nodded. 'National Trust are bastards, aren't they?'

'Pardon?'

'National Trust. I hate them. They're bastards.'

'Why?' I said.

'Why! Why! Why, you say?!'

'Yeah. Why?'

'Cause they're bastards that's why.'

I couldn't argue with facts like that so I sat back as he delivered a lengthy diatribe concerning the policies of the National Trust: how they bought up all the coastline and wouldn't let anyone do anything with it; how the land really belonged to Cornishmen, not to some institution run by people who wanted to turn it into a museum; how they didn't realise the difficulties the locals had in making a living around here; how you had only three months to make enough money for the other out-of-season nine; how it was always the little man who suffered and how Padstow would be the perfect place to build the Cornish equivalent of Disneyland.

Anyone walking these coastal paths couldn't fail to notice the enormous amounts of land the National Trust owned. It bought great stretches before the war when development threatened, and then, in 1965, Enterprise Neptune was launched in an effort to buy up what was considered to be the remaining nine hundred miles of unspoilt coastline in Britain. The aim was to negotiate for all the land one farm deep, and in the West Country the campaign had gone very well. The National Trust now owned about a third of the Cornish and Devon coast.

Slowly though, local feeling had become embittered.

No-one liked the National Trust making the rules. The locals claimed that Cornwall was now in tune with the visitors' needs rather than their own, and that they, the natives, knew how best to manage their own land.

But that seemed a spurious argument. The further south I headed, as the farmland began to be patched with fields full of tents and caravans, it became evident that as far as the locals were concerned, tourists were a crop and the more land put aside for them the better the harvest. That Cornwall depended on tourism was already clear and, of course, tourists had to be encouraged, but there came a point when this sort of exploitation became counter-productive, when the tourists would stay away because the resorts were over commercialised; not to mention the detrimental effect it all had on the environment.

In this respect the National Trust or similar bodies were essential. The Trust at worst prettified the countryside, decorated it with nature trails and notice boards; and in some places, perhaps, even conserved when Nature was desperately trying to say: 'Forget it!' But one only had to look at some of the protected properties – the coast around Tintagel, for instance, where developers have been confined to the periphery like a pack of wolves – to realise that without the support of the National Trust great stretches of these cliffs would by now be tarmac.

'I was going to open a car park but they wouldn't let me,' said my friend. 'Shame, good money in car parks.'

We walked back to the sand dunes to find a spot to camp. But every nook seemed to be occupied by couples with their hands inside each other's clothes. The evening was alive with the sound of zippers and poppers and intermittent sighs. Only after a number of apologies did I find a patch of virgin ground.

The tide was out and the estuary was a great expanse

of sand and mud; a few gulls plodded about in it, up to their kneecaps in slime. Across the river the lights of Padstow grew in intensity and brought the water to life. Around the dunes the sand grass hissed in the light breeze. Another beautiful evening, and at least warm.

'I'm twenty-nine years old and I'm warm!' I said out loud: a small achievement but the future looked bright. I could tackle those hills over the river with consummate ease.

A couple of gropers ran past giggling. They had no shoes on and sand in their knickers. I felt shocked, then indignant and finally jealous. I put my arm round Boogie. He wasn't so bad. I patted him affectionately and he eyed me with suspicion: 'You can cut that out for a start'. I wondered if he had any idea why he was here; whether he knew what all this walking was for. I wondered if he liked me, I wondered if he hated me. I wondered if he was enjoying himself and I thought he might just be beginning to. I wondered when his birthday was. He probably didn't know. He'd probably never had a birthday. I decided he'd have one on this walk. I'd just pick a date and that would be his birthday: 25 May. On that day I'd buy him a tin of Pedigree Chum and a Twix bar, and for a treat we'd watch television in a shop window.

I crawled into the tent. A hundred yards away I could hear a house party in full swing: glasses clinking and hoots of laughter. I thought about going and knocking on the door and saying: 'Hello, you don't know me but I'm walking the coast path with my charming little dog here and I was just passing your house and I thought how nice it would be to join in your party, because you look like such pleasant, kind people and I know I look messy but I'm quite presentable underneath, and my dog, despite being ugly and covered in dung, does have qualities of his own, and anyway it's my birthday so could I come in.'

Although, it was a good job I didn't. Next morning I took the first ferry over the river to Padstow. The passenger next to me was reading a newspaper. 16 May, it said on the top; a familiar date and I realised I'd miscalculated. Today was my birthday. I decided to buy some eggs and have a cooked breakfast.

I sat on the harbour wall in front of the semi-circle of slate- and grey-stone buildings which Padstow comprised. It was probably the most attractive town we'd come across so far, a subtle mixture of church bells and newsagents on this bright, Sunday morning, and I promised myself I'd come back one day and stay in a hotel overlooking the harbour and have a lie-in and breakfast in bed.

4. North Cornwall: the easy bit

'Don't you get bored?' asked the man in the rolled-up trousers, building a sand castle.

'No,' I said, defensively, 'there's loads to do.' I was sitting on the beach with my shirt off. Boogie was playing with the man's children. 'The day before yesterday, for instance, I sat and watched a snail cross the path.'

'I couldn't go walking on my own,' he said, 'I'd get bored.'

I'd lost count of the number of people who'd made that sort of remark. Don't you get bored or don't you get lonely were the most common, followed closely by, you must be mad. A few people enquired if I shared my sleeping bag with Boogie and one chap wanted to know what I did about going to the toilet.

It was difficult to explain the pleasures of the path to

these sorts. That very morning, in fact, had been a particularly rewarding one. Unbeknown to the man in the rolled-up trousers, in the five and half miles from Padstow to Harlyn Bay, I'd composed my first number-one-best-selling-hit-song.

I sang to myself a great deal as I walked. In the ten days I'd been on the move I'd run through all of Joe Jackson's albums, most of Elvis Costello's and what I could remember of Randy Newman's. It was just as I was about to start on Billy Fury's Greatest Hits that I began to whistle a tune of my own, a catchy little number, in 4/4 time with a chorus that everyone could join in on and dance to. I'd call it The Padstow Blues, or Padstow, Padstow, One Hell Of A Town. I Left My Heart In Padstow, perhaps; or maybe, It's Five And A Half Miles From Padstow To Harlyn Bay. Now I was sunning myself and trying to think of some lyrics: 'Hey hey hey, it's true what they say, it's five and a half miles from Padstow to Harlyn Bay.' Brilliant!

'When I go on holiday,' continued the man in the rolled-up trousers, 'I like to take the car and the kids and come to Cornwall and sit on the beach building sandcastles. I've been to beaches in Kent, Yorkshire, Norfolk . . .'

I wished he'd shut up. I was beginning to know how Coleridge must have felt. If this chap wasn't careful he could become known in musical circles as the Person From Padstow.

'. . . North Wales, South Wales and Devon, and undoubtedly the best sand for building sand castles is in Cornwall.' He patted the sides of his masterpiece. It really was grand. A Norman-styled keep sloping down to detailed battlements surrounded by a moat with a lolly-stick drawbridge and it was really unpleasant of Boogie to do what he did all over it.

Our progress that day was as soothing as I'd imagined it would be. Just as the little pink flowers were about to displace green grass as the official colour and plant of Nature, a crop of bright yellow things bloomed and the cliffs were the colour of rhubarb and custard. The slopes were gentle and dry, the booming surf rolled in in the distance and the beaches were now parks of bleached sand. With the wind behind me I strode along trying to keep pace with the clouds.

The most popular attraction along this stretch was Bedruthan Steps, a series of giant rocks that squatted on the beach along the curve of the coast. My guide book, beginning to show a penchant for the morbid, noted diligently the various shipping disasters the Steps had been responsible for and the ensuing loss of life. Although today, they were nothing but playthings; the surf barely reached them, gulls sat on their tops, and on the beach a lone mother and child ran down the sands to the waterline then screamed with delight as the water chased them back. I clambered down the cliffs and took out a pencil and paper and tried to draw the scene. I'd written my first song that morning. For all I knew twenty-nine might be the year my creativity effloresced. I might be a latent artist as well as composer.

But I wasn't. I caught the rocks all right, and the mother and child didn't turn out too bad, and the sea of course was easy. It was the seagulls that rather undermined the finished product as a work of art. The bird perched on the rock in the centre of the picture looked like a parked Boeing.

At Mawgan Porth I passed a campsite. The idea of a shower was irresistible and I decided to stay. I thought: campsite, campers, there's bound to be a bit of action here, and there was, not for me though, for Boogie.

Boogie had had a good few scraps since Minehead and

managed to lose them all. Fortunately, spineless that he is, and underdeveloped that he is, he can't half run when he has to. He's rather like the Tibetan dogs Heinrich Harrer was encountering as he marched ever northwards: 'lean, swift as the wind and indescribably ugly'.

But there comes a time in every little dog's life when he has to face facts and accept that, no matter how fast he can run, he's going to get swallowed whole. Such a moment of truth came for Boogie at the gates of the campsite when he bumped into the kind of beast that makes the Hound of The Baskervilles look effeminate.

It was mostly alsatian but had some shark in it somewhere, and it stood guarding the entrance, staring at Boogie, deciding whether to eat him now or later. It must have been feeling peckish. Suddenly, it was flying through the air paws and claws outstretched. I managed to grab Boogie and drag him to one side. The Neanderthal flew by, screeched to a halt, turned and charged again. Once more I lifted Boogie as a matador would a cape, and once more the beast steamed past, slid to a stop, turned, scraped its paw in the dust and charged afresh. Olé! And Boogie was still unscathed.

By now though, I'd clearly pissed the brute off. Next charge it read my dummy and a set of jaws clamped around Boogie's buttocks. Boogie yelped, fire filled the guard dog's eyes. I kicked it as hard as I could but it didn't flinch, just looked at me with one eye that said: 'Don't get cocky son, you're next.'

At this point the campsite manager strolled out of his cabin, a napkin tucked into his shirt. Before him, a scene from Conan the Alsatian.

'Whassa matter?'

'Your dog's killing mine!'

'He's only playing. Here, Fang.'

With great reluctance Fang extracted his teeth from Boogie's rump and padded over to his master in a sulk.

'Only doing his job,' said the site manager, 'I mean, you might have been a gang of Hell's Angels bent on destruction, for all Fang knew.'

The campsite was empty; Fang had seen to that. I had a shower and saw my sixth nose come off in my towel. It had been bright red for the last couple of days. Bees were beginning to land on it and dig for pollen.

Refreshed, I thought how I should celebrate my second birthday in two days. Plaice, chips and peas and four sachets of tartar sauce in a nearby pub seemed like a good bet. I ate it off one of those painfully brittle local pottery dinner plates, the sort that makes you sound like a whole restaurant, and forces everyone else in the room to huddle in a corner as far away from you as possible, gritting their teeth.

Everyone that is, except Boogie; he sat below looking into my eyes adoringly. I wondered if this newfound obsequiousness was a result of my just having saved his life or having just given him a chip dipped generously in tartar sauce. I decided against cynicism. Maybe our relationship was changing; maybe an unbreachable bond was forming between us. Maybe I should rethink the theme of my song. I'd change the tempo a little, add a twelve-string guitar and sing of the unique trust between a man and his dog. I'd call the song: Me and You and Dog Named Boogie. Hmm. Boogie. I chewed the name over. It didn't have star quality. It was a crummy name; a wimp's name. Why couldn't Sean have called him Fang or something with a bit of charisma attached to it: Hobo, or Wolf, or Elvis.

As we neared Newquay Boogie's limp, which had been on his rear right leg since Padstow – having been on his front left since Port Isaac, after a spell on his rear left from Boscastle – finally reached his front right, decided it liked it there and moved in on a more permanent basis.

'I'm a goner, sir, best leave me here. Just holding you up.'

'Nonsense old man, wouldn't dream of it. Not cricket.'

'No, no sir. Insist. Leg done for. Putting whole expedition in jeopardy. Best go on without me.'

He lay down on the grass and I examined his tendon, but again I could find no irregularity. I said: 'Looks as though we'll have to take you off to the VET!'

Quicker than Lazarus, he jumped to his feet and trotted off.

Now, we were entering surfing country proper. Everywhere were signs advertising boards for hire and all along Watergate Bay surfers sat in the water in their black wetsuits; from the clifftop they looked like flies on a pane of glass.

As they saw a suitable swell they'd shout to each other, then paddle furiously for the shore. Behind them the wave rose and as it broke they were there, meeting the crest as cars do a motorway. Their boards bobbed and they struggled to their feet and rode the white water for an all too brief moment until the swell died beneath them or dumped them ignominiously into the cold, grey Atlantic.

It seemed a lot of energy for a brief thrill, but the average surfer is a fanatical sort, and these Cornish boys had entered the spirit of it all one hundred per cent. They all had sun-bleached hair and rusty Volkswagens and they roamed the coast with their boards strapped to their roof-racks, searching for waves. It just seemed so implausible when you heard them speak in West Country accents or imagined them with part-time jobs stacking shelves in Sainsbury's. Like all American trends that spread to England, everything but the glamour of surfing had been imported. These beaches were Surf City UK but you couldn't imagine the Beach Boys singing songs about them.

From a distance, Newquay looks the archetypal urban sprawl. Once in the middle it doesn't look any different. In common with the majority of Victorian resorts it has the railway to thank for its overnight upsurgence from horrible, smelly, boring port to holiday resort. A small fishing fleet still exists in a tucked-away harbour, but the town is better represented by the large hotels that perch on the cliffs and the rabble of guest houses that fill the town with no particular style or direction.

Newquay's saving grace, though, is its beaches, which border it on three sides with a white trim and flood every corner with pale blue water. I walked along the top of Newquay Bay, past the pleasure gardens and putting green and into the town centre. I had to find a replacement gas cylinder for my stove, a straight-forward enough errand I assumed. A simple, 'Can I have a replacement gas cylinder for my stove, please?' would, I imagined, suffice. But nothing so simple. Taking off the old cylinder, a lot of French words stared back at the assistant in the first shop I tried.

'S'funny,' he said, 'never seen one like that before.' He'd not imagined that French translation would ever have been necessary when he'd opted for a career in ironmongering.

I'd borrowed the stove from the same girl who'd lent me the rucksack. I told the assistant: 'I think it may have been bought in Greece.'

He looked up at me and I knew he wanted to tell me that's where I should go for a replacement. Instead he said: 'Yeah, see, your trouble is you've got a GT 132 here. We only stock the GT 106 and then we've only got them with an S5 attachment and you've got an S8.'

'Oh,' I said, and he turned and shouted into the stores behind him:

'Dave! Where can you pick up a GT 132 with an S8 attachment?'

'Has it got a wide-angled flange?' said a voice from behind a pile of Black and Decker spares.

'Yeah,' said the assistant.

'FP 4 or FP 5?' shouted Dave.

'FP 5,' said the assistant.

'FP 5!?' said an astonished Dave.

'Yeah. FP 5.'

'Not Greek is it?' said Dave.

'Might be.'

'Oh. Dunno then,' said Dave.

The assistant shook his head. 'Course,' he said, 'you could always put a 24B adaptor on it and fit a 150 gram cylinder, but . . . hang on a minute . . . Dave! Have we got any 24B adaptors?'

'T84s or 94s?' said Dave from behind a box of Polyfilla.

'T84,' said the assistant.

'No,' said Dave, 'try Bassets in Sea View Road.'

I did. They didn't have one either.

Finding a way out of Newquay was far harder than finding a way in. The town didn't seem to have a periphery; it just meandered in ribbons. I took a wrong turning and found myself on a housing estate walking up cul-de-sacs and crescents. I asked everyone I saw how I could get out but no-one was really sure.

Eventually, I came across the River Gannel and decided to follow its banks seawards. The river bent once and suddenly Newquay was gone, vanished, disappeared, as if it never had been. Ahead was a sandy estuary and a wide empty beach curving away to the south. The sun was shining again and the scene was coloured an iridescent

green, yellow, sea blue, and sky blue. Newquay was just
around the corner and yet here it looked tropical. Well,
all right, not tropical exactly, but very pleasant anyway.

Two red things came into view in the distance as we
climbed above the silver rocks of Porthjoke. Gradually I
could make out human forms and I realised they were
walkers carrying bright red packs on their backs, like
spacemen. They slowed as they reached me. A conversation seemed imminent.

They were both about forty, one sweaty, big and
responsible for all the talking; the other, small, not so
sweaty and responsible for all the silence. They'd walked
from St Just near Land's End and were heading north as
far as two weeks' holiday from the factory would allow
them. When they discovered I was attempting the walk
to Poole, I was immediately accepted as one of the boys
and we exchanged Long-distance Walkers' talk. They told
me to watch out for the rather attractive girl who cleared
the tables in the quayside cafeteria in St Ives, and to mind
the particularly nasty clump of stinging nettles on the path
just past Zennor. I told them to watch out for the cows
in the third field east from Hartland Point, and if they
were Hell's Angels, to avoid the campsite at Mawgan
Porth. It was riveting stuff: three walkers and a dog on
a Cornish clifftop, exchanging hair-raising tales of high
adventure. After a few minutes there was a silence (which
we all blamed on the small, not so sweaty chap) then his
big, sweaty companion said: 'Well, can't stand around
chatting all day, we've got some serious hiking to do,'
and he strode off, crushing a dozen wild flowers with each
footfall.

The fine beaches continued past Kelsey Head. Holywell
Bay and Ligger Bay were both backed by sand dunes
which hid holiday camps as well as holiday camps can be

hid. But here the sands were shifting and legend had it a
local village had been buried long ago, reputedly the
Cornish equivalent of Sodom and its obliteration an act of
God. I began to wonder why similar retribution hadn't
been exacted on the holiday camp that now stood in its
place, but then I reminded myself how I'd resolved to
suffer holiday camps. I knew I'd have a number to contend
with over the next few weeks and they were after all an
integral part of the coastal make-up. They played a rôle
just as the fish factories and lighthouses did. I liked to
imagine them in a hundred years' time as museums, the
places where twentieth-century man spent his leisure time.

Along the beach before Perranporth, Boogie's limp
became more pronounced. He walked on three legs only
now, leaving bizarre trails in the sand that would've
confused any posse. I checked his legs again. They were
all there still, but his paws had no tread left, he was
walking illegally, and now I noticed a swelling on his
right front ankle. There was nothing else for it, I'd have
to shoot him.

Perranporth is a village of little distinction, a service
point for the nearby holiday camps. But it is the home of
a very pleasant young man named Alan who knows all
there is to know about vets in the area. If I went to one
in town, he assured me, I'd have to wait around all day
for an appointment. He took his dog, he said, to a farm
vet about two miles away and he very kindly offered to
drive me there in the speed and comfort of his Triumph
Dolomite.

Boogie's experience of vets is vast. In London he was
forever having to visit them to get bits of buses removed
from his intestines. On one occasion an operation left him
with a shaved back and a six-inch scar running down his
spine, the skin pinched and stitched like the top of a sack.
He looked like Dr Frankenstein's dog and every time he

shook himself a shower of blood hit the walls. Being unable to see his wound he couldn't understand what all the fuss was about. He ran into the local bakery once and seemed most hurt when everyone ran out screaming.

And yet his confidence in members of the animal profession is minimal. He wouldn't let anyone like David Attenborough near him and vets he can sniff out a mile off. As we reached the farmyard and walked through the traffic of ducks and chickens he dug his feet in the ground and began to shake.

The vet lurched out of the farmhouse, stubble on his chin, gum boots on his feet, shirt out of his trousers. He wore an old jacket of once-good quality, made to measure no doubt, but not for him. He looked at Boogie through baggy eyes and said: 'Don't tell me, don't tell me . . . it's a dog, right?' At this point Boogie wet himself.

We were led to the treatment room. I held the quivering Boogie on the table and the vet examined his ankle.

'A sprain!' he announced.

I had visions of a week in a Perranporth campsite, feeding Boogie chocolates and grapes as he recuperated.

'Best thing for it is lots of exercise.' Boogie looked at him incredulously. He demanded a second opinion.

'I'll just give him a jab,' said the vet, and he held a hyperdermic up to the light and bled it; Boogie gritted his teeth and fixed his eyes on an anatomical drawing of a horse hanging on the wall. After it was all over I asked if fifteen miles a day was asking too much of a dog Boogie's size. Behind me Boogie was nodding his head frantically.

'Animal like that can do a hundred miles a day,' said the vet, and he went on to inform me how Boogie was descended from a strain of sheep dog who, left to breed as they wanted, would continue to produce the healthiest of specimens, i.e., the mongrel, hardened genetically against every virus the animal metabolism was heir to. Only when you started to engineer dogs, to produce hybrids – to push their noses in, shorten their legs, make them rounder or fluffier, to generally tune them up – only then did they become the fragile toys that needed electric blankets, and visits to the dentist and psychiatrist. Boogie he said, would live for years.

He seemed a concerned man, with a genuine affection for animals that never veered towards the sentimental. I wanted to ask him if he could prescribe anything for excessive canine flatulence, but after what he'd just said I'd probably have discovered that Boogie's propensity to fart was some atavistic behaviour integral in the control of sheep.

It began to drizzle as we drove back to Perranporth; I dug my waterproofs out for the first time. Alan dropped me back on the path and as I set off he shouted after me to watch out for adders and old mine shafts on the stretch to St Agnes Head.

The heyday of Cornish mining was undoubtedly during the eighteenth and nineteenth centuries when the county became the largest source of copper ore in the world and firmly established itself amongst the ranks of the industrial revolution.

And yet, the extraction of metal deposits from the western coast and from the Camborne and Redruth areas had been going on for hundreds of years before then. Predictably the Romans quickly realised the value of Cornwall as a source of tin, and some historians theorise that even the Phoenicians visited the coastal regions in search of minerals as long ago as the fifth century BC.

These early enterprises extracted the metal by a process known as streaming, i.e., washing it out from alluvium deposits. Mines were dug but no-one had really grasped the technique: they used to mine upwards, a fundamental mistake for miners one might imagine, but the trouble with tin and copper is they tend to occur in vertical lodes rather than the more traditional horizontal, and miners could work their way down only until the water level was reached and the mine became flooded. The alternative method, and the one popularised, was to find an open lode, usually in a cliff-face or hillside, and tunnel up. This produced the goods, but, of course, left the wealth of the metal below untouched.

At the beginning of the eighteenth century, as British industry forged ahead, Cornwall was still a forgotten limb, a rough, tough land where men were men, boys were men, even the women were men. Living standards were deplorably low and life depended on the unpredictable pilchard harvest and the vagaries of the tin market.

It was as the demand for copper in the making of brass grew that the potential wealth of subterranean Cornwall became realised. Cornishmen, frustrated by the untapped riches they knew to lie beneath them, stayed up late at nights banging the table and trying to think of ingenious new ways to get water out of holes. This resulted in some interesting variations on the bucket, but little else. Then along came local hero Richard Trevithick. Inspired by Thomas Newcomen's crude steam engine, he developed the Cornish beam Engine, which could power a pump capable of raising water from the sort of depths the copper mines needed to reach. Their drainage problems solved, the Cornish miners did an about turn and dug down into a vein of success.

The boom continued into the nineteenth century. By 1860 the industry was at its peak, and first pack trails and then railways opened Cornwall up as the ore was transported from mine to port. Agricultural and fishing villages adapted and grew into thriving mining centres, and fifty thousand men were employed in copper extraction as the landscape took on industrial horizons.

But then, as suddenly as it had flourished, the industry slumped. New fields were discovered in Chile and Australia. The bottom fell out of the market and by 1870 copper mining in Cornwall was in irreversible decline. Some mines resumed the search for tin and they prospered briefly, but then tin prices also crashed as vast alluvium deposits were discovered in Malaysia and by the end of the Second World War only two mines, Geevor and South Crofty, remained. A revival was heralded in the Sixties when prices rose once more and a number of conglomerates prospected in the county. But history rather repeated itself and of the mines reopened only Wheal Jane was resurrected.

The stark legacy of those years of success dominated the path as it clung to the cliff around St Agnes Head. Vegetation had reclaimed a number of workings but the landscape still bore many scars. The hills were pockmarked with opencast sites and riddled with ventilation shafts, and the cliffs had an industrial hue to them. The grey rock was stained red with ore; it looked wrapped in old bandages.

The most impressive remains of all were the gutted engine houses with their stacked chimneys that stood desolately on the cliffs and in the villages where they towered over the holiday homes like brick dinosaurs. At the Wheal Coates site just north of Chapel Porth, the National Trust had bought the engine room that perched on the cliff, and largely restored it. The mine was closed in 1885 and the engine, with its thirty-five-inch-diameter cylinder, removed.

I sat inside the cold chamber, an empty space full of echoes. Suddenly a rock hit the outside wall and shattered around me. I ran out into the open and another missile landed a few yards away and ricocheted over the cliff. On the top of the hill I saw a couple of idiots playing 'Let's smash up the historic building', throwing anything they could lay their hands on. We exchanged abuse briefly and they scarpered.

For most of the day, I walked past similar, though less well-preserved, relics. It seemed strange to have such natural beauty against so industrial a background and yet wildlife didn't seem disturbed. The gulls in particular thrived on the abandonment. The coastal villages had also adapted and now, with no apparent effort, flourished under tourism. In St Agnes they'd just swept the industrial muck out of the streets, bunged in a couple of craft shops and B&B signs and left it at that, and it looked irresistibly pretty. In Porthtowan someone had made the ultimate merger and converted an old engine room into a café.

By Gwithian, the influence of the mines had dwindled to a red discolouring of the sand and some sort of processing plant next to the surfers' leisure centre. I found some dunes and camped amongst them with the silhouette of St Ives in the distance. The drizzle had persisted for a large part of the afternoon but it had been warm and ultimately refreshing rain, and now, as so often happened at the end of the day, the sun slipped through the clouds just above the horizon and took its evening dip in the sea. I fancied I was learning how to interpret the weather signs and I went to sleep that night confident sunshine would wake me in the morning.

Next morning I was woken by rain. I looked at my watch. 3.30 a.m. again; time to get up. But a lassitude had descended with the cloud. Only the thought of rounding Land's End that day got me out of bed. It was not quite two hundred miles into the journey but was the psychological halfway mark.

There were, however, a number of obstacles to cope with before then. The first was the Hayle estuary. The path diverted inland here through what, from a distance, looked like nothing but coal yards and power stations. Far more enticing was St Ives just across the river and I decided to tie my boots round my neck and wade across. The water wasn't deep or strong, at least not until I was past the point of no return and then it started to get progressively deeper and stronger. I was quickly up to my pockets in it; my money got wet. I looked around for Boogie to see him waving at me from the other bank. His natural aversion to water had enabled him to cross somehow without a drop touching him. I struggled to the other side, soaked, and he scampered off along the beach. Since his injection his limp appeared to have worn off and he'd resumed his Nimrod-like poise where no plastic bag could feel safe.

We followed the railway line towards St Ives. A train pulling two empty carriages passed in a spray of rain and we ducked under a whitewashed shelter: the Huers hut. In the days before the pilchards deserted the Cornish coasts, when two hundred and fifty seine boats filled St Ives harbour, when the ground floor of every house in the town was a fish cellar, the Huer would stand under here looking out for the shoals as they came round the headland into St Ives Bay. 'Heva, heva,' he'd shout, as the telltale red shadow appeared on the water and the waiting boats would row furiously to where he pointed, surrounding the entire shoal with their seine nets. You could imagine him sitting up on the cliffs on a summer's day: a flask of tea, a packet of sandwiches, Test Match Special on the radio. It's hard to think of a better job.

Like Newquay, St Ives has fine beaches and coves on three sides of the town, although that day they were all empty. The holidaymakers sat in their guest houses

watching the Open University, or moped around the
shops in anoraks, pressing their noses against windows.
There was talk of sunny periods, but this was just a
rumour spread by landladies. Instead, from around the
headlands to the west, a bank of cloud rolled silently into
town. It was the colour of a bruise and as welcome in the
bay as Jaws. Only one thing for it: an early lunch. I bought
a couple of Scotch eggs and a packet of Mintolas and took
shelter in an alcove opposite the Gents.

St Ives is a pastel-coloured town much lauded by the
artist fraternity, and in this half-light it looked like a
watercolour itself. It was attractively huddled, the stone
cottages were low and looked warm, the streets narrow
and cool. In fact it didn't look English; even in a cloud-
burst there was something Mediterranean about it. I
thought: I know, I'll sketch it! And over the next hour as
the rain fell, I produced a detailed drawing of men driving
round on fork-lift trucks, plastic-coated people hiding in
porches and a hamburger van doing no business. Once
again though, my seagulls let me down. The ones perched
on the church roof looked like a flock of pterodactyls.

When the downpour was over I climbed up on the
harbour wall and peered into the harbour-master's hut.
He stood inside, grinning at all the visitors being blown
along the walkways, while he had an electric fire and a
kettle and a bushy beard to keep him snug. In the window,
dials registered the weather forecast. One pointed to force
five and advised small craft to stay put. A black cone had
been hoisted at the end of the pier.

'What's it going to be like on the path to Land's End?'
I shouted through the glass. Inside there was much
guffawing and shaking of the head and general slapping
of the knees.

'Rough, eh?' I surmised. More jollity inside, and this

time the harbour-master filled his cheeks and blew, changed the dial to force six, and pointed to the black cone.

Sod him, I thought. It didn't look that bad. In fact it seemed to be blowing over, wasn't even raining any more. I retrieved Boogie, who was being beaten up by a three-legged dog on the beach and we weaved our way through the back streets until I found the path to Zennor. On the way I checked in all the ironmongers for a GT 132 camping gaz cylinder, with an S8 attachment or a 24B adaptor with a wide-angled flange-type FP 4. None of them had one.

The beach huts and back yards of St Ives quickly petered out, and beyond the first headland civilisation as we know it ceased. Inland was nothing but rough moorland, each hilltop tipped with a nipple-like granite tor, while ahead the coast line looked markedly different, the cliffs were ugly and studded with outcrops and the sea had been whipped up by the wind. Into all this I innocently plodded, trying to remain sanguine, unaware that I was about to discover how totally useless all my equipment was, how generally unprepared I was for any adversity, how there is no such word as waterproof, and not forgetting what a craven wimp I am and how I should never again do anything so rash as to act on my own initiative.

As we rounded Mussel Point, the cloud cover lowered until it was hurting my head. The wind picked up and the rain began again with a burst that made it clear this time it wasn't going to muck about. Blown horizontal each drop stung my face and passed through my 'waterproof' barrier as though I was wearing a newspaper. Within minutes all my clothing was saturated and my boots flooded. My anorak, besides welcoming the rain with open arms, back and front, somehow managed to make me sweat profusely as well, so I was also getting wet from the inside. The two atmospheric pressures were on a collision course; at the present rate a thunderstorm would break somewhere in the region between my pull-over and shirt.

Boogie decided to use me as a windbreak and he clung to my legs as closely as my trousers. We trudged onwards, having to lean into the wind at an angle of forty-five degrees just to keep upright. Another walker with a dog appeared through the rain, heading towards St Ives. He shouted a greeting but it was lost on the wind and he passed us in a flash. He had his dog on a lead and it was as though he was flying a kite. As usual only the gulls could cope with the conditions – in fact, they seemed to be enjoying themselves. They floated on the uplifts by the cliff edge as though they were on wires.

By Zennor Head the rain turned into hail. I was thinking of the harbour-master gleefully turning his dial up to force seven, when I slipped and stumbled to the ground. For the first time I started to feel concerned. There wasn't a house in sight, I hadn't the equipment to weather out the storm and now I had a grazed knuckle to contend with. I found a couple of large rocks propped up against each other and crawled between them; Boogie squeezed in with me. We crouched there, nose to nose, and I began to see the headlines in the *St Ives Gazette:* 'Coastguard finds decomposed body of walker after dog raises alarm: "death from hypothermia and loss of blood due to fatally grazed knuckle" was the coroner's verdict. The dog is now resident at the Bellevue Hotel and is looking for a new home, preferably with a twenty-six-inch colour television with remote control. Answers to name, Fang.'

I sat there and started to shiver, then took out a sodden *Seven Years in Tibet.* Heinrich Harrer was battling his way towards his dream: the forbidden city of Lhasa. One page he was sleeping rough in minus forty degrees, so cold his soup spoon froze to his lip; the next, he was wading through jungle swamps pulling leeches off himself. On every page he had confrontations with murderous robbers as a matter of course. Finally, on page one hundred and thirty-five he strode into the forbidden city and stood beneath the Potala Palace, home of the Dalai Lama, the god king, the living Buddha.

'For Christ's sake, it's only a bit of rain!' I shouted. I wasn't going to be beaten by these cliffs; I wasn't going to be eaten by the gulls; I was going to brave the storm; I was going to do battle against the elements; I was going to find my forbidden city.

I crawled out of the shelter and was immediately hit by a deluge. Someone was out there throwing swimming pools. I decided to head inland and stay in the first farmhouse I saw.

We marched over moorland for a mile or two until I saw the church tower and the few cottages that comprised Zennor. A woman stuck her nose out of a door and told me the farm at the top of the hill would put me up. Marvellous, wonderful, terrific, vicissitudinous even. I had visions of Duff Farm all over again.

And sure enough, as I knocked on the farm's front door a typically wild farmyard dog jumped over the garden wall and sank its muddy teeth into Boogie. How he'd ever survived in South London I don't know because these country mutts were beating him up with one paw behind their backs. This particular specimen was a purpose-built sort of beast, a cross between a greyhound and a tractor, with a mouth like a threshing machine. I went to Boogie's rescue with feet flying, just as the door opened to reveal the trim form of the farmer's wife: hair neatly set, apron ironed and unstained, hands clasped at her lap, a smile full of teeth and behind her a hallway that sparkled. Before her was a drenched human form, dressed in dirty blue nylon, nose dribbling, boots full of water and kicking her dog. Her smile receded to pursed lips, her hands moved instinctively to her hips. I did my best to look irresistible.

'I was wondering if you had a room for the night?' I asked, at which point Boogie stuck his miserable head between my legs.

'Eeurghh,' she squealed, 'What does he want?'

'He'd like a room for the night as well.'

She thought long and hard. Was it worth five pounds fifty to have a tramp and his scabby dog stay in the house?

'All right,' she said, at last, 'come in; it's six pounds fifty.'

We stood in the hallway dripping; all around was brass and porcelain. Boogie gave the place a cursory glance and then shook himself free of surface water, covering the grandfather clock and net curtains in a fine film of black hair. The farmer's wife looked at me and scowled, and wondered if she could get seven fifty.

The house was spotless; full of those little flowers whose name I had learnt the first two syllables of in Clovelly but had long since forgotten. Boogie was given a rug to lie on by the door.

'Stay there!' I commanded him and followed my hostess up the stairs. When we reached the top Boogie was there waiting for us.

'Until the morning, I meant,' I said and waggled a finger at him for effect.

'All right,' the farmer's wife said, 'he can sleep on the landing. She opened the bedroom door and Boogie was already in there.

'He's going to be trouble, isn't he?' she said.

'No, no, no, no, no,' I assured her, 'no need to worry about him, he just wants to sleep.' Behind her Boogie was climbing onto the bed.

'All right,' she said, 'he can sleep in the bedroom, but don't on any account let him on the bed. Breakfast is at eight, towels in the bathroom, put wet clothes on the radiator, I'm going out, and there's no evening meal.

I drew a deep bath and sank luxuriously into it with a cup of tea. I wallowed there a long while examining my moustache in a handmirror – which if viewed from a distance no greater than four inches from my face could now quite possibly be construed as an incipient beard – and thinking how odd it felt to be out on the cliffs in a storm one minute, and then locked in a stranger's bathroom the next, using their egg and lemon shampoo and patting your private parts with their honeysuckle talc.

But I liked these bed-and-breakfast places. They didn't pretend to be anything other than people's homes, and I found myself forever trying to build up pictures of the people who lived there. I'd study the bookshelves and the contents of the rubbish baskets. I'd make note of the supermarket they used, the brand of soap, the condition of the toothbrushes. Hotels were never so much fun.

Later, with hair brushed, nails scrubbed and trousers steaming, I went downstairs and found the living room. There, sitting in front of the TV with his shoes off and his feet on the coffee table was the farmer. He jumped up when I entered, a reflex action.

'God! I thought you were the wife,' he said. He had a face ingrained with earth and salt. 'Weather forecast's on if you're interested.' He pointed to a chair and then put his feet back on the coffee table. I couldn't help noticing what good condition his socks were in.

On the television, in a warm studio, some grinning weatherboy in a Hawaiian shirt and pleated trousers was announcing it would be wet and rather windy for a while. Beyond the screen, I could see the wind bending the telegraph poles outside, and hear the rain rattling the window panes.

'That's all very well for you tourists,' said the farmer, 'but what I want to know is when are we going to get us some proper rain.' Then he switched the set off and walked out.

That night I made a dash down the hill to the village pub, the Tinner's Arms. I had some Tinner's ale and ate first some peanuts and then a pasty and talked to the barmaid first about peanuts and then about pasties. Concerning the former she knew little; of what appertains to the latter, however, she was a sage.

It seems pasties grew in popularity during the mining boom. They were the miners' convenience food, enormous two-pound affairs, dropped down the shaft at lunchtime and made with great crusts which the miners could hold onto with their muddy hands and then discard when they'd eaten the filling. I told the barmaid of the evil things I'd been eating and she said the bakers today tried to experiment too much; the recipe should be kept simple, just meat, potato, onions and pepper. Some supermarket chains had tried to market a pasty with a variety of vegetables, but this was condemned as an act of pasty engineering and the Cornish Devolutionaries had had to shoot a few kneecaps off to restore order. 'Best pasties are in the WI market in Penzance,' she said, 'my Mike ate five of them in one sitting once. He was sick after, mind.'

Occasionally the pub door would open and there'd be furious sounds of weather going on outside. Human beings wrapped in layers of oiled or plastic clothing would stumble in with hats pulled over eyes and boots full of slops. They'd struggle to close the door against the gale and then stand in a pool and say: 'Cor! What a night!' or 'Blimey! What a night!' or, on one occasion, 'Struth! What a night!' Then they'd sit down with a pint of Tinner's and never speak again, just shake their heads from time to time and say, 'Ah, dearie me, I dunno.'

A man called Henry came in and stood by the bar in shiny Wellingtons. He had a funny hat and a face to match. His enormous horn-rimmed glasses gave the impression he was looking at you through a window. 'Pint of Guinness, please,' he said to the barmaid, then he turned and smiled at everyone in turn.

The barmaid stood the creamy pint on the bar. Henry put the glass to his lips and drank as he spoke, blowing froth over himself: 'I haven't got any money,' he said and emptied the glass.

Everyone chuckled. Henry lived up the road in some sort of outhouse. In London, he'd have been a vagrant without a friend. In Zennor he was the village idiot.

I ran back up the hill to the farmhouse. The light was on in the living room and I could hear the TV. I went in and found the farmer's son and his girlfriend sitting with their feet on the coffee table. They jumped up when I entered.

'Christ!' said the boy, 'I thought you were my mum.'

They brought me some coffee and biscuits and we all sat and watched Kojak with our feet on the coffee table, while outside the gale howled. The girl was anxious about her father who was a fisherman and would be out in this by the dawn. And it was stupid really, she said, the fishermen all felt they had a macho image to maintain.

Recently though, the sailors along these shores had to revise their respect for the sea. The Penlee lifeboat had gone down in a storm just five months previously and all the crew were lost. The RNLI was the one line everyone working at sea or waiting on the shore could cling to; when that too was washed away the whole community faltered.

That night I lay at the end of North Cornwall and decided that my best-selling-top-ten-hit-single wouldn't be about one man and his dog. I'd change the tempo, add a hornpipe and turn it into a shanty concerning how powerless man really is against the sea. Life on this coast had gone on in spite of it, livings had been made from it, but nothing had managed to live with it. Except for the gulls and those little pink flowers.

5. South Cornwall:
the fast bit

Boogie took the corner round Land's End on two legs
and at speed, an unpredictable end to a day which had
seen him start in familiar fashion: yawning and moaning
and given to hiding under the seats of any cars left with
doors open.

We left Zennor in thick fog and followed the road to
St Just, accompanied by the groan of the invisible Pendeen
Watch. We were back in mining country, but here was
something different, Geevor mine, an enterprise that still
worked and even thrived, supplementing its income with
a mining museum and guided tours for tourists. The beat
of the machinery was like a revived pulse and for an
instant the industry was alive, but then the fog swallowed
all and as we joined the cliffpath again at Botallack, the
redundancy returned. The Crowns mine near here had the

most dramatic setting of all the derelict workings: a lone engine house that stood on a platform under the cliff, just out of reach of the waves. At one time the mine ran under the sea for almost half a mile, the miners able to hear the pebbles being washed along the seabed above them. The situation at the Kendijack workings just along the coast was similar, although here the story is one of tragedy; the sea broke through one morning in 1893 and twenty miners drowned. Soon after, the mine was abandoned.

We stopped amongst the ruins and had lunch, and it was here that Boogie gave the first sign of an impending burst of energy. Normally, whenever we stopped to eat at this time, he would collapse in a post-prandial snooze with all the symptoms of catalepsy, the only antidote a Kit-Kat waved under his nose, but on this occasion he was scratching the ground and whining at me before I was halfway through my pasty.

I grew suspicious. Traditionally, when animals do this sort of thing it means a Cheyenne with raised tomahawk is crouched on the rock above about to pounce. I checked all likely positions but there were no indians of any tribe. Boogie whined again. Could it be that he wanted to continue for the sheer fun of it? Was this the transformation from ugly duckling to very fine swan indeed? I jumped up and got moving, finishing my pasty as I walked. Sure enough Boogie bounded off over the grass with a glide and a whistle and headed for Cape Cornwall.

This handsome headland with its ancient tin mine on top misses out on the Land's End title by only a few hundred yards and is probably all the more attractive for it. The recent auction of the last headland in Britain – which saw a million-pound offer from the National Trust outbid – illustrated the kind of big business to be made there, and I was preparing myself for the kind of gimmickry any self-respecting headland could do without.

And yet Land's End had a magnetic appeal. As we passed Sennen Cove, the last village in England, I could feel my pace quicken, and as the familiar salience of Dr Syntax Head appeared in the distance, the castellated cliffs surfaced to supply a suitably resilient buffer to the onslaught of waves that rolled forever landwards at the end of their four-thousand-mile journey.

Half an hour later we were standing on the tip, gazing out to the Longships Lighthouse stranded on its reef. It wasn't a particularly spectacular scene – the cliffs weren't high enough, nor dramatic, at least not compared to what we'd come through. But here was a milestone more than anything else; it was the turning point in the journey. Up until now I'd been outward bound, Land's End was the pole I had to round, and from now on I was heading home. I still had three hundred miles to go but it felt as though I'd reached the downhill stretch. The hard work was surely over. I tried explaining all this to Boogie, but he was far too busy buying souvenirs in the First and Last Craft Shop.

Slowly the mist cleared inland and the full extent of the development took shape. There were the predictable shops and cafés, a number of coin-operated telescopes and an austere-looking hotel further up the slope. But these were all inoffensive exploits; the worst scar was the general wear and tear to the turf. Great furrows had been dug into the cliff-top; the earth felt loose. The trouble with Land's End was that there wasn't really anything special there. Visitors strolled down from the car parks, had a look at the view, took a picture to prove they'd been, then bought a First and Last ashtray and went home. Harmless enough, but if a million people a year do it then the carpet's going to get worn out.

Behind the hotel was a service complex: a cafeteria and acres of car parking space with signposts everywhere. It was reminiscent of a motorway service area, although strangely quiet. There were more staff than customers. I went into the cafeteria, leaving Boogie outside, but a waitress told me to bring him in and I joined her and some workmates for a tea-break.

'Where are all the people?' I asked the girl who worked the cash register.

'You wait till next weekend,' she said, 'it's Bank Holiday.'

'I'm dreading it,' said the girl from the cold sweets counter.

The waitress asked me where I was going with my funny little dog, and when I told her, as coolly as possible, that I was walking the whole South-west coastal path she said: 'Kevin the breakfast chef did that last year.'

'Oh, really.'

'Yeah. He walked thirty miles a day.'

'Really.'

'Yeah. And he's diabetic or something.'

'Is he!'

'Yeah. He raised about five thousand quid for a kidney machine.'

'Did he!'

'Yeah. He said it was easy enough from Minehead to here, but then it started to get really tough.'

'Gulp.'

The girls told me where there was a telescope which was jammed and you could look through for nothing. I went and tried it and since all you could see through it was nothing it seemed like a fair price. I wanted to spy on the Longship lighthouse keeper, to see if I could catch him up to something unprofessional, but the mist obscured everything.

We pressed on. And as with all the 'honeypots' we'd passed through, one had only to walk out of sight of the

car parks at Land's End and the coast immediately reverted
to its wild state.

In fact, hardly a mile or so to the east, some of the
finest cliffs of the whole path were to be found. The
castellated granite continued, but here the rock walls were
sheer and high. They rose straight out of the water in
columns so symmetrical they appeared constructed. You
could even see the joins. In places they'd collapsed and in
one case a lifeless wreck lay wedged between the rocks,
waves bursting through its rusty shell. Further out were
little offshore islands, raw and bronze-coloured, the
exclusive domain of the gulls with the black backs. They
lodged on every sill and used the flat tops for landing
strips. Any other breed of bird that intruded was
ferociously evicted.

It was along this impressive stretch that Boogie finally
graduated to fitness. The path hugged the cliff edge here,
one false move and that would have been it, splat! no
more Wallington, and I walked five cautious miles that
evening. Boogie, however, must have covered twenty,
doubling back on himself, running everywhere and
chasing everything. As the sun reddened we stood above
Porthcurno at the Minnack Theatre, a unique open-air
auditorium carved out of rock high above the sea. Below
I could see a beach and a square of sand, which was a
bigger relief than it sounds: granite is great to look at, but
lousy for pitching tents on.

I patted Boogie with pride, so pleased he'd shown his
mettle at last and I wondered if he'd finally found his
spirit. I mean he'd hardly been the ideal travelling
companion so far. He wouldn't play cards or pocket chess.
He didn't know any games, nor even any jokes. He did
play Crazy Golf with me one time in Newquay, but he
was no good, no competition. He remained convinced
that this walk was some sort of revenge for the time in

West Hampstead when he crapped in my headphones, and he seemed to want no part in it.

I patted him again, called him a 'goo' boy,' and then picked up a stick and threw it along the path. We both watched it rise, spin and then fall, bounce once and tumble over the cliff edge into the water so far below we didn't even hear a splosh. 'Fetch!' I said and grinned at him. A crack appeared on his saturnine features. He looked up at me and sniggered. At last we had a rapport.

With its back to the Atlantic squall the coastline began to grow lush. Along the north coast every plant had had to struggle, but now the cliffs were moist, the coves were suntraps and the vegetation grew thick. The valley in Porthcurno steamed like a rain forest and on the path to Mousehole I saw a palm tree in a garden. The mist was down again and it was a morning of collisions. First, we bumped into Penberth, a National Trust fishing village, just a handful of cottages and a few colourful boats winched up on the shore, and all just a little too rich first thing in the morning. Then, a pair of charging horses almost ran us down. I could hear hooves in the distance, and didn't have to put my ear to the ground to realise they were coming our way. Suddenly two riderless animals galloped out of the mist, I leapt to one side, Boogie leapt to the other and the horses thundered by, all sweat and froth.

Mousehole had a soporific air. It was as if it was closed. The village had had an enormous amount of press coverage since the lifeboat tragedy, most of it of the opinion that the boat should never have had to be launched. A tug from Falmouth had offered assistance to the *Union Star* when it first fell into difficulties, but the captain of the doomed coaster had refused help until such time as the weather had deteriorated and the lifeboat was all that could rescue him.

But there'd also been much publicity concerning the disaster fund, which had quickly swelled to two and a half million pounds. First there was dispute over how the money should be distributed, and whether or not tax was payable. Then there was a period of investment advice and anonymous letters; all this while bits of wreckage were still being washed ashore. The village had been news around the world and now it looked as though it just wanted to be left alone.

Around the harbour the mist was soothing. The water was still and beyond the entrance it quickly turned to vapour; beyond that, a void. I peered over the edge. A wiry well-preserved chap in sandals stood nearby. He had a cat with him, on a lead.

'Don't go near the edge, Tiddles,' he said. Boogie stiffened and I grabbed him just in time. A cat called Tiddles was too much to resist.

'You a visitor?' the man asked me. I told him I was and he pointed into the water and said: 'Come and have a look at this.' I followed his finger and there, swimming through the clear, colourless pond, was a black fish about a foot long. 'Bass,' he said.

We watched it in silence for a while and then I asked him if he was a fisherman. He said he used to be, but: 'Bloody Russians came and took all the fish, didn't they?' He was, of course, referring to the factory ships from the Soviet Bloc and from Spain which came fishing in these waters with Hoovers. They were the final blow to people like this fellow who could probably just remember the last great pilchard catches when the beaches were alive with netsful of fish and every man, woman and child was involved in some way or another in the seining, salting, pressing or packing of the catch. Now, like so many ex-fishermen, he took tourists out on trips after mackerel and shark. 'If they can take a couple of mackerel home with them they're pleased as Punch,' he said. I wondered if they felt the same way about sharks.

But what he said about the Russians was interesting because whilst the majority of Cornish fishing villages, like Mousehole, no longer fished at a commercial level, the town I was approaching, Newlyn, thrived off the industry; a number of boats here led the same pelagian existence the Russians were accused of. In fact, the Cornish fishing industry had been centralised at Newlyn and in its raw state there was nothing cute or picturesque about it at all.

There must have been a hundred boats in the harbour. The water was stained with rainbows of diesel fuel, squashed fish smeared the walkways, the gulls gorged and everywhere was a smell sharp as a fisherman's socks. Around the wharf, convoys of juggernauts waited with their doors open, refrigeration units buzzing. Hitch a ride here and I could be in Billingsgate by nightfall.

The fish were all brought to the auction room and laid out in coloured plastic crates and had labels slapped on them. There were all sorts of brutes, mouths wide open and eyes bulging at the last gasp. A party of school children were being taken round, their master pointing out the various species and trying to engage the fishermen or filleters in conversation, but they weren't interested, they just sliced up the fish and talked about what they'd seen on telly the night before. Only one, a porter, offered himself: 'Wanna see a shark?' he said to the kids. They all took a step back and said 'yes please', and the porter went over to the other side of the hall and began to drag this great selachian lump across the floor. 'Ere! Where you off to with my shark?' Shouted a work mate. 'I'm only borrowing it,' said the porter. He laid the fish out in front of the children. It was about six feet long with a timid face and a lot of soft white areas. A bloody rip ran the length of a flank. It looked very dead indeed.

The porter stood proudly over it and, placing one Wellington boot on the back of its neck, he pulled open the mouth for all to see. This was a cue for the master to go to work with his ruler: 'Now, a fish breathes through its gills, here. They separate the oxygen from . . . Anthony, stop putting your fingers in the shark's mouth.'

'Is it a boy or a girl?' said a little thing in pigtails.

'It doesn't matter if it's a boy or a girl, Lucy. Kevin! Stop hitting Peter with that Lemon Sole.'

'It's a girl,' said the porter, who'd turned the fish over displaying its genitalia for all to see.

'Ah, yes, so it is,' said the master. ''First time I've seen a female shark's.'

It was the first time I'd seen a female shark's as well.

It began to rain as I reached Penzance. I looked for some-where to shelter and settled at first for a place under the blinds of a TV rental shop, where we watched the racing interspersed with news bulletins from the Falklands. But when it started to pour, I adjourned to a launderette doorway. As washers came and went I'd get hit by irresist-ible blasts of warm soapy air and in the end I slipped inside and read a copy of *Woman's Own* with a picture of Warren Beatty on the cover, while a vibrating front load automatic massaged my back.

There were the average launderette crew at work. One woman kept smiling at me maternally, another stared but looked away every time I caught her eye, an elderly couple sat and watched their laundry go round and round as if it were on television. Boogie was on familiar territory here and he did the rounds and collected a few strokes and tickles.

A lad with two bags of football togs came in and used the machine next to me. He lifted the jerseys out of one bag and showered me and the floor with dried mud. 'Sorry,' he said, then took the shorts out of the other bag and did exactly the same thing. 'Sorry,' he said again.

His team had had a muddy game last week, he explained. He played for a local pub side and they'd lost to a team from St Just 3–2. I asked him what his position was and he said, Midfield Schemer, and went on to relate how he almost scored a late equaliser: 'There I was, with just a minute to go, when I picked up a loose ball. Well, I tell you, I was so far out I didn't know whether to shoot or pass back to the goalie, so I . . .' I lost his commentary as my attention was distracted by something big and hairy striding down the aisle between the spin dryers. On closer inspection I determined it was female. She had a housecoat on with sleeves rolled up and she goose-stepped past the washers, kicking aside stretched out legs and carelessly placed shopping baskets. She was the launderette manageress – commandant if you like – the woman whose job it was to give the establishment that homely, washday touch. 'If in need of assistance, please ask,' read the sign on the wall, but anyone who so much as asked for change she'd have strangled with one hand.

She was coming our way. Boogie cowered under the seat. The footballer, preoccupied with his report didn't notice her until her shadow fell over him: 'So, there I was with thirty seconds left and eight men to beat, when . . . .'

She stood over him, the light from the overhead strip highlighting the ginger in her beard. She was staring at the little pile of mud on the floor. 'I know you, don't I?' she said to the footballer. He nodded.

'You've been in here before, haven't you?' The footballer nodded and tried to grin.

"Last time you came in here you threw mud all over
the place, didn't you?' The footballer thought about
protesting but in the end nodded.

'And now you've done it again, haven't you?' He
admitted the foul deed with a nod.

She was clearly having trouble containing herself. Her
neck had disappeared, her head had begun to swell and
her chest to heave. And that's when she saw me. In a fit
of panic I dropped my magazine and threw all my clothes
into a washing machine. At this point she erupted.

'You!!'

I looked round. 'Me?'

'Yes! You!' She pointed at me and I detected a strong
current of underarms. 'You've been reading my *Woman's
Own!'*

The launderette fell silent. I tried desperately to expel
the dreadful image I had of the damsel before me in bed
with Warren Beatty. Slowly, I bent down and retrieved
the magazine for her. She snatched it from me and
marched off. For the first time I noticed she was wearing
pink bedroom slippers.

Actually, it wasn't a bad idea to wash my clothes. Most
of them were still stained with pea soup from that jolly
night in Crackington Haven. Only my socks I kept back.
They were rigid by this time. I stepped into them rather
than pulled them on and I wasn't sure how they'd react
to water.

I sat down again, this time with a *Homes and Gardens.*

'So, anyway,' said the footballer, 'I went round one
man, sold the second a dummy and nutmegged the third
and with ten seconds remaining . . .'

'Isn't it a bit late in the year to be playing football?' I
said.

'Nah. It's the Cup Final tomorrow.'

The Cup Final!? Tomorrow!? Of course it was.

Saturday 22 May, the Cup Final, Spurs versus QPR. I'd never missed a Cup Final.

The rain stopped and I left the launderette, but the lull was brief and I soon found myself sitting in a shelter in Penzance bus station. And a very friendly bus station it was too. In quick succession I met a chap who told me what a nice lively place Penzance was out of season and how the winter closedown was a misconception invented by tourists. And then I met a woman who ran a bed-and-breakfast house and who told me what a horrible place Penzance was in the winter and that the tourists were very nice. The people who complained about them, she said, were those who had come here on holidays themselves for twenty years and then moved down to live.

Little exchanges like these were somehow very special. It was strange and often sad to meet someone for just a couple of minutes, and listen to them talk, usually about something local and frequently with great feeling, and then, afterwards, to know I'd never see them again.

'If you ask me,' continued the woman, 'I think the tourists are better behaved than the locals, and I've lived here most of my life. It's the locals that go tearing around on motorbikes, not the tourists.' And then she was gone on the 224 to Marazion.

Marazion was the direction I was headed, although first I thought I should look round Penzance a bit. But after admiring the palm trees and the statue of Davy – local inventor of the miner's lamp – I quickly lost interest in the idea. Walking round these large towns wore me out and there didn't seem any point in getting to know them unless I was going to be spending time there. I did my usual and futile tour of the local ironmongers – which were, in general, better than those in St Ives although not as good as Newquay's – then found myself in a street full of craft shops. And I was growing to hate craft shops. They all had 'Handmade' or 'Home-made' or 'Locally Made' signs hanging on everything, and yet they all sold the same collection of coloured pebbles and table mats and glass jewellery, and I was going to throw a brick through the window of the next one I came across, when there, looking at me through the glass, was a baby camping stove cylinder, type GT 132 with an S8 attachment and French writing on the side. I dashed in and bought three of them from an assistant with a fixed smile and a mission in life to ensure that no-one left her shop without buying a box of fudge.

We followed the railway line out of town, as helicopters bound for the Isles of Scilly flew low overhead. After a mile or two we reached the flooded causeway to St Michael's Mount; at its end, a beautiful combination of blue sea, yellow sand and green island with a grey chapel perched on top. I'd have liked to take the ferry over and camped there, but I thought I'd likely as not be thrown off, so instead I decided to take Boogie out to dinner.

In Marazion I found a pub where I got to drinking real ale with a couple of lads down from Colchester on a long weekend. They advised me that the pasty and chips they'd just had had come with the largest portion of chips either of them had ever seen. They were on motorbikes and had oil all over their hands and looked like the sort who would know a good chip deal when they saw one, and so I ordered a portion. They were right, it was the largest portion of chips I'd ever seen as well, and it was neatly juxtaposed with the smallest-ever pasty.

I tucked in, furtively slipping chips to Boogie under the bar. 'Do you know,' I said to the lads from Colchester, as they bought me another pint of Sidebottom's Old Stagnant or whatever the stuff was called, 'that in days gone by, pasties weighed over two pounds and were dropped down the mine shafts at lunchtime?'

They said they didn't, and after that the evening gets hazy. I remember one of them said he wanted to move down to Cornwall and he went on about the beaches and the windsurfing and the discos, and I told him he was forgetting about the wintertime and the foul weather and the cow shit everywhere, and the rotten bus service and the isolation and the perennial scrape for a living, and that he was a mug because he was moving down here for all the wrong reasons, at which point he made some uncalled for comment about the state of my nose.

I think we all had another plate of pasty and chips and then we shook hands like old buddies and I got my fingers covered in engine oil and went off and camped under the nearest tree.

After Penzance the granite coast comes to an end and the cliffs become shiny black chunks of slate with sharp edges and deep clefts. Something green with crimson flowers cascades appealingly over the rocks, and tracks lead down to caves cut off by the tide. The walker is approaching Prussia Cove and this is the land of the Moonlight Men.

Prussia Cove took its name from the King of Prussia Inn, a hostelry which once stood on the clifftops here, run by the notorious Carter family, a sort of Smugglers and Sons Ltd. During the eighteenth century they and their kind pioneered the romantic age of smuggling for which this coastline became infamous. Smugglers became stylised as Robin Hoods of the sea, rowing ashore on moonlit nights with illicit cargoes of French brandy, salt, French brandy, tea and French brandy.

In reality, of course, it was all rather different. Your average contrabandist was an opportunist with questionable seafaring sense and a tendency to consume large

quantities of his duty-free cargo on the way over from
Roscoff or wherever.

And the idea that this was the golden era of British
smuggling is nonsense. This roguish world of lanterns
and secret passages pales into insignificance, remunerat-
ively and morally, when compared to the operations of
drug smugglers today. Further up the coast in Talland
Bay – a popular place for landing undeclared liquor during
the Carters' time – 1979 saw a three-million-pound mari-
juana smuggling racket busted by customs and excise
officers. The liquor used to be stashed in the churchyard.
The drugs were stashed in the beach café.

All very interesting, but what I was looking out for on
this sunny Saturday was TV aerials.

It was Cup Final day. As I strode across Perran Sands
the pre-match warm-up would be getting under way and
John Motson would be introducing the Road to Wembley.
As I rounded Cudden Point, they would be showing
extracts from the White Horse Cup Final and the Stanley
Matthews final of '53. As I passed the crumbling Wheal
Trewavas copper mine, the teams would be being inter-
viewed in their hotels. In every village I passed through I
dallied in the hope I'd be invited somewhere with a TV,
but by the time I reached Porthleven (as they went over
live to Wembley for the community singing) I was still
without a seat.

Porthleven was a sizable port with a well-protected
harbour and lots of TV aerials. The wind was picking up.
Waves slapped the harbour wall. I sat on a bench and tried
to make friends, quickly.

The trouble was the town was deserted. Not a car on
the roads, just a few shoppers and one or two people
securing their boats. At last a man came and sat down
next to me.

'Where is everyone?' I asked.

'Don't know,' he said. 'Is that your dog?'

'Yeah. Do you think everyone's watching the Cup Final?'

'What sort is he?'

'Eh? Oh, a mongrel. It's Spurs v QPR you know.'

'Reckon there's a bit of alsatian in there. Bit of greyhound as well, and spaniel, poodle, labrador, touch of retriever perhaps.

'Yeah, a mongrel. Should be a good game, the Cup Final.'

'I had a dog once. Got run over. He was a mongrel.'

'Are you going watch the Cup Final?'

'Eh? No, I hate football.'

It dawned on me the only people I'd be likely to meet now were those without the slightest interest in the game. Anyone wanting to watch the match would already be parked in front of their telly with their cans of lager. I had one more attempt, in a supermarket, where I could hear a TV on in the back room.

'That the Cup Final on in there?' I said to the youth at the cash desk.

'Yeah,' he said, adding up my groceries. 'That's ninety-six pence please.'

'Should be a good game.'

'Should be. Ninety-six pence please.'

'Spurs v QPR eh!'

'That's right. Ninety-six pence, please.'

'I'm camping, see.'

'Are you? Have you got that ninety-six pence?'

'You going to watch the Cup Final, are you?'

'When you give me ninety-six pence, yeah!'

I wandered round the town trying to find a shop window to watch it in, but no luck. I peered through a few net curtains. In every living room groups were gathered staring at a coloured blur of animation in the corner.

The game had started. I began to feel miserable, so did Boogie, he's a Spurs fanatic, but there was nothing more I could do. I put my head into the wind and walked on.

Only when I reached Mullion Cove that evening did I discover the score: a one-all draw. A drunk told me the result. I was sitting down by the harbour when he stumbled up to me smelling of Guinness and fish and said he wanted me to go for a drink with him. He'd had a good win on the races that afternoon and now he was going to get everyone in Mullion smashed.

I thanked him for his offer but told him I wanted something to eat rather than drink and he said: 'Pub up the hill serves a pasty and chips with the biggest portion of chips you've ever . . . come back. Oi! Where you going?'

I stayed in a campsite that night, which was stupid and unnecessary. It cost almost as much as Duff Farm and as far as I could see campsites rather took the fun out of camping. I only stayed at them for company but at this time of the year they were invariably deserted, and this particular site with its hedgerows and private dustbins and Laura Ashley tents, did nothing for my few square feet of cotton and nylon but show it up for the amorphous mess it was.

I sat inside it and filled in my diary. I had two weeks' worth of entries behind me now and reading through them it wasn't difficult to detect a change in attitude. Page one contained a lavish account of Porlock Weir, full of zeal and *joie de vivre:* 'Exmoor: an ethereal landscape, moulded by the legend of Lorna Doone and the vagaries of the sea. A place where time has stood still and yet somehow moved . . .' etc. My entry for Mullion Cove, despite the offshore islands, greenstone harbour and general drama of the setting, read: 'Mullion Cove – quite a nice place'. And my social conscience, which had been so easily provoked along the north coast by any aberration on the landscape or in the community, was reduced to observations like: 'The handle has broken off my cup.'

I was becoming blasé, uninspired even. That afternoon I'd passed Loe Bar, Gunwalloe Cove, Dollar Cove, Parc Bean Cove, Halzephron Cliff, Carag-a-pilez Cliff, Poldhu Point, Polurrian Cove and many more spots, all, according to my guide book, exquisite (as well as being notable for the many boats wrecked offshore and the number of sailors horribly mangled on the rocks). And yet I couldn't remember one of them; in fact, since Land's End the coast had become a muddle of cliffs and water, green on one side, blue on the other.

The problem was clear: I was going too fast. With our newfound fitness, both Boogie and I had become lean and streamlined. We were strong and brown, I from the sun, he from liberal amounts of muck. I was asleep as soon as it got dark and up at first light and apart from occasional lapses into vats of real ale I was disgustingly healthy and striding along from one headland to the next, seeing little of what lay between.

I decided I must slow down. Tomorrow was Sunday, I'd take things easy. I'd sit and watch some more snails. Better still, I'd dedicate the day to rockpools.

Rockpools had been a source of wonderment all along the coast. To the uninitiated they can appear as mere stranded pools of water, but stick a finger in and immediately all becomes animated. Little crabs sprint from side to side, plants open, tiddlers flash from one piece of cover to another and seaweeds wave at you.

Then, of course, you've got your molluscs.

Limpets, cockles, winkles, they were everywhere. On the beaches east from Mullion Cove you could actually hear them grazing. The morning was calm, the tide out, the water flat and all was quiet but for the munch, munch of hundreds of thousands of molluscs eating breakfast.

On one beach a man and his boy were picking at the rocks and filling plastic bags. The boy came over to Boogie, hand outstretched.

'Don't go near the dog, James,' said his father.

'It's all right,' I said, 'he won't hurt.'

'No, but James will. He likes to poke dogs in the eye and swing them about by the tail. Used to give our beagle hell.'

James lunged. Boogie sidestepped. I took James by the hand and led him back to his dad.

'What are you looking for?' I asked him.

'Littorina Littorea.'

Blank look.

'Winkles. Periwinkles.' He opened his plastic bag to reveal scores of little black shells, crawling all over the place, trying to escape. 'Boil 'em up, bit of brown bread and butter, lovely.' He closed the bag. 'You can live off the sea, you know. See that?' He pointed to a tangle of seaweed and drawing a penknife sliced off a limb. 'Pure nourishment. Boil that up, bit of brown bread and butter, lovely. Put spots on your chest and get rid of hairs, that will.'

Another blank look.

'No, sorry, put hairs on your chest and get rid of spots.' He fished out a different weed. 'See this: sea kelp. One man can live one day on one pound of sea kelp.' He threw it back. 'Alternatively, of course, two men can live half a day. Full of fascinating facts like that, the sea is.'

Like so many of the schemes of self-edification which I'd promised myself I'd pursue during this trip, my plans for self-sufficiency had come to nothing. But now it seemed absurd to be living off pasties and soup when all around me the shelves on these beaches were stacked like a supermarket. I dug out a book I'd brought with me: *Food For Free*, not a guide for holding up grocery stores, but a comprehensive list of the wild foods one can and cannot eat. I turned to the shellfish section. It was true, all you had to do with any of the mollusc family was soak them and boil them. The same with seaweeds.

'Is this a limpet?' I called to James's dad, indicating one of the thousands of conical shapes that clung to the rocks.

'That's right,' he said, 'a limpet. Interesting little mollusc the limpet. Did you know for instance, the male has a reproductive organ over six feet long? Relatively speaking, of course.' He deftly slipped his penknife under a shell and prised it off the rock. Underneath the suckers groped blindly. 'Boil that up, bit of brown bread and butter, lovely.'

I prised some off for myself and collected some winkles and sea kelp. In Kynance Cove I found a fresh water tap from where I filled a plastic bag and put the lot in to soak. They would be my main course. According to Richard Mabey, author of *Food For Free*, stinging nettles were in their prime at this time of year. I'd gather a bunch later, they could be my greens. Tonight would be a rare culinary experience.

I set off round The Lizard, the most southerly headland in England and subject to the same sort of erosion as Land's End. The path was like a three-lane motorway round here and being Sunday the traffic was heavy.

From the tip of the Point, the visibility was astoundingly good, although the inertia of the morning had disappeared and in the Channel tankers rode white horses. On the clifftop the day trippers gazed out to sea through binoculars or sat in their cars reading the newspapers and having picnics. The Jimmy Saville show was on the radio. He was playing hits from 1963, and from now on whenever I hear Billy J. Kramer and the Dakotas sing 'I'll Keep You Satisfied', I'll think of The Lizard, and vice versa.

Cadgwith, like all the really pretty places, appeared suddenly, one step round a headland. It was a fishing village with all the standard features: thatched cottages, village pub, a tea shop, links with the smuggling era, coloured boats drawn up on the beach, and narrow streets trimmed with double yellow lines.

I sat on the patio of the tea shop. Since I was trailing seaweed and a plastic bag full of rattling molluscs, I had no trouble getting a table to myself. I had a cup of tea and a teacake, and a very sympathetic proprietor sold me some brown bread and butter and a can of Lassie Meaty Chunks which all looked very unappetising when put on the same bill.

I sat looking out to sea. Some fishing boats and lobster nets were attractively framed in a portico. Some of those colourful flowers which I once knew the first two syllables of were sitting sweetly in hanging baskets.

'What are those flowers called?' I asked the waitress.

'Er . . . don't know,' she said, 'Poly something, I got them in Falmouth.'

That was it! Polysomething. I wrote it down.

That night I found a sequestered spot called Downas Cove. It was wildest Cornwall. At least two miles from the nearest public telephone. A clear cold stream ran to a thin beach where waves broke heavily over rocks. All around was an abundant supply of stinging nettles. I picked about a pound, then pitched the tent by the stream on a made-to-measure patch of turf.

'Check all your specimens are alive immediately before cooking them,' warned Richard Mabey. I prodded my collection individually. They all but one flinched enough to convince me. The inactive one could, of course, have been an old campaigner and been feigning death to escape the pot, but I decided not to risk it and chucked it out. The rest I put on to boil, adding the seaweed bit by bit.

This is the life, I thought: nice valley to sleep in; warm evening; winkles, limpets and seaweed on the boil, stinging nettles to follow, they don't know what they're missing back home. I sat stirring the stew with one hand and holding Richard Mabey in the other. 'Be warned,' he said, 'limpets can be very tough and may need considerable further simmering' – and he should know, the man would eat anything: water lilies, thistles, trees – dinner round his house would be a real experience.

'Another slice of beech log, Mark?'

'Just a small one, please Richard. Want to leave room for some of that privet mousse'.

The pot boiled for half an hour. Towards the end I threw in the stinging nettles, then drained it all and peered tentatively inside. It looked very dark in there, dark and unfriendly. I plucked a winkle out and with a picker crudely fashioned from a safety pin, I dragged the little Littorina Littorea out of its shell. It looked like something you might find in your handkerchief. I decided to give it the acid test and offer it to Boogie, the dog who once ate five house plants in the time it takes to go to the off licence; the dog who once ate a Peter Gabriel album; the dog who frequently eats the Evening Standard.

He sniffed the winkle and recoiled: 'I wouldn't eat that if I was you.'

The limpets had come away from their shells and didn't require the skills of micro-surgery the winkles did. I stabbed one with a fork and the fork bounced out of my hand. Acting on information gained over twenty-nine years of self-preservation, my stomach sent frantic messages of the 'do not put this anywhere near the mouth,' variety, to my brain. Only by disguising the

limpet in a ball of bread could I summon up the courage
to bite into it. It was like eating an old tennis shoe.

The seaweed had the flavour of an iron bar, and the
nettles had disintegrated into a sludge. I tried a mouthful;
it was full of sand – the rest I threw in the bushes. Boogie's
bowl of Lassie Meaty Chunks looked delicious by
comparison. He was chomping blissfully away and a
horrible thought entered my head which, I'm pleased to
say, I quickly dismissed.

I sat in the tent and read *Seven Years In Tibet*. Heinrich
Harrer had by now established himself amongst the better
circles in Lhasa. The Dalai Lama's mother was inviting
him round to forty-course meals. He was throwing his
own parties. He'd even opened the first Tibetan tennis
club. I put the book away. The man made me feel a
failure.

Sensing my depression, Boogie came and sat by me and
we conversed until it grew dark. We covered a wide range
of topics: the films of Lassie, whether or not there was
reincarnation for dogs, and Boogie's chances of winning
anything at Crufts that year. Then we listed our top ten
favourite TV shows, who we'd have round to dinner if
we could invite anyone, living or dead, and every player
in the great Spurs double side of '61. Then I went outside
and brushed my teeth and counted the stars, after which
I took my socks off and counted my toes and then climbed
into bed and counted the sides of the tent, which tonight
was more or less hexagonal. Finally I put some Nivea on
my nose and went to sleep. That night I dreamt I was
Spurs' goalkeeper. It was the Cup Final. The score was
nil nil. Thirty seconds to go and I was facing a penalty.
The ball flew to my left. I was about to make a lunge for
it when the Person from Porlock appeared and detained
me on a trivial business matter. I pushed him aside and
he turned into a giant limpet, shaped like a phallus and

wearing a QPR scarf. In the middle of the pitch I could see my polygonal tent. I dived into it just as everything went black and a munching began.

I was woken by a knocking on the tent pole and a Home Counties accent. 'Morning,' it said.

I looked at my watch: 3.30. I was on the coast path in wildest Cornwall at least two miles from the nearest public telephone and someone was knocking at my door.

'Going to be a lovely day,' said the Home Counties voice, 'perfect for a hike. It's about thirteen degrees Celsius with a south westerly force . . . leaves rustling, feel wind on face, waves short with glassy appearance but not breaking . . . force two, I'd say.'

I stumbled to the tent flap, zipped it open and stuck my head out. There stood Ronnie Corbett.

'Hello,' he beamed.

I gawked at him in disbelief. My stomach ached. I had the feeling I looked terrible.

'You look terrible,' he said.

'Been eating molluscs,' I told him.

He nodded knowingly, and from one of the array of pockets and pouches in his anorak, he pulled a box of tablets. I took one and swallowed it without question.

'Great day for hiking. Wind picking up though. Probably force . . . leaves and twigs in motion, large wavelets beginning to break, scattered white horses . . . force three now. Want to hear the shipping forecast?'

He swung his bulging rucksack from his shoulders. It hit the ground with a metallic crash and he began to burrow into its myriad compartments. Zippers and poppers went flying as he dug out mosquito repellent, a bicycle pump, a sewing box, an umbrella, a mouth organ, a copy of the TV Times and finally, from the third pocket along, second row down, under the Kilimanjaro motif, a transistor radio.

He tuned to the BBC. An authoritative voice announced it was five fifty-five and the shipping forecast would follow. And what a forecast! There were none of your scattered showers or sunny spells here. This was proper weather, a good blast of Met. Office rhetoric consisting of force sevens off Finisterre, freezing fog off Rockall and South Westerlies blowing in from Biscay. It was all imminent or variable becoming severe and was undoubtedly read by a weatherman with a full beard, crouched over his microphone in oilskins and sou'wester while his producer threw buckets of cold water and live fish over him.

Our zone was Plymouth and it sounded marginally less terrifying than the majority: a mere light to moderate, variable force three to four.

'See,' said Ronnie Corbett, tucking his transistor back into his trouser leg, 'perfect day for hiking.' No doubt he'd have reacted the same to a hurricane warning.

He asked me where I was headed and when I told him he nodded and looked at me meaningfully: 'Trying to sort yourself out, I suppose? Find yourself, eh? Discover the real you?'

I said: 'I don't suppose you've got a rivet gun on you by any chance. The pins in my rucksack keep falling out.'

'Rivet gun?' he said, taken aback, 'no; no, sorry. Didn't think to pack a rivet gun. Silly really.'

He'd started in Plymouth, he said, and was heading for Land's End: 'I work for a shoe shop chain,' he added, as if that explained everything. I asked him what the path to Falmouth was like and he unfolded his ordnance survey map and showed me I'd have to cross a number of estuaries, some with ferries, some without, the latter requiring detours inland. At this point the worst guard dog in the West Country poked his sleepy head out of the tent.

'Ah, I suppose you're inseparable travelling companions, eh? Do everything together, right? He probably understands every word you say, doesn't he?'

I told him Boogie wasn't even my dog and he shook his head and intimated what a puzzling couple we were. I wanted to ask him if he was ever mistaken for Ronnie Corbett, but he suddenly seemed keen to get going.

'Wind picked up again,' he said, taking out a bar of Kendall Mint Cake from a pouch halfway down his trousers leg. 'Probably force . . . moderate waves, frequent white horses . . . force four now.' Then he consulted the compass that hung around his neck and headed off westwards, narrowly missing the cliff edge.

My first obstacle of the morning was Gillen Creek. My guide book told me I'd be able to wade across if the tide was right, but when I got there it was clearly wrong. I scratched my head for a while then turned to the trees behind me where two elderly men were chopping wood. They were repairing a gate. Their black and orange jackets suggested they were council workers. The words South Cornwall Urban District Council on their backs confirmed it.

They both made a fuss of Boogie and when they discovered we were heading for Falmouth and needed to cross the creek, they immediately downed tools, convinced I was in some sort of race and that delay would be disastrous. They conferred briefly in some jaw-straining dialect and then told me I shouldn't try to cross the creek here. I'd do better to turn inland to Manaccan, then make for Helford and cross the whole estuary via the ferry.

'How do I get to Manaccan?' I asked.

'What!?' said one of them, taking his hat off, 'You don't know even know where Manaccan is!?' He shook his head in disbelief. Things were worse than he thought. He replaced his hat and launched himself into directions.

I can remember every feature of that man's face: the number of fillings he had, the number of hairs up his nose, the delta-like pattern of veins that mapped his cheeks and the way his eyebrows danced making his hat wobble as he spoke. As for the directions he gave me, I couldn't recall one.

As I followed the coastline I often felt the urge to see what sort of country lay inland. The path veered away from the coast occasionally, but I was rarely out of range of the sea breeze and I was beginning to feel I was only seeing the frilly edge of Cornwall, particularly on these southern shores.

Now however, as I followed the creek inland, the smell of fresh water overpowered the salt and the scream of the gulls abated. The problem was, without the sea to steer by, my navigation suffered; I just followed a leafy lane to wherever it took me. Unfortunately, when I arrived at where it took me I still didn't know where I was and when a man on a bicycle appeared, I made a grab for him.

'Which way to Manaccan?' I shouted. The cyclist pivoted on his saddle and fought for his balance, then pointed up in the air and said: 'Straight on.' Sure enough, ten minutes later, up a hill and through some trees, was Manaccan, and a scene you could only describe as delightful: a village square, a pub, a post office, a blacksmith, a village church and, sitting on the steps, a village cove, at least a hundred and fifty years old and clutching a packet of Silk Cut.

'Which way to Helford?' I called out, disturbing his reverie. He lifted his head, grunted, looked in both directions and pointed with his stick to the one on the right. 'Blarum!' he said, which could have meant go down the lane, take the left fork, over a couple of stiles, over a stream, past a sewage works and you can't miss it, or alternatively it could have meant . . . blarum!

'Blarum!' I replied and gave a wave of thanks.

I followed a meandering path through more woods, until I came to a fork and chose left. The path began to curve, took me over a couple of stiles and a stream, past a sewage works and up a hill, and into a village strangely familiar, with a square, a pub, a post office, a blacksmith and a village church and, there on the steps, a village elder. The scene was charming, which just goes to show there is a way of describing Manaccan other than delightful.

'Which way to Helford?' I asked the same dateless fellow with the low tar cigarettes, and he lifted his head, looked in both directions and pointed to the one on the right, as before, and said: 'Blarum!' which could have meant, go down the lane, take the right fork, over a couple of stiles, over a stream, past a rusting burnt-out Volkswagen and you can't miss it, or alternatively, it could have meant . . . blarum!

'Blarum!' I said, and waved and thanked him again and strode off down the meandering path through the woods, until I came to the fork, where I turned right and climbed over a couple of stiles and across a stream, then past the rusting, burnt-out Volkswagen, until the path began to curve and climb and there was a very familiar village with a square and a pub, a post office, a blacksmith and a village church and, sitting on the steps an old man who'd aged considerably even in the short time I'd known him. The scene could be described as monotonous, which just goes to show there are many ways to describe Manaccan if you visit the place often enough.

'Blarum! Blarum!' said the old-timer and pointed his stick making it clear he'd run me through if I asked again.

I waved and nodded and thanked him and then walked

off in the opposite direction. 'Blarum! Blarum' I heard him calling, then starting to choke on his dog end and begin a coughing fit that had all the signs of being his last.

Half an hour later I reached Helford and sat in the ferry café with a cup of tea and some shortcake. A man carrying a petrol can told me the next ferry would be in twenty minutes. I phewed with relief. I wanted to get back to the coast quickly. I wasn't equipped to handle the rigours of the interior.

That night we reached Penance Point, with Pendennis Castle in silhouette across the bay and Falmouth round the next headland.

I slipped smoothly into my camping-by-numbers-drill: roll out tent, stake to ground using four metal pegs; find eight sticks with barbed ends to act as stakes for lost metal equivalents. Crawl into tent, make utter fool of self trying to locate holes for poles. Throw fly-sheet over and stand back to admire bizarre construction from Cubist school. Put water onto boil, open can of dog food, open can of soup, feed dog food to dog, put soup into pan, taking care not to get cans mixed up. Make tea, drink soup, eat loaf of bread, admire view of sunset – if available – while cleaning teeth. Take socks off and place at end of tent furthest from nose, do same with dog. Climb into sleeping bag, realise last pee is needed, climb out of sleeping bag, pee all over Cornwall, climb back into bag, read page of *Seven Years In Tibet* and fall asleep. Wake as Boogie farts blissfully.

That night, I'd reached the putting soup into pan stage when a family came strolling up the coastal path: mum, dad, two kids and a red setter going bound, bound, bound everywhere. So adept had I now become at the art of camouflage that they didn't see me until they were tripping over my guy ropes.

'Good evening,' I said, 'Come in, make yourself at home, soup will be ready in a minute.'

They started. The children buried themselves in their mother's skirt. The red setter did some more bounding which Boogie, knowing that all red setters are mentally handicapped, ignored. And then the whole family backed away and made an unsubtle detour round me. There was much whispering and I heard the word tramp mentioned once or twice.

The air was warm and still, the ground soft, and I should have slept perfectly that night. The tent was pitched on a slope of sorts but surely, I thought, not at an angle acute enough to matter. Unfortunately, gravity didn't agree with me. I spent all that night crawling up to the top of the tent and then waking up in a bundle at the bottom again, cuddling Boogie. Pathetic really. If I was a tramp I was a lousy one.

6. South Cornwall: the slow bit

Falmouth looked like the largest town we'd come to, and to celebrate our arrival I decided to have a wash.

The extent of my bathroom activities had been largely governed by the facilities available in the public conveniences en route. Although, on the whole, Cornish Gentlemen's were a credit to the county. A far cry for example from the comforts on offer in the hut marked Men under the railway bridge outside Finsbury Park station.

The little number which I chose for my early morning ablutions in Falmouth was an unpretentious pebble-dashed affair with a well-trimmed box hedge and standard council issue railings bordering a crazy paving path to the entrance. Inside, the paintwork was a tropical blue; the floor, a tropical concrete with a seashell grain. Along the north wall stood a row of six vitreous china urinals, well sluiced and bearing the Twyford crest. Opposite them, four coin-operated doors in varnished plywood, each leading to a fully-fitted cubicle with sumptuous wooden seating and equipped with a spare packet of Bronco. The feature of the west wall was a functional but lovingly cared-for hand basin with water supplied at the temperature of the bather's choice by a trusty Ascot. A towel dispenser hung nearby, and, above, a single frosted window, which cast distorted shafts of seven a.m. sunlight on an Erotica machine bearing the slogan: Plymouth three Rotherham nil, all right!

I stripped off and stuck my feet into a basin of hot water, then refilled it and did my other end. As I cleaned my teeth in the mirror, a faintly furry face stared back. My beard would surely pullulate soon. The Chris Bonington look was the one I was aiming for. When I reached Dorset I wanted blackbirds to be nesting in the thing.

The rest of my appearance grew more bizarre daily. The Penzance launderette had made my T-shirt run and now all my clothes were stained a blotchy red. My shorts were fraying, my hair slicked back vampire style, and my socks of different colours, one green, one white, not I should add out of any respect for fashion, but simply because my feet had decided that that was the most comfortable combination. I looked like a rambling punk from Transylvania and emerging from the Gents I wondered if Falmouth was quite ready for me. In the car park opposite, Boogie had made friends with a well-groomed labrador at the end of which was a well-groomed woman in tight skirt and high heels. She took a step back as I approached, but I breathed Signal all over her and she relaxed a little and directed me into town.

It was Falmouth's rush hour. Traffic clogged the streets.

A lollypop lady saw us across the road with a gang of school girls. They giggled when they saw me. 'Nice legs shame about the face,' said one. Bitch.

What I wanted in Falmouth was an ironmonger. I needed some device to fix my flagging rucksack. In·one place I was told spring clips would do the job and was sold a bagful. It was the kind of shop that doubled as a camping centre. In the window was an erected tent, a similar model to mine. Somehow they'd managed to assemble it with the poles on the outside and the canvas suspended beneath. I asked the assistant to explain:

'Ah, yeah, well, you see, you've got the FI8b model, whereas this is a TPR6. We only stock FI8bs with a P2 attachment, so I wouldn't be able to help you. 'Course, you could always have a look at the Wanderer 888. Have you got a Dolomite fly-sheet or the ordinary Saskatchewan?' I told him not to bother. One thing this journey had taught me was there's a lot more to being an ironmonger than meets the eye.

We went down to the harbour and waited for the boat to take us across to Place and the resumption of the path. Boogie sat next to one of those Guide Dogs For the Blind plaster casts. They had similar builds, although the model looked more intelligent. Passers-by smiled and pointed. One man took out a camera and lined up a shot. I smiled and posed and he asked me if I'd mind moving out of the way.

The ferry was a smart, highly polished affair, as were the young cabin crew. I asked one for a ticket to Place but there was no such route, he said; boats only went to St Mawes, which left me with another channel to cross. I sat down and sulked. A rivet popped from my rucksack and plopped into the harbour. I replaced it with a spring clip. That too popped off. I replaced it with a matchstick.

The ferry threaded its way ever so, ever so carefully

through the millions of pounds' worth of yachts anchored in Carrick Roads. The rigging played tunes in the breeze, the waves slapped against the hull and, as we pulled away, Falmouth appeared in perspective, a long, narrow town stretched along the waterfront and really very attractive.

Also very attractive was the girl leaning against a cabin door practising to be Brigitte Bardot. She was sixteen going on twenty-five and had perfected the art of eating an ice cream and pouting at the same time. Her other hand hung from her belt and her hair blew across her face in a manner which caused every member of the crew to become starry-eyed and imagine the boat was sinking and that he was saving her. Just within reach sat the girl's parents. Boys had undoubtedly been knocking on their door since their daughter was ten years old and now they seemed resigned to the fact they'd produced a sex symbol. They just read the papers and tried to look the other way.

We reached St Mawes and I strolled around the water-front trying to beg a lift over to Place. The alternative was a ten-mile hike inland, which seemed ridiculous when I could see the start of the coast path a few hundred yards across the water. I explained myself plaintively to the harbour-master and he said: 'Ask that bloke in the Wellingtons, in the old fibre glass; he's a pleasant enough sort.'

Actually, he was a cantankerous, belligerent, obnoxious, bellicose and rather unpleasant sort: 'Who do you think I am? I'm not here just to ferry people about all day, you know. I've got work to do. Bloody tourists. I tell you, if I had a penny for every person who's asked me to ferry them across to Place I'd be a millionaire.'

The temptation, of course, was to ask him why then he didn't charge a penny a trip, but I chose diplomacy:

'Sorry,' I said, 'The harbour-master said you might take me over, that's all.'

'Did he!? Did he!? Did he, now!? . . . Huh! . . . Well, all right then, just this once.'

Boogie and I jumped in and he started the outboard with a piece of string. His boat was like a lawn mower only not so watertight.

'How much?' I said as we climbed out in Place, but he waved his arm dismissively and told me to keep my money and to get lost and not waste his time because he had a living to make

Three weeks out, and a diurnal pattern was beginning to emerge. I wake and get moving at three thirty each morning, stopping for breakfast when I was warmed up. During the morning we'd walk about ten miles until midday when we'd stop in some suitable town or village and frequently embarrass ourselves with the amount we'd eat. Whole loaves and lettuces and boxes of Winalot would disappear, accompanied by pasties and slabs of cheese, tomatoes, apples, chocolate and pints of milk.

After that we'd stop for lunch and then relax during the afternoon with a variety of activities. Boogie's favourites were seeing how long he could stare at the sun without going blind, or else chasing flies. Me, I was beginning to take a healthy interest in rubbish.

I've always enjoyed beachcombing. You never know what you're going to find: a lump of the Armada one day, a bit of orange peel the next. Most of what I was finding on these shores, however, was plastic bottles.

I'd noticed litter along the strandline throughout Cornwall and just assumed it to be the usual picnickers' debris. But picnickers don't bring bottles of shampoo and washing up liquid down to the beach with them; at least they don't bring Russian or Spanish brands, but that's what these were: pieces of international rubbish, obviously thrown overboard from ships steaming along this marine motorway. I quickly learnt the Polish for Head and Shoulders, and experienced the thrill of finding my first bottle of Brazilian disinfectant. Actually, there was something exotic about it. It was jetsam from a land of sun-kissed beaches and clean drains. I cherished the thought of a Brazilian walking his dog along the strand in Rio, and clutching with equal fascination an empty bottle of Harpic.

We'd begin walking again in the late afternoon, buying food in the last village of the day, then keep going into the evening; they were growing longer and warmer now and were good times to walk, and we'd not camp until the sun had but an hour left in the sky.

The day we passed through Falmouth, that last village was Portloe. Charming, I noted in my diary later, noting also that, as had happened with the sky, the search for adjectives to suitably describe fishing villages was putting a strain on my vocabulary: delightful, cute, enchanting, idyllic, picturesque, exquisite, nice, I'd used them all. I decided to adapt the Beaufort Scale of wind speeds and apply it to charm. Twelve different levels, registering ferocity of enchantment.

Portloe was about a force six. A fish factory converted into a holiday home and a local antediluvian sitting on a wall, ruminating, were its main strengths, although it lost points on its complete lack of an antique shop called The Spinning Wheel.

I walked up the main street and quickly found the post office stores. Since St Mawes I'd trekked over St Anthony's Head, spent the afternoon among the coves of St Nares Head and now I was striding towards Dodman Point to complete my hat-trick of promontories for the day. I was tired and I was weathered, but above all I was hungry.

'Can of mushroom soup and a can of Kennomeat, please,' I said to the lady behind the grill. She clasped her hands and shook her head. I scanned the shelves behind her. If I'd wanted a TV licence I'd have been all right, but soup and Kennomeat, in fact sustenance of any sort, was right out.

'But I was told you sold provisions here,' I said; the thought of another night on limpets and nettles injecting a hint of desperation into my tone.

Again she clasped her hands and shook her head. I decided on a more hysterical approach.

'But, but, but, look at my poor dog, he's been walking all day and he's starving.'

Her face crumpled as Boogie laid his head on the counter and, sensing the gravity of the situation, drew from his vast wardrobe of expressions the 'been walking all day and now starving,' mask.

Then the woman had a brainwave. She'd phone her sister who kept a small store in Port Holland, the next village along the coast. She'd stay open for me until six, she said. It was two miles. I had half an hour. It was going to be close.

If Heinrich Harrer had found himself in a similar situation there'd have been none of this panic, of course. He'd simply have eaten his dog. As I strode along the cliffs I tried to banish the thought. I mean, what could I tell Sean – I ate his dog because the post office was shut. Hardly gallant. It wasn't as if Boogie was a particularly tasty looking dish, anyway. He was stringy, probably tough and sinewy, all dark meat, the kind of dog Amundsen would have left on the side of his plate. Mind you he might taste better if I barbecued him, put him on a spit over a driftwood fire. Hadn't I seen a Chinese recipe for cooking dogs, recently? 'How to Wok Your Pekinese,' or something.

I wondered if he'd put up a fight. I mean, how would I do the dastardly deed? Push him off a cliff; maybe just club him, or stab him with a tent pole; better still run one through him, then he'd be all ready to go on the spit. It wasn't that I didn't appreciate the sacrifice, but there was no room for sentimentality. This was the ultimate altruistic act for a dog, and I should make sure I made the most of the gesture. I'd try and make him last over a few days. Eat him leg by leg, in a goulash on Wednesday, curry on Thursday, dog supreme on Friday, and in sandwiches or cold with cranberry sauce and salad over the weekend when I didn't want to have to cook. I was contemplating a bowl of thin but nourishing dog soup, when Port Holland came into view: a row of cottages, a telephone kiosk and the stores.

The sister was waiting for us. She stroked Boogie affectionately, told him he needn't have worried. She wouldn't have let him go hungry, then offered him a choice of Pal, Chappie or Lassie Meaty Chunks. She checked he had enough milk and biscuit for the morning and before she closed up she even sold me a can of soup.

We pressed on towards the Dodman. In the distance a lone figure strode towards us; the path bringing us inevitably together. I had about five minutes to think of something to say to him. But something original for Heaven's sake. I was getting tired of saying 'hello there' or 'nice day for it,' or 'morning,' 'afternoon,' 'evening' or 'can you direct me to the nearest ironmongers, please.' I wanted to say something different. I could even be someone different. This fellow knew nothing about me. I should celebrate my anonymity. I could be Bjorn Gullfoss, Icelandic tourist. I could be Sir Dorian Putney, eminent botanist and Olympic hurdler. I could be Stig Wilson, bass guitarist with the Cruds. Charlie Expo, mime artist, Sid Barrington, International jewel thief. I could even be Nigel Blund, tobacconist and newsagent, 21 Elm Ave, Basingstoke.

The man grew closer. Our paths crossed.

'Evening.'

'Evening.'

I camped in a hollow that night, where the views to the east stretched for miles along a chain of bays and headlands. The sky was clear and crammed with stars; the weather was turning, and this time for the better. Suddenly, in the southern skies, a UFO burst across the night. It left a brief silver trail and then vanished. Actually, it might have been a shooting star. It didn't hover or make strange noises or anything. Come to think of it, it could have been an aeroplane, or maybe just my imagination. Yeah, that was probably it. Whatever, I made a note of it in my diary, also noting that I'd been in Cornwall two weeks now and eaten thirteen pasties.

My weather forecasting was improving. Next day, not a cloud in the sky; the sea and the heavens merged into one shade of blue and after the rains of the previous week the fields were virescent. The dandelions, I noticed, were particularly yellow that morning.

I sat on the quayside in Gorran Haven and had some Weetabix. A couple appeared wearing rucksacks and hiking boots. They were German. The man spoke English, the woman didn't, so she sat and tried to work out the offer on the back of my cereal packet while he told me how they came from Düsseldorf and that they thought England was prepossessing: Kent was prepossessing. Yorkshire, simply prepossessing. Cotswolds, no other word for them but prepossessing. He knew England better than I did. Mind you I had been to Düsseldorf. I told him so and that I'd found it . . . well . . . prepossessing. He laughed. I laughed. He translated and his wife laughed. Then his eyes narrowed and he wanted to know why, if I'd been to Düsseldorf, didn't I have a sticker on my rucksack saying so.

It was only on the rare occasions I took my shirt off that I realised the limits of my suntan. My face, arms, and, to a lesser extent, legs, looked as though they'd just spent four weeks in the Caribbean. My torso, however, suggested I'd spent the last four years in the cupboard under the stairs. If I was hoping in any way seriously to promote the rugged image, I had some heavy-duty sunbathing to do.

With a protective pebble balanced on my nose I lay flat out on the grass and conjured with the lyrics of my song. I'd dumped the sea shanty idea – not commercial enough. Instead, I was concentrating on the theme of UFOs, shooting stars and things in general that fly about in space and make lots of money. I'd play some tapes backwards and compile a load of weird sound effects, then come up with some interstellar love story about a time traveller from Alpha Centauri destined to wander the galaxy. He breaks down somewhere between Padstow and Harlyn Bay. He likes it there, finds a job, settles down and falls in love with a local girl, but she won't go out with him because he's green and can unscrew his head. Usual sort of science fiction stuff. A shuffling in the grass interrupted me. I spun round to see a quartet of cattle, lined up like a Tamla Motown group and using Boogie as a microphone.

After our previous altercation with the beasts of Hartland Point, I was very wary of cattle, particularly so in this case when, on closer examination, I noticed an acute shortage of udders. From this I deduced they were male, although even further study revealed that to all intents and purposes they were neutral.

My pulse slowed. They were harmless, as Boogie had already discovered. He sniffed them, they sniffed him. He licked the nose of the lead singer who responded by rolling out a great pink and grey oral organ and slapping it heavily on Boogie's head like a wet vest. I hurriedly took out my pad and tried to sketch the scene. I'd never really looked at cows close-up before. They had such sad, drawn faces with eyes black and moist, and ringed with flies. Each had a number clipped to his ear on a coloured tag and their flanks were caked in dried mud.

They were also large and my problems with scale persisted. My impressions started off with life-size heads then tapered off into really thin animals with pointed behinds as·I ran out of paper. Cows, like seagulls, I needed to practise.

And talking of seagulls, I was about to enter Seagull City, otherwise known as Mevagissey. Here the birds swooped down the alleyways in squadrons like something Barnes Wallis had designed, dropping their bombs with a white splat on the pavement. Fortunately, these didn't bounce, but in a place like this, it was only a matter of time before one was hit.

And now I realised that scabby brown and white birds were in fact, the young of the ubiquitous grey gulls. The adults had a red spot on their yellow beaks which, as spring turned into summer, began to appear on the young. They had only to lose their motley feathers and some of their awkwardness and they'd blossom into fully fledged scavengers. And in Mevagissey these birds really meant business. They weren't timid in the least. Like Trafalgar Square pigeons, gangs of them would strut up and down the waterfront with their hands in their pockets, chewing gum and demanding titbits or else. They knew if you lived round here you could only get fat while the season lasted.

I bought some cockles and whelks from a stall, just to see what they tasted like properly prepared. These came in a polystyrene tray complete with a little red fork and napkin, and all the trimmings: lemon juice, vinegar, black pepper and salad cream. I popped a cockle in my mouth. It still tasted disgusting.

But eating molluscs was obviously the virile thing to do. Whilst all the girls squealed and squirmed at the very thought of swallowing anything as disgusting as a whelk, the boys were having competitions: 'Last one to eat fifty is a poof', and that sort of thing. In fact Mevagissey was a fine example of how the fishing industry and tourism could be successfully merged. There were many working boats in the harbour, but all those that could, took tourists out on fishing trips. The fishermen were far more likely to be asked to pose for photos by their boats, than for a list of what fish they had for sale.

Rather different was tourism's relationship with the china clay industry whose territory we were now about to enter. The extraction of china clay from the area just north of St Austell coincided with the tin and copper boom of the eighteenth and nineteenth century, but, unlike its more fashionable contemporaries, clay survived the industrial depressions, its traditional use in the manufacture of porcelain, superceded by its rôle in the production of toothpaste and fertiliser and an assortment of goods which may not look so good when displayed on a mantlepiece, but have ensured that the industry has flourished over the years.

No clay was ever mined from coastal areas, but the ports along the shores of St Austell Bay were vital for the export of the raw material. They still are and they haven't felt obligated to prettify themselves for tourism. Not that this has bothered the tourists. The eight-mile stretch of coast east of Mevagissey is an incongruous collection of dusty harbours, processing plants and oblivious caravan sites.

Pentewan and Charlestown are both pretty ports. The former is silted up now, choked by the very stuff which gave it life, but the latter, with its sea water lock and ghostly complexion, is still very much in business. Two boats a week manage to navigate the right-angled turn into the harbour and fill up with clay from the ancient shoots that stand on the quayside.

But these two were and are small concerns compared to the English China Clay processing plant in Par where the bulk of the exporting is done. This is an impressively pale industrial zone comprising steaming chimneytops, settling tanks, dockyards, railways, dumper trucks and giant sheds, all neatly slotted between the Cornish Leisure Centre and the Par Sands Caravan Park.

We could see it from a long way off as we walked across the adjoining golf course. A thin white film of dust vegetation and as we turned into an enclosed walkway encircling the works, Securicor signs appeared and the path became garnished with dog dirt.

I couldn't believe that people would come on holiday here but at the far side of the plant was a caravan site full of campers from all nations. They stared out of their caravan windows or else lay outside and tried to sunbathe, although with the dust in the air, they most likely went back inside paler. It was a bleak scene of washing lines and faded beach huts and when I saw a village tucked into the cliffs on the other side of the bay, I put my head down and walked towards it at a pace.

The village was Polkerris and arriving there after the hike from Mevagissey was like walking out of the fog. It was a charming force seven, with old pilchard cellars and an attractive stone harbour wall. A pub, the Rashleigh Arms, was its communal point, but 'No Dogs Allowed' ordered a sign on the door. Boogie refuses to go in anywhere he's banned, so I placated him with a bowl of milk and left him outside to guard my rucksack.

The pub was a rendezvous for yachting sorts. Like the one in Padstow there were pictures of ships and all things nautical hanging on the walls. Unlike the one in Padstow the customers were talking about boats, although that's just as boring as talking about cars to someone who knows nothing about them, and besides I was far more interested in the vaguely familiar noises coming from the restaurant in the background. They were the sounds of people in clean socks talking to friends and eating things that weren't pasties or soup.

I had a drink and the landlord bought me a second. He asked where I'd walked from, and when I told him of my journey through the north and my quest for Poole Harbour and the species of my travelling companion, he said he knew of a producer at TV South West who was always on the lookout for human interest stories and if I phoned him he'd surely come out on the cliffs and make a film of me: a man and his faithful dog walking five hundred miles of British coastline would, he reckoned, make irresistible television.

Outside my faithful dog was being anything but irresistible. He'd deserted his post and was sitting on the beach, legs at an impossible angle, licking his pudenda. A horrible sight and hardly TV South West material, but it couldn't spoil the lovely evening. The sun was sinking behind St Austell and the cliffs were that dreamy grey green shade of dusk. I had a swim off the harbour wall and then found a low cliff and a lone tree to pitch a tent on and under. Since seeing that model in the shop in Falmouth, I'd experimented with one or two poles on the outside of the canvas, but it still looked like a deflated cake when erected. I was beginning to think I hadn't got all the bits with me. Either that or I'd got too many.

That night a knocking sound woke me. I checked my watch: 3.30. I thought of Ronnie Corbett: surely not?

Maybe it was a badger. Maybe it was burglars. I banged back, hoping it would go away. It didn't.

At the bottom of the tent, nose up his bum, slept my irresistible dog. I woke him and unzipped the tent flap in the hope he'd charge out all terror and teeth and have done with whatever was out there. Some hope. I pulled on my trousers. 'I'm just going outside and I may be some time,' I said to him. He didn't flinch.

The wind had picked up and was sending a branch of the tree slapping against the tent, that was all it was. I sat on the grass and smoked the remains of a thin cigar I'd bought in the pub. Across the bay the lights of the processing plant glowed red and white, and a few metallic clunks drifted across the water. Behind, the white clay mountains of St Austell were luminous under the clear sky. Looking up I saw the Plough and I thought how it didn't look like a plough at all. In fact, it better resembled a saucepan. So why didn't they call it the Saucepan? Probably for some astronomical reason far too complicated for laymen like myself to ever understand; or maybe naming constellations after kitchenware was considered demeaning. Fascinating, the stars are.

Higher in the sky was the moon, just a fingernail, but waxing now. I thought back to that first night in Minehead spent under a full and frosty corona and it seemed I'd covered continents since then.

I stubbed the cigar out resolutely. I had just decided that when this journey was completed I would donate my socks to the Royal Geographic Society.

The Gribbin is a proud old English headland, built in the days when they still knew how to build them. From aerial pictures it resembles a paw, a paw with its claws dug in the sea. Stuck on its top is a landmark for seafarers: a red and white beacon nearly a hundred feet high. In keeping with every other landmark for seafarers along this coast, irrespective of size or colour, Boogie cocked his leg on it and we continued.

Another lovely day and we marched with our heads up, up the Fowey estuary and into Fowey (pronounced Fowey).

I found a piazza furnished with flower tubs and benches and set about laying the table for breakfast. A elderly man sat down, the next contestant in 'Guess That Pedigree'.

'That your dog?'

'Yep.'

'Mongrel is he?'

'He's got some mongrel in him.'

The man shook his head. 'Looks like a pointer in there somewhere, to me. Course his ears are a bit small, and he's a bit on the skinny side; face is too square as well, and his colour's a bit dark. His tail's not right either, and he's generally smaller and his paws aren't splayed as they should be, but otherwise, yep, I'd say that's basically a pointer you've got there.'

'How do I get across the river to Polruan?' I asked.

'Ferry,' he said, and pointed to where there was no sign of a ferry.

'It'll be here soon,' he said. 'Goes every half hour.' I asked him if he'd watch my rucksack while I made a phone call.

Together with public conveniences, the other big cultural difference between London and Cornwall is the telephone boxes. In Cornwall they all work, and don't have pools of urine or vomit in them, nor jammed coin slots. I phoned TV South West and spoke to the aforementioned producer. I told him I'd been speaking to the landlord of the Rashleigh Arms in Polkerris who had mentioned how TVSW was always on the lookout for human-interest stories, and that I was walking the coastal footpath and that my cockney doggie was with me, and that we'd set out in Minehead and were heading for Poole Harbour, and that we were going to cover five hundred miles, and we were living off Kennomeat and limpets; and the producer said words to the effect of 'Big deal', and that's the story of my career in television. And Boogie's.

We crossed the river and spent the morning striding over wild, open country, taking detours down to swim. These were the finest beaches we'd seen, clear, clear water and slender curves of sand.

Even Boogie contemplated a dip. He stood on the shore and paddled for a while, but then found an empty bottle of Italian hair conditioner for problem hair and contented himself playing with that.

But this litter business was getting beyond a joke. It had gone from being interesting to being boring to being downright annoying. I'm sure it all happens quite innocently – Able Seaman Tar looks over the side of his boat and all he sees is miles and miles of blue briny surrounding him, and there he is with a bagful of rubbish, and he thinks: Hang on, just a minute, hold your horses, what's the point in storing this; I'm wasting valuable crude oil space, so he lobs it over the side. The problem is that while the sea will break down a large amount of refuse, it's stumped when it comes to nonbiodegradables. They'll float around the oceans forever, although, inevitably, they get washed up on some beach. Sure, there are more urgent pollution problems, litter in this respect will never irrevocably alter the environment, but it's thoughtless and it's an eyesore – like dumping your garbage in a park. It also shows what an inordinate amount of time sailors spend washing their hair and cleaning the bathroom.

The path continued through a great chunk of National Trust property. No roads came near the coast here and all was unspoilt. The sun shone, the sea sparkled, the birds

sang and the fields were full of buttercups and dais . . .
Bang! I'd walked smack into Polperro.

To begin with, Polperro looks like a totally authentic
fishing village. There's a neat harbour, a rim of whitewashed cottages, fishing paraphernalia is strewn around
the quays and there are no cars. On closer inspection
though, it becomes noticeable that not a lobster pot or a
scallop shell has been randomly placed, every fisherman
has a beard and smokes a pipe and every pub has a nauti-
cally inspired sign: the Three Pilchards, the Blue Peter,
the Fox and Halibut. And the further you venture into
the village, the thinner the charade wears; it is, in fact, a
Disneyland version of a Cornish fishing village and if you
treat it as such, then it's very effective.

Like St Ives, Polperro is a town popular amongst artists.
You can't turn a corner without tripping over some
Bohemian with an easel and a thermos flask. Not wanting
to be left out, I sat on the harbour wall and pulled out my
soup-stained sketch pad. I hadn't been there five minutes
before an entire art class joined me.

They sat down and held their thumbs out in front of
them and then drew, with great concentration. It was as
though they were doing portraits of their thumbs.

Soon a shadow fell on me. Behind my shoulder stood
a man in a white jacket and cavalry twills; he was trying
to peer at my sketch. I moved round so he couldn't see,
so he peered further over me.

'Wonderful light,' he said

'Wonderful.'

'Subtle.'

'Very subtle.'

'Yet somehow sharp.'

'Sharpish, yeah.'

'Reminds me of Seville.'

'Me too.'

'Those seagulls are big aren't they?'

I wanted to tell him that that was how I saw them, that seagulls to me symbolised strength and resilience, they weren't subservient to the sea like other creatures on the coastal plain. I'd drawn them big because they were big, bigger than the land, bigger than the sea. The trouble was these were really big.

What was wrong with my gulls? Perhaps it was a common fault. It's a little known fact, for example, that in Venice, despite the enormous feral cat population at large, the Italian Renaissance painters, the same artists who so wonderfully captured the architecture, canals and ethereal qualities of the water and light in the city, never came up with a decent drawing of a pussy between them.

I looked at the other artists' work. Their gulls seemed okay, they weren't bigger than the fishing boats or anything. Maybe I had seagull block.

I packed up and found a grocery store and sat outside until the lunch hour finished. The day was growing really hot. My nose was throbbing. I closed my right eye and squinted at it. Surely, it couldn't be peeling again? I closed my left eye and checked the other side. Yep! It looked like an old bill poster. I stared at it in the shop window, prodded it. It was exfoliating at a rate of once every three days. It really needed some sort of protection. One of those false-spectacles-nose-and-moustache combinations would do the trick.

A girl in a sunhat and shorts and with very brown legs had sat on the wall. She had a poodle in tow. People say that dogs tend to look like their masters or mistresses. The girl looked like Faye Dunaway, the poodle like Ernest Borgnine, which just goes to show that a lot of what people say is rubbish.

But, the poodle was a bitch and Boogie sidled over. Meanwhile I turned my attentions away from my nose and towards the girl in the sunhat and shorts. The next few minutes illustrated perfectly the subtle differences in mine and Boogie's approaches to the opposite sex.

Boogie is of the Cyrano de Bergerac school: 'Give me five minutes to explain away my looks, and I could charm the Queen of France.' So whilst I talked about the opening times of grocery stores, the advantages of wearing shorts and the sense in a sunhat Boogie preferred to smell every inch of the poodle's anatomy and then, foreplay over with, set about cementing the relationship. I hurriedly turned the conversation from sunhats to mating seasons.

'Is your dog on heat?' I asked.

'S'not my dog,' she said, and then three events occurred simultaneously: the grocery shop opened, Boogie leapt on the poodle, and from around the corner came a woman who looked very similar to Ernest Borgnine, showing that, in fact, there's a lot of truth in what people say.

'Pompom!' she shrieked (all right, I admit it, I can't remember the poodle's name) and Boogie gave a salacious shudder as Pompom scurried off to her mistress.

Boogie looked up at me: 'Typical bloody pedigree,' he said. 'Never on the first date.'

On the path to Looe there were many dogs similar in nature – though not in season – to Pompom; all pedigrees from good homes, who waddled and pranced along at heel, and glanced superciliously at Boogie, as if he was a teddy boy. They looked like dogs that had taken early retirement; overweight and lethargic, they were dragged out once a day to do their duties and then spent the rest of the time gazing out of bungalow windows at the sea view. All had studded identification collars and were on the latest style of lead: a spring loaded, retractable device which allowed the dog to run off to a specified distance and then, at the touch of a button, be catapulted back to base, throttled.

But if there's one animal synonymous with Looe then it's the shark. The Shark Fishing Club of Great Britain is based here and really you can only feel sorry for the creatures, such is the hammering they get. There's a sort of shark fever in the town. The boats that haven't been successful come back with glum faces, pretending they were after mackerel or something. Whereas, the successful crews chug back into harbour, whooping and punching the air. The great grey and red fish are hauled onto the quayside then hung on the scales. There's more whooping and punching the air and then nobody seems sure quite what to do next. They probably chuck the things in the bin, or chop them up and feed them to the cat.

Two boys sat on a bench smoking the same cigarette. I asked them if they knew anywhere secluded nearby where I could pitch a tent, but they said I'd get lynched by the police, the residents' committee, the neighbourhood security patrols and VAC (Vigilantes Against Campers) if I camped anywhere in Looe outside a campsite. So I continued to Millendreath Beach which was nothing but grey sands and a holiday village which had actually managed to look like a barracks with verandas.

Music pulsated in a big white complex near the beach. It was the camp social club and inside was a disco, dark and loud, with an impressive array of sound equipment, a rampant DJ, a food bar, a drinks bar and one of those ultra-violet lights that always make you wish you'd worn your white shirt. The only ingredient the place was short on was people, i.e., it was empty. A nervous man stood at the doorway, looking at his watch, a full book of tickets in one hand, an empty cash box in the other. He looked me over: I wasn't the sort of customer he wanted in his disco no matter how bad business was.

'Know anywhere round here I can camp?' I asked.

'No,' he said, making it clear that that was the only syllable I was going to get out of him.

Boogie and I turned inland until a track took us off the road into some woods. There, in the dying light, I erected the most pathetic excuse for a tent I'd ever seen. There was more room between the canvas and the fly-sheet than there was inside. Surrounding cowpats suggested this track was a thoroughfare for cattle, but I wasn't bothered any more. I now treated the countryside with the equanimity of a man who hadn't washed a lettuce since Ilfracombe. A herd of cattle running through the tent in the night wasn't going to worry me until it happened.

On the morning of 28 May, the campers and caravanners of Seaton were treated to a rare sight: Boogie immersed in water.

Having been on the move now for three weeks his grooming was unlikely to win him any lucrative advertising contracts. His underbelly played host to a jungle of parasites, mostly tics, which reappeared as fast as I could pull them off. His feet were the texture of Brillo pads and his coat a compost heap of birds' nests, brambles, soup, Kennomeat, mud and dung from any of the following: sheep, pig, cow, horse, hedgehog. You name it and he'd rolled in it. Never one to leave anywhere without a souvenir, as we left our campsite in the woods he opted for an early morning roll in a good-sized cowpat of nauseous viscosity. It was more than I could bear. It was time he had a bath.

Easier said than done.

Boogie's hatred of water is legendary. The only method devised to get him into a tub is too complicated to explain here but suffice to say it involves a straitjacket and both sets of neighbours.

I sat on Seaton's grey beach and stripped off to my shorts. Boogie sat on the sand, nose raised, tuned into some bacon frying in a distant caravan. Whistling nonchalantly, I strolled over to him and in a flash I'd grabbed a leg and was dragging him seawards. If I wanted him to go somewhere that badly, Boogie deduced, then chances were he didn't want to go there, and he dug his three remaining heels into the sand like anchors. Risking a mawling, I picked him up and struggled into the sea up to my knees. I dropped him and he was back on dry land without disturbing the water. I ran out and chased him over the beach. Lunging, I caught the end of a slippery tail and pulled myself up, then, gripping him in a bear hug I returned to the water. This time I didn't risk releasing him, I just rolled over and held him under. We rolled over again and he held me under. By now campers were appearing at the top of the beach clutching fried egg sandwiches and watching the contest. A woman trotted along the shoreline on horseback. 'Morning!' she called and beamed.

'Morning!' I replied, going under for the third time.

When the battle was over, I lay on the beach, panting. Boogie studied his body, now ninety per cent dog and only ten per cent muck, having been inversely proportioned ten minutes previously. At the water's edge a little boy stood wearing a rubber ring and contemplating the turbid slick that now floated on the surface.

Past Seaton the path was the road and we were on a hogsback: on one side the coast, on the other the arteries of Plymouth Sound. And the two couldn't have been more contrasting. The Sound sheltered man and beast, a restful scene of yachts and ships at anchor, and pasture sloping down to muddy creeks. The coast, on the other hand, had teeth. The entrance to the Sound was miles away and there was no harbour before. You could imagine boats in the days of sail running from the storm, desperately trying to reach ʰhe safety of Plymouth.

The verges were all freshly cut here and ʰead I could see a man at work with a scythe. He worked methodically and swung his edge deep, but somehow managed to leave all the heads on the flowers. His jacket hung on a gatepost nearby, a lunchbox poked out from a pocket.

'Nice day for it,' I said.

'Nice day for what?'

'Nice for . . . for scything.'

'S'all right.'

He took off a flat cap to reveal a head exactly the same shape underneath.

'See any snakes?' I asked him.

'See all sorts of things if you know where to look,' he said, a shade enigmatically. I didn't know it, but I was talking to Cornwall County Council's answer to Tonto.

Over the next fifteen minutes and without walking more than twenty yards from his jacket, he made me feel as though I'd walked from Minehead with my eyes closed. He pointed to some little holes in a bank – the work of bank voles, he said, which was one of the reasons why there'd been a tawny owl in the trees most of the day. On a gatepost were some bird droppings, ordinary black and white deposits to most of us, but the scratch marks on the wood identified a bird of prey. In some mud he found a footprint which apparently belonged to a fox. I said it looked just like a dog's but he pointed out the grained effect: foxes have hairs on their feet, dogs don't. He'd only been working on this stretch of road a couple of days, and yet he already knew each animal intimately.

I took out a melting Twix bar and we all shared it, I asked him if he knew the name of the little pink cliff flowers and he said;

'Ah, you mean Sea Pinks.'

I tried not to look disappointed and asked him what the name of the gulls with the black backs was.

'Great Black-backed Gulls, they're called.'

'I see,' I said, beginning to get suspicious, 'and how about the gulls with the grey backs?' If he said Great Grey-backed Gulls I was going to take back my Twix and leave.

'They could be either Common Gulls or Herring Gulls,' he said.

'They're everywhere.'

'They'll be Herring Gulls, then. You don't see many Common Gulls.'

Ahah! Natural history obviously wasn't as straightforward as it first appeared.

Plymouth was growing in the distance and there seemed to be an awful lot of it. However, a poor road link had meant that Rame Head had been bypassed, and Kingsand and Cawsand, the last two villages in Cornwall, were two of its least affected. There was one hotel between them and a couple of B&B signs but no other deference to tourism at all, not even a craft shop.

On the beach I met a boy scout sucking an ice lolly, and we skimmed stones together for a while. In fact, Kingsand and Cawsand seemed to be populated entirely by boy scouts sucki . .ce lollies. They had a camp in Edgcumbe Country Park, a suitably Ransomesque estate full of tunnels of vegetation and gnarled trees. They'd pitched a camouflaged marquee in a clearing and were spending two weeks cooking a billion sausages and practising their first aid. Union Jacks flew everywhere, the air was thick with the smell of burning lard and in the middle of it all stood a diminutive Akela stirring a big pot of beans, oblivious to the young boys performing tracheotomies on each other all around her.

As I left the camp arena, an angelic pre-teenager, dressed

in all the regalia and sporting a pair of impressively green knees, popped his head out from behind a bush. I gave him the scout salute. He returned it and then said, 'Got a light?' and produced a shiny red packet of Dunhill.

At the quayside in Cremyll I finally ran out of land and camped among bushes by the water's edge. Across the Sound, Devonport and Plymouth effused electricity, and searchlights swept across the naval dockyard. So many great voyagers had set sail from here: Cook, Darwin, Drake, The Pilgrim Fathers, now grey warships slipped through the black water; this city waited for news from the Falklands more than any other.

After a warming can of Cream of Tomato, I adjourned to the local pub, the Edgecumbe Arms, a convivial sort of place, where I met a man in a cravat. He was an introspective fellow, although the more he drank the more garrulous he became, and unfortunately the less sense he made. At one point he touched my arm and after a glance over his shoulder pledged his allegiance to Mebyon Kernow.

Before now, I'd only read about the Cornish devolutionary party. In wilder parts of the county when I'd broached the subject, people had looked at me strangely, narrowed their eyes and made highly emotive remarks like, 'What?' And yet here, with Devon in sight, a fractious little man in a cravat was campaigning for a return to the pure Cornish way of life (which basically meant a ban on carrots in pasties and the reintroduction of the Celtic language, plus an immigration policy involving the deportation of all foreign, i.e., non-Cornish, residents). As gently as I could I broke the news to him that if all but the indigenous folk were thrown out of the county, the residual population would hardly be large enough to get a cricket eleven together.

7. South Devon: the red bit

Heinz make twenty-two different flavours of soup, ranging from traditional favourites like Oxtail to tastes of the exotic such as Mulligatawny. I walked the first three hundred miles fuelled by a can a day. I knew the labels off by heart. I'd lie awake at night thinking of the cooks at work in their big kitchen in Hayes, Middx UB4 8AL pouring in the modified starch and the hydrolised protein, unaware of the all-important rôle they were playing in powering my legs towards Dorset.

By the time I reached Plymouth, however, I was sick to death of the stuff. I'd planned to mark this re-entry into Devon by washing my socks, but decided that could wait until Exeter. Instead, Plymouth would be where I'd shop for the gourmet evening I had in mind. Tonight would be an Italian night. I'd cook Spaghetti Carbonara and follow it with a Macedonia. I'd buy a bottle of wine. I'd buy Boogie a can of Pedigree Chum. I'd invite a few friends round. We'd make whoopee!

Plymouth was extensively bombed during the Second World War and is a bright, new city with wide streets and good acoustics: a clarinetist busked outside a department store and you could hear him blocks away.

It was a hot Saturday, short sleeves everywhere, making for a fine display of naval tattoos. I found an ironmonger (good selection here, better than Newquay's, in fact) and bough some replacement tent pegs, then entered the milieu of Tesco.

I never took my rucksack into shops with me. It tended to knock over pyramid displays and poke the eyes out of any shopper under seven foot. Instead I'd leave it outside with Boogie. Anyone foolish enough to attempt theft would be severely ignored.

As I perused the wine shelves I could see Boogie and rucksack through the window. He'd made friends with a Jack Russell, a chirpy little chappie, with a highly mobile tail and advanced myopia, and having smelt my rucksack, he proceeded to treat it in the manner dogs normally reserve for lamp-posts. I banged on the glass and shouted, attracting with ease the attention of five hundred shoppers. Then, thrusting my basket of groceries into the arms of the assistant manager, I barged through the queue at the checkout and emerged at a sprint, to find a dark stain on my luggage centred around the Athens Is For Lovers badge, and a small yellow puddle on the pavement.

I found a Gents under the bus station and hosed down the polluted patch of material. Halfway through the operation, I was approached by a young man with an unbelievably badly knotted tie. The thin end reached his trousers, while the fat bit was stumpy and pointed upwards. He caught me totally off guard by asking me if I wanted a job.

'What sort of job?' I said, fascinated that some one should recruit personnel in a public convenience.

'National and international factoring.'

'I don't know how to factor.'

'Soon pick it up.'

But I didn't fancy the idea of working for someone who'd employ someone who looked the way I did, so I resisted the chance of settling down in Plymouth and took a bus to Newton Ferrers. A pleasant journey, throughout which the couple in front of me discussed the relative merits of Jimmy Tarbuck and Bruce Forsyth as comperes. Personally, I think Les Dawson is in a class above both.

Newton Ferrers is a village stuck up a backwater of the River Yealm. It's all flowers and antiques in bay windows, and is above all else the domain of yachting folk.

On this bank holiday weekend they were all out pottering around their craft. As a crowd they seemed a predictable lot; they wore the same coloured clothes, talked in the same funny voices, and called their boats by the same names: Calamity-Jane, Emily-Jane, Emily- Sue, Calamity-Sue, Salcombe-Sue, Saucy-Sue, Saucy- Salcombe, Suzy-Calamity, Calamity-Jane, and so on.

But the activity itself looked wonderful. Nothing was as elegant as these beautiful white boats cutting through waves. I watched them for a long time from the cliffs, gliding out of the shelter of their estuary and suddenly sparkling in the salt water and sunlight as they struck the swell of the sea and caught the breeze.

We walked on through the simmering afternoon, the sun beginning to scorch my right shoulder. Every so often we'd stumble across picnickers sitting in the shade. Boogie would detour to investigate and introduce himself with his, 'Hi, I was just passing and was feeling peckish and I thought maybe . . .' expression. Sometimes he'd get a crisp, sometimes a clout.

And this was real Devon clotted cream country now. Spring had been pushed aside by summer and all around was a great expanse of lazy green, freckled black and white by dairy herds. Soon we came to the mouth of the River Erme and I decided to spend the rest of the afternoon sitting on the grass and watching the water level drop until I could wade across. I liked the idea of being the victim of a colossal chain of events: the difference in gravitational attraction between the celestial bodies and the centrifugal acceleration of their rotation, had combined with the relative distances between the sun, the moon and the earth and their relative masses and volumes, and the end result was me sitting on this river bank waiting for the tide to ebb.

Beyond Bigbury, however, was another estuary, that of the River Avon, and this was going to be more problematic. I thought of trying to wade it, but a fisherman warned me otherwise, drawing his finger across his throat and making drowning sound-effects. I asked him how I might cross and he said: 'Walk up the river bank until you see a sign for the ferry and shout, "Ferry!" '

'Shout ferry?'

'Shout ferry.'

Fair enough, I thought and toddled off up the bank. Soon I came to a low table of turf and sand. I could hear gunshots not far off and assumed I must be on some sort of private estate, but there at the water's edge was the sign for the ferry.

I read the timetable. The next boat was due in . . . two days . . . hmmm. This was a pleasant spot, but sitting here for that time could get boring. On the other side of the river there was a boat house. Rather self-consciously,

I called: 'Ferry!' which resulted in a total lack of activity of any description. I cleared my throat, took a good breath and in a style Norman Wisdom fans would instantly recognise, bellowed, 'Ferry!'

'What you shouting ferry for?' said a grim voice behind me. I spun round to see a man wearing plus fours with a shotgun broken over his arm.

'Just trying to get across the river,' I said.

'Next boat's Monday. You'll have to walk round. It's eight miles.'

'You don't know anyone with a boat, I suppose?'

'No. You'll have to walk. It's eight miles,' and he gestured with his shotgun, like a sheriff throwing an undesirable out of town.

'What are you shooting,' I said, trying to get pally.

'Rabbits.'

There was a silence. I couldn't think what to say next to a forty-year-old walking round in plus fours at dusk, shooting rabbits.

'Think I'll camp here for the night,' I said and immediately wished I hadn't.

'Private property,' he said, 'I'm the gamekeeper. He won't have campers. You'll have to walk round. It's eight miles.'

'Yeah, yeah, I know.'

Draconian git. It seemed incredible that here was someone going round shooting at anything he fancied, on land that had a public thoroughfare. I let him get out of sight, then walked deeper into the cover of the bank. I'd camp somewhere in the recesses of the cliffs. The sun would be down soon, he wouldn't shoot rabbits at night, surely, then tomorrow I'd find someone to take me across.

Under the cliffs I could see lights on in a pretty white timber bungalow. I peered through the bushes and through some French windows, into a living room lit by table lamps. A few people stood in flowing clothes and drank from cocktail glasses.

I rapped on the window. The party turned, jumped in fright, lost control of their jaws and then clutched their chests. The man among them was pushed towards the window to deal with the tramp. 'Now, look here, old chap . . .'

'I wonder if you could fill my water bottle?'

'What . . . eh . . . oh . . . yes . . . all right.'

Holding my water bottle in two fingers and at a distance he repaired to the kitchen. I stood on the doorstep grinning at the ladies, who had now moved closer together for security. They all looked so comfortable in their nice clothes, sitting half in light, half in shadow. The smell of dinner drifted through the room and ice cubes clinked in glasses and I wanted to join in, desperately. So, obviously, did Boogie. Arriving late on the scene he slipped easily into his cow-eyed, orphan-of-the-storm act. His tail disappeared between his legs. A little paw lifted and rubbed his eye. There might even have been a real tear in there. The reponse was instant. All the women let drop their defences with a long 'Awww,' and ran over to him with arms outstretched.

We exchanged the usual where are you going? Where have you come from? Does your dog carry his own luggage? What's happened to your nose? pleasantries, and I explained how we needed to get across the river because a man with a shotgun was after us. At once they offered to take us across in their boat, and the man of the house led me down to their little outboard which putt-putted us across the river in a minute. He said he liked my dog and I said I liked his house, then he putt-putted back to the party. I was left standing on the bank, thinking how good it was that I'd got across the river, but how much better it would have been if I could have stayed on the other side and drunk gin and tonics all evening.

I put the tent up on a grassy nook overlooking the river. The perfect spot to camp and the perfect spot for young lovers with no home, no local Gaumont and no car back seat to go to. One such couple fought their way through the bushes to their usual Saturday night rendezvous, only to find me there breaking up spaghetti into two-inch pieces.

'Evening,' I said and raised a glass of Soave. They turned and fled, the boy screaming as the girl dragged him through the nettles.

The logistics of cooking Spaghetti Carbonara in one pot aren't excessively complicated, but timing is all important. First: feed the dog; a step you won't find in most classical Italian recipe books, but necessary in this case. Two: cut up onions, mushrooms and bacon, ready for sautéing. Three: grate cheese and have egg and black pepper at hand. Four: put oil in pan. Five: put pan on stove. Six: switch gas on. Seven: reach into side pocket of rucksack for matches. Eight: pull out sodden lump of phosphorus and doggie urine.

It was a calm, sweet-smelling evening. The moon laid a line of interference across the river. A lone canoist paddled upstream through the water that parted like ink, and I sat by a cold stove struggling to digest a sickly dosage of raw onions, mushrooms and egg with parmesan.

Boogie lay quietly by me, raw bacon bits now resting on top of the Pedigree Chum in the corner of his tum. Across the water in the white beach house, the glasses still clinked and the lights shone on the trees. I began to feel angry. It seemed unfair that they were over there having a party and telling amusing stories to one another, and eating and drinking merrrily while I wasn't. I drank the Soave and tried to get pissed and failed miserably, and if anyone had come along that evening and made any clever remarks about rubbing two sticks together, I'd have been very rude to them indeed.

The wind was freshening as we walked to Hope Cove the following morning. Folk sat in deck chairs on the beach dressed in swim suits and pullovers; windbreaks had been erected but hats and Sunday papers flew across the sands.

I stopped for a while and watched an extremely one-sided game of cricket between a father and son in which the father cheated madly and slogged every delivery his boy bowled at him halfway to France. 'Good shot, Dad,' said the boy running after each ball enthusiastically. Eventually he was given an innings and was out LBW second ball. 'Well bowled, Dad,' he said and handed the bat back to his father who began belting off-drives out to sea once more.

Bolt Tail to Bolt Tail is a spectacular high stretch of cliff, with steep combes and bull-nosed headlands. At the viridescent Soar Mill Cove, a man and his dog walked slowly along the grassy ledge above the beach. He was a military-looking sort with a fine ginger moustache and a pair of field glasses perched on his stomach. His dog was a senile black labrador with drooping jowls and stumbling motion, not to mention a bladder condition that caused him to cock his leg once a minute.

'Finest cliffs in the South of England, these,' said the military gentleman, 'except perhaps for Land's End; and of course those white jobs at Dover. Seven Sisters are pretty impressive as well. Still . . .'

A pheasant rose with a mad clap of wings, and he swivelled and shot it with an imaginary gun. Next to him his dog's legs buckled and the poor old thing had to lie down for a minute. Their car was parked just up the hill, but it looked doubtful if the dog would make it back.

'Old campaigner,' said the man, 'damned leg's playing him up.' He spoke as if the dog had a shrapnel wound. I stroked the poor animal and he struggled to his feet; his colourless eyes had great sacks under them and his face was excruciatingly sad. Dogs aren't supposed to understand the concept of death but at this fellow's age you'd think they'd get the hint.

In mid-afternoon we reached an estuary with a mouthful of sandy coves and the path turned inland to Salcombe, another sailing centre. The wind had made the boats unmanageable and the quayside was full of families gathered around their cars, watching their craft straining at anchor like tethered animals. It was an innocent bank holiday scene of egg and tomato sandwiches and colouring books but was about to turn into an afternoon of degradation and terror, not to mention abhorrence, as from afar the rumble of motorcycles grew, reaching a crescendo as a convoy of faceless bikers turned onto the quay and wove their way through the rows of parked cars to form a semicircle by the waterfront.

I could remember this sort of situation well from days in Swanage when gangs of Hell's Angels or Rockers or Greasers or whatever they were called, gathered in the town and spent the day wandering around looking mean. They'd go to great lengths to look grubby: never cleaning their shoes before they came out and covering themselves in oil. They had German helmets and studded denims; one or two of them even had motorbikes, the rest came in on the bus and they all mooched around bumming fags and trying to scare old ladies with their tattoos. More often than not they'd end up in the amusement arcade playing air hockey or riding on the dodgems and for this they earned themselves reputations as Animals.

Unfortunately for the gang of bikers who rode into Salcombe that afternoon this notoriousness still travelled with them. They were mostly over forty, with balding pates and were members of some club or other. Gone were the names of the past: there were no Slashers or Grippers or Killers, they were Georges and Hedleys with one or two Stephanies, and they spoke in Surrey accents, not a consonant dropped anywhere. They were the kind of hooligans a sharp word from a traffic warden would have sent packing, and yet as far as the average tourist was concerned they were a bunch of barbarians out for an afternoon's destroying and maiming. As they arrived, children were called in and property locked.

The bikers stayed about half an hour. They read the Sunday Times and one or two of them tinkered with their bikes, then they had a cup of tea and some biscuits, put all their rubbish in a bin and rode off to terrorise another town.

I bought an ice cream which self-destructed on the first lick and then caught the ferry across the estuary to East Portlemouth. In the Gara Rock Hotel I asked the receptionist if she could fill my water bottle and she took it without a word, leaving me in the lobby to look at the notice board. It was covered in advertisements for all sorts of attractions: the River Dart Country Park, The Totnes Motor Museum, The Dartmouth Steam Railway, Buckfastleigh Abbey, bird sanctuaries, zoos; the choice was enormous and it struck me how I'd managed to avoid all such diversions in the four weeks I'd been on the move, and how now, with everybody involved in the bank holiday, I felt strangely left out. The best times on this walk had been when I'd met people randomly; when they'd had the time to spare and I'd just sit and listen to them talk about anything. But on crowded days like the last two – and no doubt tomorrow would be the same – everyone was preoccupied. I was just another visitor. The ice-cream girl in Salcombe was the only person I'd spoken to all afternoon.

'Ice cream please.'

'Twenty-five pence.'

'Thank you.'

Riveting stuff.

If I was going to be on my own, I thought, I might as well get right out on the cliffs again. Besides, the crowds were making me appreciate the solitude I'd found hard to cope with in the beginning. Now I looked forward to that period in the early evening when I pitched the tent and brewed up and cooked something – after the Carbonara fiasco, I'd quite happily returned to soup. Cream of Chicken tonight, yippee! And I'd begun to camp in the wildest places. In that last hour of the day I'd come to feel the path was my own and I didn't want intrusions. I liked to sit and watch the moon grow.

We walked for three hours that evening through more high and untouched country. The wind had dropped, the mist slowly slipped in and the path threaded a blind passage through the outcrops of rock.

And then, just after Prawle Point, where the cliffs recede and the fields slope gently to the shore on a raised beach, I witnessed what I thought I'd never see.

Boogie had disappeared into a patch of briars and when he emerged, backside first, I could see he had something flopping about in his mouth. It was a rabbit, a real one with fur, ears and everything. He came bounding up to me shaking the unfortunate creature from side to side: 'Take that and that and that.' Then he dropped it at my feet: 'I'll have it casseroled in a white wine sauce with broccoli and new potatoes.'

Although he'd have been unwise to eat it. It had probably been dead a week. Its eyes bulged, and its belly was swollen. Myxomatosis looked an unpleasant way to go.

But that wasn't the point. The point was, after five years of tinned food Boogie had heard and answered the call of the wild and that night as I pitched the tent in a remote cove at the back of Start Point, I began to realise how he'd become a changed animal over the last few weeks. This walk was his now, not mine. He was the star, I was just accompanying him. This rabbit was merely the first step in the realisation of his true potential, and I could already feel him pulling away from me. Tomorrow night he might bring a buffalo back to the tent and I'd be powerless to rebuke him.

I slipped into a bout of the Minehead Blues. I felt beaten and dispirited, and I think I might have despaired had I not looked heavenwards for guidance and seen out of the corner of my eye a perfectly erected tent. After four weeks of distortion, the canvas was now stretched tightly over its poles, the ground sheet hadn't a crease, the fly-sheet stood independent of the canvas, not a loose end fluttered.

We sat on a ledge in the cliff; below, a seal wallowed in the water by the shore. I put my arm around Boogie and pulled a tick off his chin, and we talked about how we'd had to take the rough with the smooth, how it hadn't always been a bed of roses, hadn't always been plain sailing; how we'd had to grin and bear it at times; how we'd had to buckle down and pull our socks up and keep our nose to the grindstone. But against all the odds we'd pulled through. That night was our night of triumph and what we felt for each other was respect.

It didn't last long though. At 3.30 the next morning, 31 May, Boogie began to moult.

It started off with the odd hair. The first I found on my toothbrush. Soon though, they were everywhere. The tent was carpeted with them; my clothing quickly turned from red to black. If Boogie shook himself the sunlight faded, and as we strode around Start Point the following morning, he left a hairy trail on the path. At the rate he was going he'd be bald by lunchtime.

From the lighthouse on the Point, a wide bay curved away to the north, calm and bright as a mirror. Conditions were perfect and we quickly reached the ruined village of Hallsands, pinned against the cliff by the sea. At one time a hundred people lived and fished here; the beach kept the sea at bay then, and the villagers could cope with their exposure. But when, at the end of the nineteenth century, a developer carted away tons and tons of shingle to build the new docks at Devonport, the village was left defenceless. During a storm on a January night in 1917 the sea undermined foundations and the population watched from the cliffs as their homes collapsed. There's little left now, just a few timbers and broken walls; the beach has completely vanished.

The neighbouring village of Beesands had also been threatened that stormy night, but had survived. Now, a great line of boulders protects the seafront, although the houses still look ridiculously vulnerable. Boogie and I sat on the beach and had breakfast. In my bowl three black hairs floated in the lane of milk between the Weetabix.

A large and anaemic caravan site was the next feature of the morning. The day was going to be another warm and sunny affair and yet, no matter what the weather, these sites always looked miserable. Here the caravans were old and sun-bleached, the curtains faded, the paint peeling. Many had wheels and were called mobile homes, although most of them would surely have fallen apart like garden sheds if they'd been moved.

From here on the bank holiday took over and I was carried along on the current. Cars were everywhere. In fact, at times, one could only admire the levels of indolence the drivers achieved. I'd come across tracks that llamas would have thought twice about following but there, halfway along, there'd be a Ford, picnic laid out on its bonnet, the Radio One Road Show on full blast.

At Torcross the path petered out and we had to follow the coast road. For a while I managed to lose myself amongst the reeds of Slapton Ley, where I caught up with a party of naturalists out collecting specimens, butterflies, I think. They all had nets and notebooks open, and were clearly of the mind that insects were omnipotent and just biding their time until they made their move for world domination. 'Look everyone!' cried a little man with a big moustache, 'a green fritillary,' and he dived gleefully into the undergrowth.

But soon I was back on hot, soft tarmac. The traffic was heavy, there was no pavement and, when I came across a bus stop in the village of Strete, I gave up.

I consulted the timetable. Bank holiday buses were about as common as green fritillaries; every asterix applied; as far as I could work out, buses came every twelve hours in months with the letter J in, unless the driver was on holiday.

I sat on a wall and waited. A steady stream of cars passed: adults in the front, kids in the back, grandma strapped to the roof-rack. A Hillman pulled into the bus lay-by. The back window was decorated with stickers: 'Hired car, XJS being resprayed.' 'This car is slow and temperamental; just like men.' 'I may be going slow but I'm in front of you.' Inside was a man and a woman, and two children, either bored stiff or heavily sedated. The man got out and lifted up the bonnet. He unscrewed the radiator cap and immediately set a new world record for the reverse long jump, as a blast of steam shot out and melted everything it touched. His much-freckled wife stuck her head out and shouted something along the lines of: 'I told you so, oaf!' Her husband muttered a reply that included the words, 'little pieces,' 'bury' and 'hatchet,' then he poured a kettleful of water into the radiator. I asked him if he had enough and he said he wasn't sure, so I added what I had in my bottle.

'Thanks,' he said.

'Any chance of a lift?' I asked cheerily.

'Well, I don't know, there's not much room in . . .'

'Only I've run out of water, see.'

He could hardly refuse.

Mind you, his wife could, but by that time I'd pressed the two kids up against the window, thrown Boogie on their laps and climbed in myself with my rucksack laid out over the lot of us.

'See, loads of room,' I said, and we slipped back into the traffic flow.

Relations between husband, wife and siblings weren't good. They were all suffering from Bank Holiday Syndrome. Dad wanted to go to the Totnes Motor Museum, Mum wanted to go to Powderham Castle, the kids wanted to go on the Dart Valley Steam Engine. After two miles all I wanted to do was get out, partly because we'd just flashed past a signpost pointing back to the coastpath, but also because an enormous six-wheeled lump of polished metal, bearing the words Wallace Arnold, was heading straight for us.

Everyone's foot hit imaginary brake pedals, even Boogie's. The car shuddered to a halt and a collision was somehow avoided, although I'd never seen a Wallace Arnold coach this close up before. It was crimson and cream, fifty per cent metal, fifty per cent glass and full of sweaty people eating food out of boxes.

'Well, I'm not backing up,' said Dad, very bravely I thought, since the coach driver had adopted a madcap expression and was slowly edging his vehicle towards ours. Dad held out until we could all count the flies on the coach's number plate, then he fired a fusillade of profanities, bracketed by the words Wallace and Arnold, and reversed at speed into a hedge. The coach passed and Mum and Dad announced they were going into Torquay to find a Pay and Display car park for the day. I asked to be let out, and I crawled from the car, so did Boogie, leaving the kids covered in black hairs.

The coast path led us quickly into Dartmouth, another port up an estuary, and like Falmouth, Fowey and Salcombe before it, seen at its best from its river. It was full of trees and had an elegant waterfront and like the others seemed such a sensible place to build a town.

A ferry crossing took us to Kingswear and we walked along the road for a while then came down to the water's edge and to a fine view of the Royal Naval College. A man lay nearby in swimming trunks, sunbathing. I sat down and took out my lunch: turkey paté.

Things aren't what they seem. The paté turned out to be mushroom. The man, when he stood up, turned out to be a woman sunbathing topless. I looked at the paté. I looked at the woman. I calculated I'd reach Poole Harbour in six days.

Four hundred miles into the journey and I was beginning to take an active interest in spiders.

Like gulls and snails, spiders were omnipresent; they'd become an everyday part of my lifestyle, or rather I'd become a part of theirs. Each morning I'd find a network of webs strung across the tent and the path; at first I'd walked through them without a thought, but after a while I began to feel guilty, webs looked like pretty tricky things to construct no matter how many legs you had, and I got into the habit of stepping round them or unhooking them and tying them up again when I'd passed.

And then, after a while I began to notice which spiders spun which webs; the brown podgy members of the species wove an untidy mesh of silk resembling a laddered stocking, whereas the long, thin, mean-looking variety spun orbed webs that caught the sun and the dew, and looked so beautiful flies leapt into them as if they were swimming pools.

On the path to Man Sands, I lay down in a field and found myself staring into the eight eyes of a little black spider with a head shaped like a tractor. I went to pick it up and it jumped spectacularly out of my reach. Incredible! Fantastic! A spider that could jump. I reached to pick it up again, and again it leapt out of the way. So it wasn't a fluke; it could actually jump. For every film star black widow or bird-eating tarantula there was one of these jolly little arachnids pogoing about its field unnoticed. I'd discovered a star. I could be its agent. We could have our own TV show. If only I could catch the slippery little monster.

In the distance, a spider was what Boogie resembled, as he scuttled up a hillside. Having caught his first rabbit, he was now riding on a wave of self-sufficiency that carried him far ahead of me and struck fear in other animals: beetles had to be quick on their feet when Boogie was around, particularly disabled ones, and no ant in the vicinity could relax. The couple of holiday-makers on the path above St Mary's Bay didn't look too happy either as he bounded up to them.

'Call 'im off!' screamed the girl, and hid behind her young man who tried to look aggressive by thrusting out his chest, complete with medallion.

'Bloody thing ought to be chained up,' he shouted and they hurried off before Boogie could lick them.

'Look at those flowers,' said the girl just before they slipped behind the fence back to Pontin's. She was pointing to something yellow growing out of the cliff; without a thought for his own safety her beau clambered down the slope, plucked a clump out by the roots and climbed up to the clifftop again. He presented the flowers to her with a bow.

'Eeurgh!' said the girl. 'They've got earf on 'em.' She chucked them back over the cliff and they walked into the holiday camp, arm in arm.

I pitched the tent in a field not far away. Camp residents passed me on evening strolls; they stopped and stared in bewilderment: Who was this man covered in dog hairs, crouched in a tent and reading *Seven Years in Tibet*?

On a visit to the monasteries of Debrung with the Dalai Lama's entourage, Heinrich Harrer describes his room thus: 'the overpowering smell of rancid butter and unwashed monks had sunk deep into the stone walls.' I looked around my own walls. One could have drawn comparisons with Debrung if one wanted to be unkind. Maybe I'd redecorate; some vinyl wallpaper, a coat of varnish on the ground sheet, cheese plant in the corner, couple of nice prints on the wall, few bean bags. I could put up a partition, have a spare bedroom; I could do Bed and Breakfast.

I climbed into my bag; Torquay tomorrow. 'Torquay tomorrow, Boogie,' I said. But he was lying motionless, quietly moulting in his sleep.

A cuckoo started to sing at 3.30. It sounded wonderful. About an hour later it was still singing and sounded quite average. An hour after that and I sat up intent on silencing the thing, for good. But it reached a sudden high note and was then heard no more. A Great Black-backed Gull probably got to it before me.

I waded through the sea of hairs and peered out at the morning. The English Channel had gone, Pontin's had gone, the cliffs, sky and grass, all but for a few feet around the tent, had gone. The world had ended during the night and no-one had told me. A foghorn groaning on Berry Head explained the situation.

I felt my way along the path until I reached tarmac. A milk float passed like an apparition. After half an hour I bumped into something hard. Running my fingers over the surface I worked out it was a house. I had reached Brixham.

A pamphlet claimed that Brixham was the premier fishing town in the country although it was hard to believe. The town may have been seminal in the development of the industry around the nation's shores – the Brixham trawler, built during the eighteenth century, was the most efficient boat of its sort ever developed, and the vessel used by the Brixham fishermen when they colonised the east coast ports around Hull and Grimsby – but now pleasure craft occupied a large number of moorings and surely somewhere like Newlyn landed more fish.

I bought a pasty from a bakery on the quay and sat and watched men throwing baskets of fish up from boats. The novelty of the harbour was a full-size replica of Drake's ship, *The Golden Hinde*. In an identical craft Drake had circumnavigated the globe in the sixteenth century, and yet it was no bigger than most of the fishing trawlers anchored around it. It was painted as if it belonged in a fairground, and in fact there was something surreal about the whole of Brixham that morning in the fog; its edges were blurred, the harbour mouth and the cottages on the hill loomed in shades of purple and grey, the voices of the fishermen carried eerily, and there was a smell of curry in the air. Madras unless I was mistaken. Come to think of it I could taste the stuff. I examined the pasty I'd just bitten into; it was full of a strangely coloured substance that had already burnt its way through the paper bag and was now staining my fingers. That'll teach me to buy a Cornish pasty in Devon, I thought. I gave the remains to Boogie. He swallowed it whole. Poor animal hadn't had a curry in weeks.

Some old naval minesweepers had been converted into passenger ferries and we took one across Torbay into Torquay. Another tourist pamphlet I'd picked up quoted Tennyson's impression of the resort: 'The loveliest sea village in England,' he'd said, and with good reason, no doubt. Unfortunately, in the fog, there's little difference between the loveliest seaside village in England and, say, Stoke. There were supposed to be palm trees here, yacht marinas and flashy hotels, but all I could see was a stream of motorcar headlights.

An arc of tracer lights chased each other round a dark, low entrance and I ducked inside to find an amusement arcade like the Tardis. It was tunnel-shaped and with the aid of mirrors stretched away into infinity. Lines of sinister black cabinets whirred, buzzed, flashed, and exploded along both walls as the Horror Monsters from Argon waged unending war against The Metal Eaters from the planet Zuck.

In a change booth in a dim alcove sat a Venusian holding a mug of tea and reading the *Daily Express*. A hundred-weight of keys hung round his neck and he looked as though he'd not seen sunlight since he was twelve. I asked him where I could find the coast path and he said he'd never heard of it, in fact, he seemed confused by the word coast.

I stumbled round the town bumping into department stores and assorted obstacles. Eventually I found a bus station and jumped on a double-decker to Babbacombe. I'd wanted to do the seaside bit in Torquay, to spend a day on the sands with a bucket and spade and a stick of rock, but being unable to find the beach, this would have proved difficult. I'd save it for Weymouth.

For the rest of the day I walked through mist and an intermittent drizzle. A muddy red path followed the sandstone cliffs over Babbacombe, Oddicombe, Watcombe and Maidencombe. I grew sick of combes. I couldn't see the sea and I couldn't see inland. All I could see was my feet. I grew sick of my feet

Between Babbacombe Bay and Labrador Bay I came up with an idea for a trilogy of novels, a stage play, a TV series, a feature film and an opera, all based on my feet. A sort of boy has feet, boy loses feet, boy wins feet back again, saga. Then I started to count things. Not many people know this, but there are five hundred and eighty-six trees between Watcombe and Maidencombe beaches. Finally I drew up the definitive guide to ironmongers in the South-west (coastal regions).

In this fashion I reached the bridge over the River Teign and crossed into Teignmouth. This stretch of the Devon coast is known as the English Riviera, although it seems ridiculous when you think of the Mediterranean version. A couple played bowls in the thin rain, and the lines of coloured lights strung between lamp-posts glowed faintly. I followed the railway line past the terraces of off-white hotels, and after a few minutes the town had completely vanished.

Actually, if I'd thought about it, I'd have taken the train over this next stretch, not just because the path was boring and along the road for a good way, but because of the railway itself. For this was part of the trail that Isambard Kingdom Brunel blazed as he engineered the Great Western Railway ever westwards towards Plymouth. From Exeter to Teignmouth, the line followed the slim raised beach that formed a convenient natural platform between the cliffs and the sea. In places where the beach had been swallowed and the water met the land, he had simply tunnelled through the cliffs and the line was one of the most spectacular I'd ever seen. Not that I could see any of it that day, but I remember vividly a jigsaw of the line I was given one Christmas. There was blue sea, red cliffs and an engine bursting through a tunnel, pouring steam. There was an engine driver waving from his cabin, as well. We got to Dawlish and I rested in some gardens and watched the trains run along the front. In Victorian times a railway line running between your hotel and the sea was an attribute the town could vaunt; now it just looked odd.

On the jetty opposite the station some schoolboys were fishing. They were at the conkers, gobstoppers and frogs-in-pockets age and there was a spirit amongst them oblivious to the gloom. One of them told me I'd catch good pollock there, and I decided to have a go. He even lent me a live ragworm to bait my hook with.

I sat there, damp and sniffing, feeling myself nodding off. I didn't even notice the twitch on the line that gradually grew more frantic. It was only when I saw a rainbow flash beneath the surface that I realised I had a bite. I jumped up and pulled in the line with a sharp tug, landing a rusty-looking fish about four inches long. It squirmed and glinted on the concrete and I wondered what the hell I was supposed to do next. All the boys were looking at me. Not wanting to appear soft, I picked up a rock, turned away and bought it down on the fish's head. I missed. I swung again, and it was dead.

I'd done it. I'd caught a fish. On a miserable June afternoon in Dawlish I'd caught my first fish. I called Boogie – he must see this. I'd cook it tonight, fry it in butter and make an anchovy sauce. Alternatively, I could have it stuffed and mounted. Boogie arrived and sniffed the corpse with indifference; so did the boy who gave me the ragworm.

'You were right,' I said to him, 'I've caught a pollock.'

'No, you ain't,' he said and threw his eyes up. 'It's a wrasse.'

'Fine, fine,' I said, 'I love wrasse, one of my favourite fish.'

'The legal limit is ten inches,' he said with disgust and took back what was left of his worm.

I stared at the baby fish I'd just murdered. Its expression was twisted. A trickle of blood ran from a gill. I wrapped it in a newspaper and dropped it in a bin on the station, along with my fishing line. From now on, I vowed, I would be vegetarian.

The path continued alongside the railway line. Trains passed kicking up water, lights on in the carriages and faces peering through the condensation. Then we were back on tarmac; hurrying past go-kart tracks and holiday camps with the occasional housing estate for variation.

At the mouth of the River Exe we turned inland along the estuary to the ferry terminal for Exmouth, but it was past six o'clock and the last boat had gone. There was only one word for the village I was stuck in and the word was – horrid. I stood in a bus shelter and decided to get depressed.

A bus pulled up, wipers slapping, and on the front, printed in dirty white letters, the destination: Exeter. The doors opened with a hydraulic hiss and I was suddenly tempted by the thought of a night in a city. I'd find a B&B, I'd have a bath, I'd wash my socks. The driver was getting impatient. Was I or wasn't I? It was too much to resist. I looked round for Boogie but he'd disappeared. Then I saw him – third row from the back, window seat.

The bus trundled inland. After two miles the wipers were switched off. After three the fog was a mere haze.

As Exeter appeared in the distance we emerged under a sunny blue evening sky. And it had been like this all day. Only the coast had lain shrouded.

I'd been to Exeter before. A coach load of us from Poole Technical College had gone to see a production of *Hamlet* at the Northcott Theatre. The prince was played by a young actor named Derek Fowlds. He gave an impressive performance. So impressive he next surfaced on the Basil Brush Show as the wise-cracking fox's straightman.

I remembered little about the city, but now, walking round the centre, it seemed like a town planner's showpiece. Maybe it was my newfound rustification but all I noticed was underpasses, roundabouts and precincts, and a number of secluded little road works.

I crossed a set of mini roundabouts and followed a one-way system round until I came to a hill with a cluster of B&B signs. I chose the first I saw and marched down the pathway. As I knocked on the door, a very attractive and smartly dressed girl arrived at the gate carrying a suitcase. She smiled at me like an air hostess. I smiled back and tried to cover my nose. I had the evening all planned. We'd see a play at the Northcott, dinner in town, an evening stroll along the Exe and then back to . . . The door opened. A woman in slippers stood there. Before her was a very elegant air hostess, a man in his late twenties, looking late-fifties and covered in black hair, and a dog with a tongue reaching her doormat and little hair at all. There was one room vacant and no prizes for guessing who got it. My offer to share didn't go down well with anyone.

I walked on to the next establishment, reflecting how this trip had hardly been a sexual success story. I mean, I hadn't been expecting a Sex and the South-west Coast Path extravaganza, but in all the travel books I've ever read, the lone wanderer always has at least one romantic encounter, or some similar euphemism. In a book I'd read just before leaving, a man and his dog had walked across their native USA and he'd recorded a romantic interlude every ten pages; he'd even come back with a wife (the dog got run over, by the way). I suppose I'd got on quite well with that waitress in the cafeteria at Land's End, but it was hardly the sort of incident Jack Kerouac would have written home about. My problem was, I had a strong libido and even stronger socks. I took solace in the knowledge that Heinrich Harrer had had an equally celibate time in Tibet, and he was into his sixth year!

The second door I knocked on gave the same verdict. The town lodging houses weren't as all-embracing as their country cousins, or maybe they weren't as hard up. I told the landlady Boogie would be very good and wouldn't make a mess, and she looked at me as if to say it wasn't the idea of Boogie staying in her house for the night that she objected to.

Over a pelican crossing, through an underpass, round the one-way system again and over another set of mini roundabouts and I found myself in a street behind the city prison where one or two houses had accommodation signs in the window. I tried one and a little girl answered and said that her parents were out, but of course I could stay and so could my little doggie. She was about ten years old and could have managed a Hilton with ease.

The room had a television, a kettle and a double bed. Through the window I could see a flowering garden in one direction and the gaunt walls of the prison in the other. I took off my boots, switched on the TV and slumped into a chair. The Falklands dominated all programming. I'd not looked at a newspaper or television properly for weeks, and I'd not realized the extent of the crisis. I'd seen a few car stickers, telling the 'Argies' to get out, amongst other things, and I'd caught a few headlines, but in general people had spoken about it little. Few wanted to acknowledge that such a conflict could happen and I'd noticed no effect on day-to-day life, not even in Plymouth. And yet, here on the news, there were stories of four British ships being sunk in the last ten days, Argentinian aircraft falling from the sky in drones, fierce fighting on the islands and hundreds of men already dead. The whole affair seemed too fantastic to be real beyond the screen.

I never thought I'd let myself get this much out of touch. I'd never have thought it would be possible to get this much out of touch. But now, even looking at myself in the mirror was a shock. I was unrecognisable. My hair and eyebrows were bleached white. My skin, creased and bashed about by the weather was brown, but in a way which just served to highlight the white bits. I'd lost a lot of weight: my wrists were lean, my trousers bunched around my waist and my legs and arms reduced to muscle. Even my face was thinner; its tan made my eyes look very blue and my tenth nose of the journey very red. The disguise was completed by a fragile, fluffy, undistinguished and patchy thing that clung to my face like a cobweb. It was a beard. Just.

I decided to celebrate. It's not every day you grow a beard. I had a bath, fed Boogie and left him to watch the television, then hit the town.

Exeter was quiet. Really quiet. A few boys played football in a subway but otherwise the pedestrian precincts were deserted, just rows of sleeping shops. A pub by a multi-storey car park seemed to be the only source of activity. Inside was a bunch of students having after-exams drink-ups. They were singing and having drinking games, but in the background, discernible above it all, were the baleful strains of a different sort of song. I followed the sound through double doors, down a passageway, through more doors and into a dimly lit room where, standing on a low stage before a semi-circle of semi-occupied chairs, was a young man dressed entirely in denim. He had his hands in his back pockets, his eyes closed tight and his head straining upwards as he sang, unaccompanied, a three-hundred-verse-long epic concerning a seventeenth-century Irish potato famine. I had stumbled across a folk club.

He was a floor singer and was quickly followed by a series of similarly styled artistes who all sang about the highland clearances or shipwrecks or unrequited love. The interesting thing about them, however, was not so much the content of their material as the places they put their hands when delivering it. The second performer sang with one hand on his hip, and one resting against a pillar. The third began in the conventional arms folded poise but then alternated between the hands in front pockets, hands in back pockets and hands behind head, positions. The fourth, a booming Scot, had solved the hand problem by hanging his guitar around his neck and holding onto it. The fact that he couldn't play it didn't seem to bother anyone, least of all him, and he launched himself into a series of songs sung in an indecipherable highland accent which gave coherence to about one word in sixty. 'Everybody sing,' he called out at the start of each chorus.

Next came a pregnant lady who sang in her anorak and rested her hands contentedly on the plateau of her tummy. She was followed by a morbid young man dressed entirely in brown, who climbed on stage clutching his pint pot and delivered a monotone dirge that began: 'I fill my glass up to the brim and through my glass my life looks grim.'

After that lot, the guest singer, the guy who was actually being paid to sing, didn't stand much of a chance. The audience clapped politely as he stood up on the stage and took out a battered guitar from a battered case and introduced his first number: a two-hundred-verse concept song concerning the wreck of the good ship something or other. But then he did something very strange for a folk guitarist; he tuned up, and from that moment he was as good as dead.

In the other bar the students had reached the pouring beer over each other stage and were debating whether to go for a curry. 'Eight pints of lager and a vindaloo,' they chanted as they careered, arm in arm towards some poor unsuspecting immigrant's restaurant. I found a fish shop and ordered a large fish and chips and ate it outside. Not until I was halfway through did I remember my resolution made earlier in the day concerning vegetarianism, but the cod tasted so good I finished it and went straight back in and had the same again.

I could see the prison lights on top of the hill and I walked slowly back towards them. As I waited at a set of pedestrian traffic lights two girls approached me. They were both dressed for a disco and were giggling.

'It's my eighteenth birthday,' said one. 'Will you give me a kiss?'

'Certainly,' I said, and we puckered our lips and smooched briefly. She tasted of lipstick and Pernod and I undoubtedly tasted of fish and vinegar. They ran off holding hands and I wondered if I'd just had one of those experiences that travelling is supposed to be all about.

The next morning I had breakfast with a telephone engineer. The little girl served us as her parents were out. The telephone engineer said he'd been staying there a week and hadn't seen the girl's parents yet. He had this theory that she was running the business on her own and without her parents knowing. It certainly seemed a possibility; after breakfast she quickly cleared away the tables, took my money, wrote me out a receipt, and then asked me if I'd be so kind as to vacate the room by eight-thirty as she had to be in school by eight forty-five.

It was a day of caravan sites. Boogie and I took the bus back to the coast at Exmouth. The fog was gone, the sea had returned to its former metallic blue and the cliffs were a vivid orange capped with green. Refortified, we strode over them to the top of Orcombe Point and right into the jaws of the Devon Cliffs Holiday Camp.

From one side of the valley to the other and as far back as the eye could see, there were caravans. But not the ramshackle boxes of previous sites. These were modern and multi-coloured, with crazy paving around them and herbaceous borders. Each had a TV aerial and its own parking space, and they came in a range of models with names like Ambassador and Executive Deluxe.

I managed to thread a path through them and reach the tranquillity of Budleigh Salterton, but then the same thing happened. Having been assuaged by the iridescent beauty of this classic Devon seaside village, I'd only got as far as the next headland before another dirty great caravan site blocked my way forward. I mean, I'd been very good about all this so far. I'd entered into the spirit of things. I'd tried not to moan. But it was all beginning to get out of hand. I was going to start being unpleasant about caravans soon. I mean, Executive Deluxes could get pushed off cliffs, you know. I wouldn't have minded so much if there'd been an effort to blend them in with the countryside. Surely someone could come up with a more rustic design than the current two-toned shoe box idea. They could be painted black and white and given udders, for example.

The day grew hotter, the cliffs grew redder and we came down to the beaches at regular intervals to swim. Since his initiation the previous week, Boogie had rather taken to sea water and splashed about whenever I did. At first I thought he was responsible for the earthy scum that floated just off shore, but it was nothing more noxious than detritus from the weathered sandstone. So susceptible to erosion was this stretch of coast that stacks of rock had been left stranded in a number of bays, and the cliffs themselves crumbled at a touch, leaving the hands stained orange.

There was a caravan site visible either fore or aft almost all day, although I suppose after a while I just grew used to them, the way you get used to a bypass that's built outside your front window where once there was a meadow. But my Greenpeace spirit was merely in abeyance, any further discrepancies on the landscape could easily tip the scales. The fisherman in Sidmouth, crouched in his boat and depositing rubbish on the beach as if he was bailing out, did just that.

Now, I've always considered myself a conservationist. I watch Wildlife On One, and put the right coloured bottles in the right coloured holes down the bottle bank. Sometimes I feel really sad when I remember I'm never going to see a dodo, and I worry when I watch TV and see men with explosive harpoons chasing what could well be the last whale on the planet, but generally I'm of the impression that as long as nature has men like David Bellamy on its side, then it will pull through.

Of course, it's all a bit different when the action is on your own doorstep. I mean, where are the Friends of The Earth when your front garden is chosen as the site for London's fourth airport? Over the last few weeks I'd come to consider the coast as my backyard and while I could, perhaps, learn to live with caravan sites, gratuitous littering called for action.

Not that I was going to threaten the fisherman with one of his own boat hooks or anything uncivilised like that. I was just going to pick up all the litter he'd deposited on the beach, hand it back to him, and tell him I'd been walking along the coast for a month now and had been amazed at the enormous amount of ship's rubbish littering the beaches. I'd explain how it was a needless eyesore and how I was worried that sooner or later it would have some adverse effect on the marine environment, and so would he mind curbing his habit of dumping rubbish overboard and use one of the many receptacles along the sea front.

As I got nearer to his boat I noticed there were two fishermen at work, and as I grew nearer still I noticed what big fishermen they were. I stopped and considered for a moment how two muscle-bound six-foot sailors with beards like bushes and hands like mallets would take to a five-foot-eight-and-a-half conservationist, with a derisory amount of facial hair, pushing rubbish in their faces, and that's when I decided to write a letter to the local council instead.

Past Sidmouth the path started rollercoastering again. I was hot and damp from sea water and sweat, and flies seemed to have taken to the taste of me. Only the woods above Branscombe offered respite from the humidity of the afternoon. We sat there peeking at the village below through the trees: a church, some farm buildings and a fractured collection of cottages; the whole scene looked studio lit. There was a hum of traffic in the distance and of insects nearby.

Not far from here I came across a landslip: a section of the cliff had subsided about six feet. It was inconsequential really, but was the sign of larger slips to come, the ones that I knew lay to the east in the Dowlands Undercliffs. They were the largest and reputedly the most spectacular in Britain, and I planned to reach the start of them that night, camp just outside and walk through them early the following morning.

Then suddenly, I was in a pub. I was just walking along the promenade in Seaton, minding my own business, when I was approached by this ruddy-faced, ebullient individual who pushed me into a glass and formica bar and insisted on buying me a drink. He was a fisherman, he said. I looked at his flowered shirt, slacks and sandals somewhat dubiously, but he said he'd had the day off. The boat had gone without him that morning and so he'd embarked on a day's drinking which had all the signs of continuing through the evening.

He was peripatetic sort of workman. He'd begun the year fishing out of Plymouth but hadn't stayed there long because, he said, he couldn't get on with the people he worked with. Instead he'd gone to St Ives, but had had an altercation with his boss and had left to work for a boat out of Newlyn. There, he couldn't get on with the people he lived with, so he'd decided on a sojourn in Mevagissey, which he'd liked a lot, he said but he'd fallen out with his workmates, and when the chance of a job in Seaton had come up, he'd taken it. He liked it here he said, although he wasn't getting on very well with the rest of the crew: 'That's the third time this week the bastards have left without me.'

A shame really. His problem was he was crazy about fish. He wrapped his enormous hands around his pint pot, making it look the size of a medicine glass, and started to wax sadly about how fish were his only friends. Mackerel he had a particularly soft spot for.

'They enjoy it really, you know,' he said.

'Enjoy what?'

'Being caught. Having a hook shoved through 'em. It's all fun for 'em, a game. I'll never forget the first mackerel

I brought home. I was six years old; war was just over
. . .'

I was going to get the full life story, I could tell, and I
wondered if I was beginning to get tired of talking to
strangers in pubs.

The television made noises in the background. The
news was on, followed by the weather forecast. While
listening to my friend recount how he caught not only his
first mackerel but also his first flounder, his first bass, and
not to mention his first mullet, I couldn't help but hear
phrases like: 'thunder from the west', and 'storm force
eight,' and 'stay indoors tonight', coming from the screen.
I turned to it in disbelief. The weatherman was moving
little arrows about so that they were all pointing at Seaton.
How could he do this to me? Didn't he realize with my
equipment I could drown in weather like that?

He continued relentlessly. Every isobar and low
pressure on the chart was converging and heading this
way. 'Since records began' was the phrase that did it. I
thanked the fisherman for the drink – 'But you haven't
heard about my prize-winning turbot' – and went outside
to survey the sky.

It looked beautiful. A pool of faded blue with a wisp
of thin cloud, the sea just a murmur, the wind non-
existent, and soon a moon would appear, almost fully
inflated again. A perfect summer's evening and yet inside,
on countless TV screens along this coast, a little man in a
kipper tie was telling us that all was about to dissolve in
a crack of thunder.

We crossed the River Axe and climbed up the hillside
to the east of the town. Then over a golf course, dodging
the little white missiles that whizzed overhead in the half-
light, and back onto the cliff path. After mile or two we
reached a sign informing us we were about to enter the
Axmouth to Lyme Regis Undercliffs National Nature

Reserve, that the walk through was five miles long and had no intermediate escape routes, and that there was to be no lighting of fires or camping, or cooking of soup.

I pitched the tent just to the legal side of the sign and secured the poles, pegs and guyropes with uncharacteristic care. Before I turned in I took one last searching look at the western sky. It was still blank, in fact so blank it was unsettling. I imagined large amounts of weather mustering off Land's End, great banks of ugly and unpleasant black things rolling inexorably towards Devon, ripe with water and powered by wind.

Inside the tent another ugly and unpleasant black thing, also powered by wind, slept oblivious to the warnings of weathermen. I lay beside him, unable to sleep, checking the tent structure every half hour, and waiting for the deluge.

8. Dorset: the hot bit

But I never felt a drop. I woke at first light and leapt to my feet all prepared to bail out. But there was an unnerving sense of normality around me. The tent was still firm, everything was dry and, crawling outside, I saw a clear and calm morning sky. The world had turned and I stood in the chilly dawn watching the daylight spread quickly from the east, and enjoying the simple satisfaction of having survived another night.

In fact, simple satisfactions were what this journey had been all about. I'd felt the pleasure of a Mars bar for breakfast, the prospect of a whole day ahead of me with nothing to do but walk and the comfort at the first sight of the valley in which I would sleep. I'd not discovered anything revelational about the universe or myself, but I had discovered how everything depends on the weather, I'd gained a sense of distance and I'd rearranged some priorities. Things that I'd once taken for granted, I now knew better the true value of: spoons, for example. Wonderful things, spoons, indispensable on trips of this nature and yet rarely given the credit they deserve in the annals of exploration.

The landslips around the coastal areas on the Devon and Dorset border are caused by the variety of levels of permeability of the geological strata: rain water passes quickly through the chalk and greensand, but is diverted towards the sea when it meets the impermeable gault clay. This tends to wash out the greensand, and the result is subsidence.

A number of slips have combined to form the Axmouth to Lyme Regis Undercliffs but undoubtedly the largest and most dramatic occurred over Christmas 1839, when twenty acres subsided. This opened up a chasm, a case of the earth dropping its trousers for all to see, and over the years a wooded wilderness has grown up inside. Walking through it is the closest you'll come to experiencing unexplored jungle in Southern England.

Pushing aside the brambles, I followed a thin, steep path that wormed through the trees and undergrowth, past fissures in the earth and sheer walls of rock. The sea was barely visible through the foliage and the sunlight only pierced the forest roof in shafts that hit the ground with a splash. The flap and panic of pigeon wings was all that disturbed the silence.

For three hours we followed the path seeing no sign of human interference other than a ruined cottage – oh, and I think we passed a sewage pumping station. These undercliffs are a rare wildlife habitat and although we saw nothing in the flesh, I knew that every scent, every broken flower, every track in the mud and every trail through the leaves meant something significant. Unfortunately, I didn't know what.

Then, as suddenly as the canopy of trees had begun, it

came to an end and we emerged on farmland. Ahead, was the curve of Lyme Bay, in the distance the bulk of Portland and I knew I was in Dorset.

Lyme Regis had recently become famous worldwide as the location for the film *The French Lieutenant's Woman*. At the end of the sea wall here Meryl Streep had stood dressed in an ankle-length black cape, giving meaningful looks no-one could understand the meaning of. The town was made up heavily for the film, although in reality it has its own period-piece elegance. The colour-washed promenade and the steep main streets fill the narrow valley the town sits in so that it can't be developed further, and has managed to retain intact its original Georgian seaside façade.

The stone harbour, The Cobb, is Lyme's focal point, as it snakes out into the bay protecting the town like a hand shielding a face. I walked its length past the usual collection of pleasure and working boats. A couple of young fishermen sat on their decks, gutting fish, and leering at the visitors. One combed his hair into a lank slick, the other clicked his tongue and displayed the slogan on his T-shirt proudly: 'I'm not a tourist, I live here.'

But if Lyme appears to be an attractive spot now, then you should have seen it during the Jurassic period. In those days it lay near the shores of the warm shallow sea that covered large areas of Britain. The West Country was then tropical, the vegetation that of a rain forest, and Devon and Cornwall rose into a range of mountains over eight thousand feet high. It was your actual tree-lined tropicana, the sort of place they'd make Bounty commercials.

Unfortunately, in common with all good things it didn't last long. Within a couple of million years the Cretaceous period had muscled its way in like a firm of contractors, everything got covered in chalk and from then on the place went rapidly downhill. The dinosaurs left, three or four ice ages rearranged the scenery and within a geological fortnight the first craft shop had opened.

As luck would have it, however, those balmy Jurassic days didn't sink without trace. Conditions then were apparently perfect for fossilisation and over the millions of years that followed the land around Lyme Regis hardened into a unique fossiliferous record of the flora and fauna of the period. As a result, the town has become a Mecca for amateur collectors and learned palaeontologists alike, and most weekends the beaches around here echo to the tap-tap of geological hammers on mudstone.

All around the town the story of local girl Mary Anning is legend. At the age of eleven she unearthed the first fully articulated ichthyosaur – literally, fish lizard. If an eleven-year-old could do it, then so, I thought, could I. In the fossil shop I bought a guide to collecting in the area and with my heart set on a tyrannosaurus rex, I set off for the beach.

The sun reached its zenith; my arched back sizzled. At Black Venn, to the east of the town, the cliffs dripped and crumbled, and the piles of shale and mud at their bottom were evidence of frequent landfalls. A fossilised dinosaur could, I deduced, be just as dangerous as a live one if it fell on your head from a great height, and so I stuck to the shore, where the man in the fossil shop told me the sea washed up perfectly preserved specimens daily.

By midday I'd found half an Access card belonging to Heather Mitcha something and an empty bottle of German shampoo, price M3.50. I was beginning to get fed up when along the beach strode a lad with a satchel slung over his shoulder and a hammer sharpened like an axe.

'Found anything?' I asked him.

'Bits and pieces,' he said, and delved into his bag. 'Dug

up this Asteroceras Obtusum back there.' He handed me
an ammonite of some sort, 'And there's this Penta Crinus,
of course, and I reckon this could be a skull plate from a
Pholidorsu Dapedium.' He had enough for a rockery.

'Well done,' I said.

'Not really, I was after a bit of plesiosaur. How about
you?'

I showed him my half Access card belonging to Heather
Mitcha something. He had a look at it, but I could tell he
wasn't impressed, so I didn't bother him with my German
shampoo bottle. I just watched amazed as he picked up a
rock by his foot and cracked it open with a single blow
to reveal a veritable family plot of ammonites.

'Just as I thought,' he said. Then he handed me the
rock, said I could keep it and wandered off up the beach
picking up bits of saurian reptiles like litter.

I studied his gift. The ammonites looked a bit small. I
wondered if, as with wrasse, there was a legal limit to the
size of fossils you could take home. Anything under a
certain diameter perhaps you had to put back and wait for
a millenium or two. No-one was looking so I slipped
them into my pocket.

I'd been looking at the distant dark cliff face and yellow
sandstone peak of Golden Cap all morning and now, as I
lay on the grass at its base, I found it had even impressed
itself on the back of my eyelids.

It was the highest cliff on the south coast, as every
pamphlet, guide book, signpost and person we'd come
into contact with since Lyme Regis had gone to great
pains to point out. But, like all climbs with reputations,
Golden Cap could be conquered with the right tactics,
i.e., walk a few yards, stop, have a drink, a hunk of
chocolate and a little lie down, then walk another few
yards. An hour and a whole bar of Galaxy later, I finally

scrambled up to the summit. There to meet me was a group of very red picnickers.

I always felt rather peeved, having climbed a particularly steep incline, to find people on top lounging in their Luxury Recliners, cars parked a few yards away. This foursome were surrounded by plates of sandwiches and a tin of Peak Freans. 'How do!' said one of the males. He came from Yorkshire. Boogie went over, all charm and falling hair.

'How far have you come?' said the second male, giving everyone a fine view of his mashed cheese and tomato sandwich.

'Four hundred and fifty miles,' I said, pretty nonchalantly, I thought.

'Well bugger me,' he said, 'give his dog a custard cream.'

They all held their arms out to Boogie and fed him not only custard creams but chocolate digestive, bourbons, jam splits and wafers. Me, I didn't get so much as a Rich Tea. I was about to point out that I was the one carrying all the luggage and doing all the navigating, when without warning the scene slipped easily into surrealism.

From the other side of the hill surfaced a wide assortment of about twenty walkers, supported by a wide assortment of about forty legs. They all had packs piled high on their backs; most walked with unfolded maps in their hands and clearly the ascent of Golden Cap had been the climax to weeks of careful planning and training. Now they stood on the top amongst the sandwiches and biscuits and shook hands, slapped each other on the back and took pictures of each other. The chap at the front, who had no luggage and could therefore safely be assumed to be the commander, took a head count; all present and correct and with a wave of the arm he led them off on the descent.

The picnickers from Yorkshire sat in silence for a while

but managed to go on eating. None of us were sure if we'd just dreamed the interlude.

'Have you really walked four hundred and fifty miles?' said one woman eventually.

'Yes,' I said.

She thought about this for a moment.

'That's like walking from Sheffield to here and back,' she said.

But with hundreds of miles behind us and only tens to go, a growing number of people were impressed by our efforts. In West Bay, the old harbour of Bridport, the woman in the grocery store wouldn't let me leave:

'Well, I think that's fantastic! Who said the youth of today haven't got it in them; that's the Falklands spirit that is. That's what this country needs, more people walking from Minehead to Bridport. Cedric! Come out here, there's a lad and his dog walked from Minehead . . . Where is Minehead, by the way? Cedric, come out here! Fantastic, I call it.' But Cedric was watching telly and anyway, he was one of the not-impressed brigade. So were the members of the steadily growing queue, waiting for ice creams, behind me.

All afternoon the beaches were a splash of coloured towels and costumes, and cars filled every valley. They flashed in the sunlight, their metal hot to touch; one Cool Cat, dressed only in the briefest of swimwear, jogged athletically up to his open-topped MG and sprang into it without using the door. His bare legs touched the black seat and his carefully crafted image shattered in a scream as flesh welded itself to molten plastic.

As the sun slipped behind the headlands for the day I camped in some tall grass behind the shingle at West Bexington. Gnats were out in force and I hid in the tent with Heinrich Harrer whose sojourn in Tibet was drawing to a close. A mosquito motored around my head like a by-plane and I chased it, knocking over pans of tea and soup as I swatted wildly. I trod on Boogie's tail and he yelped and joined in the fun. I'd like to have seen it all from the outside as the canvas bulged amidst thuds and barks. Eventually, the mosquito landed on a tent pole. I swung, the tent tilted and the yellow cover of *Seven Years In Tibet* had a black and red stain splattered over it.

That night I dreamt of the killer caravans. A herd of them were chasing Boogie and me along the coastpath. We leapt over a stile and into a field only to discover it was a Pay and Display car park and full of Wallace Arnold coaches. They began to chase us too. We scrambled down the cliff and onto the beach but the caravans and coaches appeared lemming-like on the clifftop and tumbled down in a landslip. We ran into the water only to be met by the Person from Porlock who detained us on a trivial business matter. I pushed him aside but he turned into a fully articulated ichthyosaur wielding a geological hammer. I was woken by a mosquito roaring round the tent on a motorbike.

Next morning I sat outside in 3.30 a.m. sunshine, eating breakfast and contemplating the ten-mile trudge over the Chesil Bank ahead of me.

For generations geologists have been puzzled as to why the pebbles on this unique bank of shingle should grow progressively larger as they extend eastwards from West Bexington to Weymouth. I tried to work it out over three Weetabix and a bar of Bourneville, but couldn't come up with the answer either.

The path followed the beach to begin with: a soul-destroying, exhausting slog with no visual respite except for the occasional on-shore fisherman who sneered at anyone who came near.

But then at Abbotsbury the trail turned inland, the

constant sucking of the waves on the pebbles ceased and a pastoral peace returned. Ahead was a monastic-looking building perched on a hilltop, and two girls with rucksacks perched on a fence.

Like most pairs of walkers these two were complete opposites. One hefty, one slender, one dark, one fair, one silent, one chatty. They were walking and busing it through Dorset on their hols and were waiting for the Abbotsbury Swannery to open. Like everything in Abbotsbury, the swannery is a legacy of the powerful Benedictine abbey that presided over all this area during the Middle Ages. The monks slaughtered the swans for meat; today it's a reserve and a popular attraction and I could remember going there on a school outing when I was about nine and being severely reprimanded by the warden for feeding the cygnets home-made almond tarts from my packed lunch. As I related the incident to the girls a van appeared in a cloud of dust. On its side, the words: 'Abbotsbury Swannery', and inside, the warden. He parped and pulled to a halt as he reached us. Surely he hadn't recognised me. No, the girls had arranged to meet him there at eight o'clock and they all disappeared through the gates. I was excluded because I had Boogie with me and the warden was of the opinion that Boogie would have treated the swans in much the same way as the monks did.

It was no matter anyway. For the rest of the morning there were swans everywhere, as the path detoured to the north of the Chesil Bank and followed the banks of the lagoon that contained the River Fleet, turning what I thought would be a morning's routemarch into one of the most serendipitous stretches of the whole trip.

The river meandered drunkenly and we doubled back on ourselves repeatedly, passing delapidated jetties at the end of which sat delapidated fishermen. I could hear one couple long before I could see them. A discussion concerning the musical convolutions of the Beatles came drifting over the reeds.

'See, I think the Revolver album showed the split in their personalities, the way the imagery competed against itself.'

'Yeah.'

'But then that was probably due to George Harrison's emergence as a songwriter . . . Pass us a maggot . . . Ta.

'Never recorded any songs about fish, did they?'

'What?'

'The Beatles.'

'Nah . . . Pass us another maggot, that last one burst . . . Ta . . . *Michelle ma belle, sont les mots...*

The midday heat drugged everything. Swans plodded slowly across the mud looking for shade and all sorts of furry and feathered creatures sat in corners on the brackish water. I walked on mindlessly, and was quite unprepared for the caravan site that suddenly pounced on us out of the bushes. It was an immature one though, easily shrugged aside, and anyway, it meant we were near Weymouth, the first town on the journey I was familiar with. I was going to sit on the beach with a knotted hanky on my head and eat Ninety-nines until I passed out.

We took to the road, past rows of orange terraced houses, over roundabouts and one-way systems, through underpasses, under overpasses and across bypasses. Past traffic lights, speed limit signs, stop signs, no entry signs, major road ahead signs and no parking 8.30 a.m. to 6.30 p.m. 31 May to 1 Oct. signs. All these things I'd come to see in a new light since Exeter. I decided my top-ten-best-selling-hit-pop-song wouldn't be about spacemen in Padstow, it would be a folk song concerning mini-round-abouts and contraflow lanes in urban areas; in fact it might even be a concept album. Walking through traffic systems instead of driving through them, I felt I was seeing them for the first time; perhaps they were really beautiful rather than functional, maybe they had cultural qualities, maybe there was something spiritual about them, maybe I'd been in the sun too long.

George III was about the best thing that ever happened to Weymouth. His first visit to the town, in 1789, was on the advice of the royal physicians who suggested that bathing in sea water might be therapeutic for his various ailments, indigestion and madness numbering amongst them. There's an amusing cartoon drawn by John Dixon, a caricaturist of the day, depicting the first royal dipping. The monarch is shown going walkabout in the sea, supported by a number of nubile handmaidens who have their hands all over him, and by a band of local and humble musicians standing waist-deep in the water, giving an impromptu rendition of 'God Save The King'. Poor George hangs there limply, utterly depilated and wearing a detached expression that indeed supports the diagnosis that he was suffering from indigestion and madness, but mostly madness.

However, the publicity from this and subsequent visits quickly provoked an 'If it's good enough for George III then it's good enough for me,' reaction and the resort has been perennially popular from Dixon's time right through to Giles's. As Boogie and I emerged from the town onto the beach, before us was a scene of chaos and human sacrifice as rows of etiolated bodies were laid out under the sun. Amongst them people were burying each other, games of football were being played, kids were eating sand, and screaming redheads were having calamine lotion slapped all over their shoulders. Only the elderly opted out. They sat in the shelters along the promenade, safe from frisbees and nudists.

I spread myself out on a deck chair and waited for the attendant, but he was busy making advances towards a dark-eyed girl in a white bikini who could have had her deck chairs gratis for the fortnight if she'd played her cards right. They mooched around at the water's edge. Beyond them bathers were discovering that although the day had warmed up in only a matter of hours, the sea would take another couple of months before it reached a comfortable temperature.

Some braves, of course, just charged in with a scream, a splash and a coronary; others preferred to enter on tiptoe, arms aloft, somehow managing to elongate themselves as the water neared the danger area around the crotch. A third category stuck a foot in and suddenly remembered they'd just eaten.

Above all this George III presided in statue form. In his day bathing was a competition to see who could be the most modest; now he gazed down on acres of wobbling flesh and he didn't half look bored.

Mind you, I liked it. I liked to think of all the seaside towns we'd passed through since Minehead doing good business on this lovely June afternoon. I thought of them all in Ilfracombe sitting on the harbour with their trousers rolled up; in Sennen Cove, riding the surf; in Torquay, sunbathing topless. It was the sort of day on which you couldn't imagine wanting to spend your holidays anywhere but Britain.

I'd never been in any danger on this trip, not consciously anyway. I may have been one step away from a hundred-foot mine shaft and not known it, or I may have camped in a valley which was hit by a meteorite the following evening, but, as far as I was aware at least, my survival had never been in jeopardy.

Neither had my health ever faltered. I'd had the regulation blisters but no sprains or breaks. I'd suffered no appendicitis in isolated coves, nor contracted any terminal disease from excessive amounts of canned soup. I did have a sore on my shoulder but as long as that didn't turn gangrenous over the next couple of days, I was confident of reaching the finishing post, intáct.

And then . . . snakes!

Yep, snakes. There was a rustle in a bush, a slither on a rock and a little viperous head popped out from under a stone. It made a face at me that said: 'Oh, oh!' and then vanished.

I jumped back instinctively, but then curiosity made me look behind the rock. I parted the grass and there was a nest – a mother, presumably, with offspring, although not babies by the look of them, immature perhaps. They hissed and writhed in a suitably anguine fashion when they saw us, at which point Boogie made a hasty retreat. Something in his metropolitan makeup had warned him to approach no closer and he was probably right, for these I'm sure were adders. They were black and brown with diamond tattoos on their heads and oblique markings down their backs. And yet they hardly looked fearsome. In this open nest in the grass they appeared quite vulnerable. I felt as though I should cover them with something.

'Just seen a nest of adders up there on the cliffs,' I said to the barman in The Smugglers at Osmington Mills, and immediately the bar went hush. Faces turned, mothers put their arms round children. I thought I might add that I'd recently read somewhere that only two people had died from adder bites in this country in the last thirty years and then only because they were allergic to the antidote, but there didn't seem much point. Snakes, like motorcyclists, had a reputation to live up to.

I took my drink out into the garden and sat by a bed of poly somethings. Boogie went crisp collecting. Almost everyone contributed – only a man with a pint of Guinness and a packet of pork scratchings proved unforthcoming. He would have to be worked on. Boogie stuck his head in the man's lap and challenged him to a staring competition.

A couple sat down at my table. The man seemed to be taking a more than casual interest in my feet. He studied them, closed one eye and scrutinised them, weighed them up from every angle, put his hand over his mouth, sat back in his chair and nodded. I crossed my legs selfconsciously.

'See you've got Skywalk Specials,' he said.

'Pardon?'

'Skywalk Specials. I thought I recognised them.'

'What?'

'Your boots. Skywalk Specials. Leather uppers, synthetic soles. Made in Italy.

I looked at my boots. They were well worn-in now. The leather was creased and scuffed, the laces broken and knotted, the eyes rusty; but they were as comfortable as a pair of bedroom slippers.

'Woman in the shop told me they were revolutionary,' I said.

He smiled sympathetically. Behind him, Boogie had just hypnotised the man with the packet of pork scratchings.

'Just bought a pair of K2s, myself,' said the man at my table.

'Really,' I said. What the hell were K2s?

He asked where I'd walked from and when I told him Minehead, he looked astonished.

'Minehead?!'

'Yeah.'

'What, in a pair of Skywalk Specials?'

'Yeah.'

'That's incredible.'

His wife felt she had to explain. Her husband's somewhat unusual preoccupation with boots stemmed, she said, from the fact that he was preparing to walk Offa's Dyke in September. Flowers were his real interest.

'What are those things called?' I asked, pointing to the poly somethings.

'Polyanthus,' they said in harmony.

'Thanks,' I said.

Behind them, the man with the pork scratchings tossed one in the air. Boogie knocked it up once with his tongue and caught it on the rebound.

Saturday morning and nothing but fog. The lighthouse on Portland Bill woke me. I peered out of the tent. A flower that wasn't a polyanthus or a sea pink, proliferated nearby. A seabird that wasn't a Great Black-backed Gull pierced the grey curtain, screamed once and wheeled away. I hated walking in the fog, but there was nothing else for it. I packed up and swung my rucksack over my shoulder. A rivet popped out and lost itself in the long wet grass. I replaced it with a matchstick.

Having lost vision the world continued on sound only; the chatter of waves on pebbles just reached us as we followed what were, presumably, high cliffs. At one point a fox ran across the path and Boogie gave instant chase immediately disappearing down the slope, where I knew, and surely by now he knew, that more often than not there was a suicidal drop. I shouted after him but his name just bounced back at me off the fog. I dumped my rucksack and ran down the hill. There was no sign of him, just a sudden end to the grass and then an abundance of nothingness. The fox reappeared and trotted off inland, and as the air breathed in and the fog momentarily dissolved, I could see the water hundreds of feet below.

There was a time once in London when we thought we'd lost Boogie for good. He was gone for nights on end. We searched everywhere for him, all over Hampstead Heath, Golders Green and Kilburn. We put notices up and asked in all his haunts: the pub, the betting shop, the local branch of Rediffusion. We didn't really have much hope when we went to the Battersea Dogs' Home, but there he was whining like a lost child, rattling the bars of his cage. He'd barked himself hoarse and lost a lot of confidence, but after a takeaway curry and a night at home he quickly recuperated. So quickly, in fact, he was gone again two nights later. The reason, we later discovered, was a bitch on heat just off the Finchley Road, but this time we went straight down to the Dogs' Home. There he was, fast asleep in his usual room, a lot more relaxed about the procedure this time. Sean banged on his door, Boogie lifted one eye, got up, stretched, yawned, farted and strolled back to the car.

Now, I sat on the hillside feeling helpless. How could this happen after the rigours of Cornwall, the pains of North Devon? I lamented how badly I'd treated him. How I'd made him sleep next to my socks, how I'd forced him to break his moral code and have a bath. And then I remembered: I'd forgotten his birthday. I'd told him we'd celebrate it on 25 May. I'd promised him a party. I'd even mentioned Pedigree Chum.

So full of remorse was I that I failed to hear the rustle in the grass behind me. I just felt a shower as a sneeze exploded on the back of my neck, and there sat the filthy little reprobate, his tongue swinging low, his lungs gasping. God, his breath smelt awful.

Since the air had cleared where I was but was still thick with fog on both sides I decided to sit for a while and wait for conditions to improve. I put the stove on for elevenses and took out my sketch pad.

Since the ignominy of Polperro, my style had changed. I'd abandoned my eye for detail and turned to landscapes and seascapes. Rock and wave formations were now what caught my imagination. I'd entered my minimalist phase, or at least one that didn't include seagulls.

And Durdle Door was the perfect subject: a natural limestone arch worn by the sea, the hole growing ever bigger. Unfortunately, in my interpretation the process was very much in reverse, and the more I worked at it the smaller the hole became. Soon, it was just a pinprick. Finally, I filled it in altogether and called it Durdle Door 20 million years BC.

Eventually, the fog lifted and we pressed on to Lulworth Cove, where the beach had been invaded by funny little men in black skintight suits with webbed feet and iron lungs on their backs. I phoned my parents and asked if someone could meet me at South Haven Point the following afternoon. My mother said she'd arrange for the press to be there, plus family and friends, there'd be a reception party, nothing flash, just a bottle of champagne and some mushroom vol-au-vents.

I walked off round the perfectly pincered cove, already feeling lightheaded. I was on the home straight. At the other end of the beach, I came to some barbed wire fencing. There was a red flag and a red signpost informing me there were bombs and unexploded shells in the vicinity and that they could kill me. I was entering the Lulworth Ranges and from here on I knew every step.

We'd passed a number of MOD properties en route, although none of them as beautiful, as emotive, or on the same scale as the Lulworth Ranges. This seven-thousand-acre tract of land is used to train tank personnel and evidence of the military's activity is there for all to see. Besides the ubiquitous red flags and warning signs, the fields are cratered and in places littered with empty shells. Rusting tanks lie on the hillside like dead animals and

tucked in the valley behind Worbarrow Bay sits the evacu-
ated village of Tynham.

This was the third 'lost village' we'd passed, but
Tynham seemed to arouse more sympathy than either of
the others. The villagers of Port Quin in Cornwall left to
find work, those of Hallsands in Devon fell victim to the
sea. The villagers of Tynham left voluntarily, as an heroic
but naive gesture to aid the war effort.

It was six days before Christmas in 1943 when the 225
inhabitants packed up and moved out. D Day was six
months away and the allied troops desperately needed land
to rehearse manoeuvres. The cliffs and beaches around
Tynham suited their needs perfectly. As the villagers left
they pinned this note to the church door: 'Please treat our
church and houses with care. We have given up our
homes, where many of us have lived for generations, to
help win the war to keep men free. We shall return one
day and thank you for treating our village kindly.'

But they were never allowed to return despite a government pledge to the contrary. In 1952 the land was bought
compulsorily and the village and valley were strictly out
of bounds until the mid-Seventies when a scheme of resto-
ration and improved access was drawn up. Unfortunately
this came too late for much of the village and many of
the houses are just ruins. And whereas the church and the
school have been beautifully restored the effect is largely
one of a museum – the final stage in the exorcism of the
village spirit.

By the lectern in the church there's a book for visitors
to log their reactions. The messages are predictable: 'Army
get out,' 'Give land back to rightful owners,' etc. But the
writers are people from all over the world. Few local
people would go back to live there. They've come to
value the employment the army gives civilians, the way
the army wages are spent in local towns and the support

given to the local railway and schools. And, of course, the paradox is that the army have become conservationists, albeit unwittingly, for, free from land management and intensive farming for the past thirty years, all wildlife on the ranges has thrived, and whilst it is undeniably sad that such a beautiful corner of countryside should have such limited access, the saddest part of all is that it's taken an army to preserve it.

We followed the range paths along the top of Gad Cliff and then down into Kimmeridge, past what was, until the extensive fields five miles away at Wytch Farm were discovered, the largest on-shore oil well in Britain, which sounds very industrial and intrusive but in fact is nothing more than a nodding donkey, painted green. Once a day a green tanker drives onto the site driven by a man in a green uniform. He fills up from the green-painted pipes and drives away again. His name is probably Mr Green.

I'd walked these paths so often and yet each time they looked different and each time was the best. They changed with the season and with the weather and even with the time of day. For most of that afternoon the fog had slipped in and out, and in the evening, as I camped high on Hounstout cliff, I was above a great bank of cloud as though in an aeroplane. I sat there picking the dog hairs from my Cream of Celery as, like an extractor fan, the sea began to suck the fog from the valley below. The hills and cliffs cleared. The shoreline became distinct. The sun set brilliantly and a full white moon emerged. It had taken me exactly one lunar month to walk from Minehead.

I ate my last brace of Weetabix in a hole in the cliff at Winspit where the Thames embankment used to be.

From these cliffs in the middle of the last century the stone was cut and shipped to London in what proved to be the largest enterprise undertaken by Purbeck stone.

The industry was then at its peak. Four hundred local men were employed in a hundred quarries. Now sixty men work a handful of opencast concerns, and the legacy of the boom years is just so many holes in the ground.

At Hedbury I knew of a path that led to an old cliff quarry. I followed the thin track down the hillside to a letterbox opening in the rock and crawled through into a short tunnel. Scrambling over some rubble I emerged in the dark, main chamber. The ceiling was fractured, thin pillars of rock had been left as supports. The air tasted dank, the floor was covered in muddy puddles and on a wall someone had written 'Happy birthday Fiona,' which was thoughtful. The only sound was the echo of dripping water.

'Hello,' said a voice from the shadows.

I spun round, heart pounding. There, in the corner, was a man doing up his fly.

'What are you doing?' I said rather stupidly.

'I'm on holiday,' he said. 'Nice caves these, aren't they?'

They're not caves, you buffoon, I wanted to say. Instead, I decided to educate the man, and I led him off on a tour of the quarry, into deeper, darker chambers where the quarrymen spent most of their lives chiselling away at the bedding planes, working by candlelight. Then out onto the cliff where there were remains of the whims that lowered the stone into waiting boats, so precarious an operation that cliff quarrying was only possible during the summer. Finally, I gave him a potted history of the industry, how during the boom years Purbeck stone was building cities all over the country, some even ending up in the Vatican, and how now the survival of the stonemerchants rather depended on the sale of birdbaths and assorted garden ornaments.

Actually, it felt good to be imparting knowledge for a change. Over the last four weeks I seemed to have been listening most of the time. When I'd finished he said, 'Thank you,' and dug his hand into his pocket. I thought he was going to tip me, but he pulled out a camera and took a picture of me, then asked me to take one of him standing outside the quarry. He made note of each picture in a little book. 'Number 138,' he wrote, 'cave near Swanage.'

One of the many monuments to Purbeck stone in the Swanage area is The Globe, an enormous world of stone, set high on the cliffs above the old Tilly Whim quarries and surrounded by tablets engraved with gems of knowledge pertaining to the world's perpetual motion: its circumference, its volume, how long it would take a pigeon to encircle it, etc. It was one of the more outlandish tourist attractions we'd encountered since Minehead, but only a taste of the eccentricity of George Burt, the man most featured in the annals of Swanage. Burt was a man of vision. His masterplan, to convert a Victorian quarryman's quagmire, i.e., Swanage, into a fashionable resort, required that the boats which transported stone to London be ballasted on their return voyage with any number of defunct and movable London monuments and ornaments. These he would then use to redecorate the town. As a result, a walk round old Swanage today is like a walk down Holborn – lamp-posts are marked 'City of London', bollards come from boroughs throughout the capital, columns, statues, a clocktower and an archway were all imported. Rumours that Burt's death interrupted a deal concerning Big Ben and the Houses of Parliament, are, however unfounded.

In the centre of the town is John Widdowson's delicatessen. He was doing good business on a sunny Sunday, and I joined the queue, hoping I might embarrass him into giving me a free lunch.

'Hello,' I said.

'Hello sir, and what can I do for you?' he replied, slipping into his Victor Mature impersonation, the one he reserves for trying to be nice to customers. 'A pork pie, perhaps, only forty-eight pence, freshly . . .'

'It's me!'

'. . . baked . . .' He studied me for a minute. 'What's happened to your nose?'

'It's peeled . . . a lot.'

He served another customer without taking his eyes off me. Boogie watched from the window as slices of ham slapped onto greaseproof paper.

'Your mum's just phoned,' said John. 'She says she's going to meet you at Studland.'

'Are you coming?'

'You bet. She's bringing champagne and mushroom vol-au-vents.' Then he narrowed his eyes and said 'Have you really walked five hundred miles?'

'Yeah.'

He nodded. 'Have the pork pie on the house then.'

We ate it on the beach watching the Punch and Judy show. I had the meat, Boogie had the pastry and jelly. All around us Punch was provoking hysteria; a terrifying character in a terrifying production, one for the purists, with roles for Scaramouch, Pretty Polly and Jack Ketch the Hangman; only Kevin Keegan had been thrown in for popular appeal.

Ballard Down was the last hill of the journey and memorable for the size of the fly I swallowed near the top. Normally insects would stop at my teeth which acted as a windscreen, but this one burst through the gap in the front line and hit the back of my throat like a Messerschmitt. I doubled up in a fit of expectoration not unakin to the performances tramps frequently give on the Circle line, and uncertain passers-by made detours dangerously near the cliff edge in an effort to keep clear of me.

Other flying objects of interest on these downs were the seabirds. There were a number of those low-slung, oily-black birds that seem to be ninety per cent neck and tend to fly low and fast over water. And on the grassy swards on top of Old Harry Rocks I saw a species of gull I'd not noticed before. They were smaller than the average seabird, white with black heads, like minstrels, probably known as Black-headed Gulls.

But it was the activity on the water that really caught the eye that afternoon, as a myriad boats filled the twin bays of Swanage and Studland. A speedboat sounding like a chain-saw skimmed from crest to crest. I could see the driver clearly from the clifftop. He had a steering wheel in one hand and a screaming blonde in the other. Also given to screaming were the windsurfers he toppled in passing. One minute they were tacking gracefully across the blue, the next they were clinging to their wreckage, lungs full of water.

I could see Poole Harbour now. It cut inland like the one piece missing from a jigsaw, and there at its entrance was South Haven Point and my champagne and vol-au-vents. I glanced at my watch: 3.30. I was ahead of schedule, so in Studland I bought a Midnight Mint choc ice and sat on the beach. Boogie finished off the Winalot and I finished off *Seven Years in Tibet*. The Chinese had invaded. The era of Tibetan feudalism was over. Heinrich Harrer sailed away down the Kyichu River in a yak-skinned boat. He had three pages left to meet a Tibetan girl and have his romantic interlude; I had one and a half miles, likewise Boogie, but unlike Heinrich Harrer and myself, Boogie was going to do something about it.

A section of the beach to the north of Studland has been designated a zone where naturists can roam without embarrassment – embarrassment, that is, for those people who keep their clothes on. To one side of a notice, ladies and gentlemen sit in deck chairs. They change with towels wrapped tightly around them and get their nudity from the tabloid newspapers. To the other side of the notice, naturists sit on rafia mats. Pubic diamonds, little bald willies and bosoms of every shape, size and colour abound. Everyone is happy and free and reads the *Guardian*.

It was into this latter section that Boogie wandered, stating clearly which side of the fence his political interests lie. The first I knew about it, however, was when a man, woman and child who'd been splashing about in the water and saving a fortune on swimwear at the same time, suddenly starting gesticulating madly. I followed their fingers to a beach towel where, in the time it takes to read three pages of *Seven Years in Tibet,* Boogie had seduced a rather attractive collie, and was about to do what, if Lassie let her co-stars do to her, would earn her films 18 certificates. The collie obviously belonged to Mr and Mrs Naked and family who were now halfway up the beach at full sprint, knowing full well that their dog was a pushover in her present condition and that animals like Boogie didn't take precautions.

I yelled at him but he wasn't going to leave the West Country without something to tell his mates back in town, and besides he was at the stage where his eyeballs had crossed. The Nakeds arrived on the scene. They tore Boogie and the collie apart. I'd never seen so many quivering genitals. The collie was bundled into the back of a Datsun Cherry and Boogie was left in a state of coitus interruptus with everyone shouting at him to clear off. I put him on the lead and dragged him away in the sitting position.

We turned the last corner of Shell Bay and into the

harbour mouth. Here all the boats came inshore to navigate the narrow entrance and for a while they were sailing alongside us. I felt like Sir Francis Chichester coming home until a great container ship with the word 'Truckline' emblazoned along the side ploughed a passage through the sails and rather ruined the flotilla effect.

And then I could see a figure ahead of me, crouched over a camera tripod and frantically waving his hands. At first I thought it was a man from the press but then I noticed the lens cap was still on the camera and realised it was my brother, a keen amateur photographer. Alongside him stumbled a small woman, and getting smaller all the time as she sank into the sand under the weight of camera equipment. This was my brother's wife, not so keen on the activity.

Beyond them I could see the reception committee. I waved, they all waved back. I waved again and someone else who thought I was waving to them, waved back at me. I returned the wave. What the hell, I'd just walked five hundred miles, I'd wave at anyone.

I reached the Sandbanks ferry terminal and the official end to the path. A champagne cork popped, echoed by the last rivet on my rucksack as I swung it from my shoulders.

'Don't worry son,' said my father, 'a matchstick'll fix that.'

There followed a lot of hugging and remarks about my nose and my odd socks and the colour of me and the amount of weight I'd lost, although no-one mentioned my beard. The champagne went straight to my head, and I came over all British and sentimental and began to spout about how these had been the best five weeks of my life, how Boogie and I had reunited ourselves with nature and developed a telepathic relationship in the process; how Britain had the richest and least understood countryside

in the world and how it was daft taking a cruise round
the Caribbean islands for your holidays when you could
walk the coast paths of the South West. And later, when
a reporter from Twin Counties Radio asked me why I'd
made the journey, I said, through a mouthful of vol-au-
vent, 'To impress a girl I met at a party before Christmas.'

But it was then I realised what my real motives were.
I'd done it because I'd wanted to know the name of the
gulls with the black backs and the flower whose first two
syllables were poly. I'd done it to teach myself how to
put up a YHA tent, to read *Seven Years in Tibet* by Heinrich Harrer and to try all the flavours of Heinz soup except
for Lentil. I'd done it because I'd wanted to write a top-
ten-best-selling-hit-pop-song (which on the last stretch, I
decided would not be the basis for a concept album
concerning traffic flow, but a musical biography of the
Person from Porlock). I'd done it because I wanted to
experience personally the wealth of ironmongers that the
South-west coast has. I'd done it to see how long a pair
of socks has to be worn before they take root, and I'd
done it to see how many noses I had (twelve). In which
case the walk had been a complete personal success and I
wished I'd thought of that lot before I left.

As for Boogie he was given a bone and refused to give
interviews. We went back to London the next day. I
called round to see Jennifer but she'd moved, run off with
someone who'd walked the Pennine Way. Then I took
Boogie home. Sean tried to look pleased to see us but
failed miserably: 'No, no, please, I've just Hoovered!' In
the time it took Boogie to walk across the room and turn
the TV on, the floor was black.

But he was in no mood for mischief. He crawled under a
table and lay there, peacefully. It was 7 June. He resurfaced
towards the end of September.

Boogie up the River

Boogie up the River

One Man and his Dog to the Source of the Thames

Mark Wallington

For Catherine

Contents

1. I'll See You on Tower Pier at Eleven

I made a lot of phone calls that evening. It was the eve of departure and I was getting desperate.

I was standing at the window with the receiver pressed to my ear and I remember thinking how the clouds were wound around the brown sky like a river. But everywhere I looked I saw a river. I had rivers on my mind.

I rang my friend Douglas. I told him I was about to set off on a long journey, a journey by boat to the source of a great river, a journey to the source of the Thames. And he said: 'So what; doesn't impress me.'

So I went straight to the point. I said: 'I want you to do me a favour. I want you to look after Boogie.'

It was a reasonable request. I had after all looked after his stick insects when he went windsurfing in Turkey. .

He said: 'Boogie?'

'Yes.'

'Your dog?'

'Yes.'

'The dog that ate my stick insects when I went windsurfing in Turkey?'

I didn't pursue the matter. Douglas clearly has a better memory than I have. Instead I phoned Clive. I explained to Clive that I was about to row to the source of the

Thames, that I was setting off in the morning and that my craft would be an antique camping skiff, and he said: 'Big deal! I've just come back from a desert safari in Tunisia.'

'I was wondering if Boogie could stay with you while I'm gone,' I said.

There was silence, then Clive said: 'Boogie?'

'My dog.'

'The dog you brought round here once?'

'That's right.'

'The dog that ate my computer?'

Actually that's not true. It was Clive's computer software Boogie ate rather than the computer itself. I didn't pursue the matter though, instead I phoned Sarah. But Sarah said she couldn't look after Boogie either. She said she was going to South America on business. This surprised me since she works behind the counter at Sketchley's, but I wished her a pleasant trip and then phoned Kevin. Kevin is an old friend. Kevin has a dog of his own. Kevin had even looked after Boogie once before. But when Kevin answered he reminded me of the stain on his ceiling, the enormous phone bill, the dent in his Vauxhall Astra, and the paternity suit filed against his own dog, all consequences, he claimed, of Boogie's visit. I thought the man was over-reacting, personally, but I didn't pursue the matter.

I went through my address book once more. Marsha was my last chance. As I dialled, Boogie came into the room to watch the new Australian mini-series on TV. He glanced at me. It was a glance that said: 'Here, you know that new frying pan?'

'Yes.'

'The Teflon job?'

'Yes.'

'I've just been sick in it.'

Marsha answered. I felt confident Marsha would help me out. Marsha loves all animals. She particularly likes monkeys. In fact she's monkey crazy. She has monkey-pattern wallpaper. If you visit her and she gives you a cup of tea the chances are the cup will have a gibbon on it. Marsha also likes dogs and so I said to her: 'Marsha. I'm going on a rowing trip up the Thames. I'm going to solve the mystery of its source once and for all. I'll be going uphill for a hundred and forty miles on a journey through the wilds of the stockbroker belt.'

And she said: 'You should take a chimpanzee with you.'

So I explained how I didn't want to take any animal with me and that the reason I was phoning was because . . .

'You're not going to ask me to look after Boogie, are you?'

'Yes.'

'Boogie, your dog? The dog that came round here once?'

I could vaguely remember taking Boogie round to her house once before. She gave him a bowl of water; I think the bowl had a gorilla on it. 'You remember him,' I said.

'How could I forget him? He tried to seduce my hamster.'

I didn't pursue the matter. I put the phone down and patted Boogie. He belched, and a miasma of curry and Winalot wound around the room like a river. I could never understand what all the fuss was about. He was charmingly noisome, that was all. Beneath his earthy exterior was an honest animal simply trying to unload his traumatic childhood. All he wanted was to be understood. Normally I took him with me on trips like this, but that was out of the question this time. This time Jennifer was coming with me.

Outside the daylight was stretched. It was the beginning

of May, the time of year when you begin to forget that the days were ever short, and I could feel the mounting excitement of an imminent journey.

I made one last effort: I called Mrs Matheson.

'Hello,' said Mrs Matheson. 'Sit And Stay Boarding Kennels.'

'Hello, this is Mark Wallington.'

'We're full!'

The problem is Boogie has a reputation on the kennel circuit. He's known as a bad influence on the other guests. He's like Bilko in kennels – he organizes poker schools and plans escapes. The last time he stayed with Mrs Matheson even the other dogs complained.

'But you're my only hope, Mrs Matheson. I've tried everywhere else. I'm going away tomorrow.'

'We're full until Christmas.'

'I'd take him with me but I'm going with a friend and . . . well . . . she hates him.'

'And I've just remembered we're full until the following Christmas as well.'

'It'll be a disaster if he comes with us. Couldn't you keep him in the fridge or something?'

'In fact I really don't think we can fit him in this century.'

Before I could pursue the matter she hung up.

On the Australian mini-series the heroine stood in the shade of a gum tree and told the hero she loved him and Boogie licked his armpit. Hadn't I heard stories of how cat owners went away for a week and left their cats seven tins of cat food in a row?

Boogie looked at me and grinned. He's the only dog I know who has a can opener attached to his collar.

There was nothing else I could do. Jennifer would just have to grow to like him; she'd have to make an effort. I called her and spoke to her answering machine.

'Hello, it's Mark . . . um . . . I just called to tell you . . . well . . . just to say . . . to say about tomorrow . . . nothing really . . . just meet me at Tower Pier at eleven . . . and . . . well, see you there.'

I couldn't tell her over the phone. Informing someone that they're going to spend a lengthy period in an enclosed space with Boogie should be done to the face. She'd find out tomorrow and then it would be her problem.

I packed nervously. As I zipped up my bag Boogie came over and gave me his 'going somewhere, are you?' look. I sighed, unzipped the bag and squeezed in his bowl. He wagged his tail and knocked over an inexpensive ornament that didn't break, then gave me his 'and you simply couldn't bear to leave me behind, could you?' look.

Then we sat down and watched the end of the mini-series. But I couldn't concentrate. I kept seeing rivers everywhere.

2. All Right, The Prospect of Whitby at Eight

A journey to the source of the Thames wasn't my idea; it was Jennifer's. Not that I'm holding her responsible for what happened – that would be unreasonable, there were far too many people involved to blame one individual. Even the manager of my local branch of The Sock Shop played a part. If he hadn't arranged his window the way he did that evening back in March things might have been very different.

I remember the occasion well. I was on my way round to Jennifer's flat in Docklands. We get together now and again. We have poetry evenings. She reads me her poems and asks for comment. She says I'm the only person she could possibly do this with. She says I'm different from her other friends. She says they all have Porsches and cufflinks, while I have sensitivity. They live on their stock market knowledge and their nerves, while I live on a whim.

I don't know where she gets this idea from but I'm certainly not going to discourage her. If anything I try to cultivate the image. I stare out of windows a lot when I'm with her. I appear preoccupied, as if I'm hiding something. I dress plainly on the surface but like an El Greco underneath. For this reason when I saw the green and yellow viscose creations in The Sock Shop window, I thought: Those socks talk. Quite what they said I wasn't sure, but Jennifer is a woman who likes to be kept guessing. She said to me once: 'The two things in life I love most are poetry and money.' She's an enigma, a contradiction; it's just a shame her poetry is so dreadful.

I changed in the lift on the way up to her apartment. It was the first time I'd ever been to a poetry evening with a dirty pair of socks in my pocket. I sat on the floor as she read me her latest work. When Jennifer reads poetry she lets her hair down and then spends the evening throwing it back off her face. She takes her shoes off and sits cross-legged and tries to sell me the poem as if it were gilt-edged stock. It's most effective.

' "Rubble lies like flesh in the streets, and my mind wanders picking at the bones . . ." ' she read, and then she stopped and pouted and said: 'It's awful, isn't it?'

'No . . . no . . . it's . . . promising, definitely promising,' I said, and then the telephone rang.

I went to the window and gazed out over London. Jennifer's flat is in one of the development schemes that rise every week from the mess that was once Wapping. She doesn't say much about her past but I have a feeling she's known the Docklands since she was a child. A lot of her poems are based around them – the word rubble has appeared more than once. She bought the flat for the price of the bricks and now if she sold it she could buy a Lincolnshire market town. She says she doesn't think about it. She means she doesn't like to think about it.

Across the river among the warehouses the new silver buildings reached for the sky like fresh tombstones. In the street below, an Audi Quattro rumbled over the cobblestones past a line of builders' skips and estate agents' offices.

I kicked my own shoes off and my socks hit the white

carpet like a spilt drink. But the shag-pile poked through the viscose and irritated my feet and when Jennifer came off the telephone I said: 'I've got really itchy feet.'

She smiled and her big eyes widened and slipped into that faraway look she has and she said: 'You're not planning another trip, are you?'

'What . . . ?'

'That's what I like about you. Nobody owns you. You look out of a window, become inspired and off you go. What far-flung corner are you heading to this time?'

The problem with Jennifer is that she likes to charm people but doesn't like much to be charmed herself. When she gives you her faraway look she threads your eyes and she takes control like a puppeteer. She makes you feel you are the only person who really matters. She even makes you forget about the other ten people she has made feel exactly the same way already that day, and I knew I would never be able to forgive myself if I admitted that when I mentioned itchy feet I was commenting on my new socks rather my wanderlust, so I said: 'Well . . .'

On a pier a police boat gargled into life. On the bank I was sure another slim building had appeared since I last looked. Through it all rolled the mighty Thames.

'. . . I think it's about time I went on a journey to the source of a great river.'

This wasn't altogether untrue. Every spring I think about going to the source of a great river, or the top of a great mountain, or across a great ocean, or to the heart of a great continent. I spend the winter locked in the den of my body. I leave the curtains drawn and windows closed and I eat things out of packets. Then the clocks go forward and I'm struck down by impatience. I pull out atlases and I read books like Charles Sturt's *Narrative of an Expedition into Central Australia*. I listen to the shipping forecast. I throw open the windows and see the blossom and I take deep breaths and say things like: 'I think it's about time I went on a trip to the source of a great river.'

Normally I'm on my own when I behave like this, and within a few days it's all forgotten and there's no damage done. But this time I was with Jennifer, and Jennifer has this idea I'm the last of the great adventurers. She's excited by the thought of me swinging through trees to get a story. She doesn't realize I spend most of my life sitting in my attic looking out over the gas showroom. I keep meaning to tell her but whenever I'm on the verge she says: 'Why don't I just pack up all this work business and go on an adventure with you?' and I'm helpless. On this particular occasion she stared downstream towards Millwall and said: 'I'd love to go to the source of a great river as well.' And I panicked and replied: 'Name your river and we'll travel together to its source.'

I quickly followed this with a nervous laugh in the hope she'd think twice before committing herself to a raft on the Orinoco with a nautical buffoon. But she just stood there watching a balloon bearing the name of a building society fly over the water. I could see the globe in her eyes. I could see the word Amazon on her lips. Then she turned to me and said: 'The Thames.'

'The what?'

'The Thames.'

'The Thames.'

'Yes. The Thames.'

'You mean . . . The Thames?'

'Yes. The Thames.'

'Let me get this right. You want to go . . . to the source of the Thames?'

'Yes.'

'Why?'

'Because it's here.'

'You mean because it's there. The phrase is: because it's there.'

'No, because it's here. Because it's here, right outside my window.'

'Oh.'

The rest of the evening we dedicated to Thames poetry: ' "Sweete Themmes! runne softlie, till I end my Song," ' read Jennifer from the Spenser collection. ' "Earth has not anything to show more fair," ' read I from the Wordsworth. Later she dug into a drawer and read me one of her own poems about the river. She stroked her hair back and said: ' "When I lie on your bed I see greyness and strange stains. When I lie on your surface, I just see greyness, I'm sinking into . . ." It's awful, isn't it?'

'No, no. it's . . . promising,' I said, and then the phone went again.

It wasn't until I drove home and found myself driving along the Thames Embankment that I began to think seriously of what she'd said. By Blackfriars Bridge I parked and peered into the black and gold water and I felt I was looking at the river for the first time. As it rolled through the city I could sense the power of an enormous history, and I began to understand Jennifer's distraction. The Thames *is* here rather than there. The Thames is our river — Britain's river. The Thames coils like an intestine through the belly of the nation. A voyage to its source would be an important journey.

So I began to make casual inquiries. Popular opinion had it that the source of the Thames was near Cirencester in Gloucestershire. But then I met a man in a pub who said: 'Bollocks!' and went on to explain that the source was undoubtedly at Seven Springs near Cheltenham. I passed this information on to the woman in the library and she said: 'The source of the Thames? It's in Crudwell, everyone knows that.' Then I brought the subject up at a dinner party and was amazed at the silence it inspired. And so I began to wonder: had I stumbled across a geographical riddle? Could a river as well charted as the Thames really have a disputed source? It didn't seem credible. I intensified my research and consulted my AA atlas of Great Britain. I followed the course of the river as it wound out of London as blue as a motorway, headed on through Berkshire and the Goring Gap, and turned north to Oxford. As far as there it was a regular ribbon of water but then as it set out through open country it gave the first signs of the strange behaviour to come. It took to wandering drunkenly through nowhere in particular. Somewhere it slipped unnoticed into Gloucestershire, and passed Lechlade as if it were lost. Finally it reached Cricklade and there things got out of control, as, without warning, the river split into a frayed end and veins ran off like leaks from a pipe. It seemed to me that any one of these could have been the source. I put my maps down and wiped a tear from my eye. It was time, I decided, that someone settled the dispute once and for all.

A fortnight later I saw Jennifer again. We arranged to meet in the Prospect of Whitby in Docklands. She was forty-five minutes late. I watched her as she parked her TVR outside and snarled at a youth who leant against a lamp post. As she crossed the road to the pub a vagrant shuffled towards her and asked her for money. She gave him ten pounds and kissed his head.

In the pub we sat underneath a photograph of Dennis Waterman and George Cole being pally with the landlord. Since I'd last seen her Jennifer had been to Munich once, Bologna twice, and had had lunch with Adam Faith. I'd spent a fortnight in my attic writing about Shropshire. She said to me: 'I like meeting with you. You lead such an exciting life,' and I smirked when I sensed the desperation in her voice. Jennifer is a woman who wants to be reached and I suddenly knew I'd have no better chance of reaching her than by travelling with her on a long journey, so I said:

'I've been thinking. You're right. We should go to the source of the Thames together.'

She went straight to the bar and came back with a bottle of champagne and said: 'Shelley did the same sort of journey in the summer of 1815, you know?'

Then she kissed me and I felt that this would be the trip I'd always wanted to make. It wasn't until the end of the evening as we parted that she said: 'Before we go, promise me one thing.'

'What's that?'

'You won't bring that horrible little dog of yours along, will you?'

3. Listen, I'll Have to Meet You in Hampton Later

Boogie isn't my dog. Boogie isn't anyone's dog. Boogie is a freelance.

He was found abandoned as a puppy, and taken home to a darkened room in south London and fed crisps. There he grew up the hard way, a London mongrel, devious and streetwise with a strong sense of survival and little in common with other dogs. He would never fetch sticks, only hubcaps.

He came to stay with me in north London a while ago for a weekend and never left. I still don't know how long he's here for. We live our own lives, Boogie and me. For this reason I never thought leaving him behind while Jennifer and I went on our trip would be a problem. To be honest I assumed he'd make his own arrangements.

Besides, my attention during that pre-departure period was directed in other areas, mostly in the search for a boat. I had quickly decided there was only one sort that would suit an expedition to the source of the Thames, and it wasn't an eight-berth fibreglass tub with a chemical toilet and bedside lights and magazine racks in the saloon. I wanted something classical, and I wanted something beautiful. I wanted a camping skiff, and nothing else would do.

Skiffs are low wooden boats based on the design of the traditional passenger craft of the Thames, the wherry. They first appeared on the river in the mid nineteenth century when messing about in boats became a popular pastime and a more stable and forgiving hire-craft was needed. With a canvas top they were easily converted into campers; the upper Thames was there for the exploring and no boat represented the heyday of the river better. In these days of fibreglass, however, skiffs have become an endangered species and I'd all but given up hope of finding one until I came across Mark Edwards, a man who restored old models at his Hampton boatyard. I phoned him and explained that I was planning a trip to the source of the Thames, that I wanted a traditional camping skiff and that I understood he was my man and he said: 'You're lucky you caught me, I was just off down the pub.'

I asked him if he had a boat that would suit and he said: '*Maegan. Maegan* is the perfect skiff for what you have in mind.'

'What's so special about *Maegan*?'

'She's a hundred years old.'

'So?'

'So whenever people sitting in their gardens by the riverside see you, they all go: "Look at that boat!" Then they ask you in for champagne.'

Maegan sounded ideal. She slept 'eight at a squeeze, two comfortably', and came fully equipped right down to tupperware. It was only when I explained I wanted to start the trip from Tower Bridge that complications arose. Mark said he could arrange for *Maegan* to be taken down, but then he pointed out that for the inexperienced waterman the tidal river up as far as the first lock in Teddington could prove to be tricky. It was prone to sudden tidal surges and unpredictable currents. It was a commercial as well as a pleasure craft's waterway and we could well find ourselves rowing alongside battleships. We'd need to know what we were doing.

So for the next week I spent a lot of time round at Jennifer's flat studying tide timetables. And there is nothing like tide timetables for dampening one's enthusiasm. Jennifer yawned and asked how long the trip would take and I said that that would depend on where the source was, but I imagined in the region of three weeks. Since Gloucestershire is only eighty miles away this astounded her and she suggested we take a speedboat and do it in an afternoon. I explained to her about locks and other delays, including the four-miles-an-hour speed limit on the river, and she explained to me about the ten thousand pounds in salary she would lose by being away from work for three weeks. At this remark I protested and said that it didn't appear to me she was entering into the spirit of the expedition. I told her that three weeks was hardly a long time in which to unravel a geographical riddle and that, to be honest, I was surprised she hadn't resigned from her job as a gesture of her commitment. Then the phone went and she had to go back to the office.

I persevered though, and each evening stayed up late reading information from the Port of London Authority, reading reports from river pilots and studying navigation manuals. I learnt that a blue and white flag means scuba divers are in the vicinity. I learnt that a bale of hay hanging from beneath a bridge means Men At Work above. I learnt that boats give way to other boats on their starboard bow. I learnt all sorts of codes and practices, and I learnt a variety of regulations and rules. Then one night Jennifer said she'd learnt that a pleasure boat with a sun-deck and a cafeteria selling teas, coffees, alcoholic drinks and an assortment of light refreshments chugged up from Tower Bridge to near Mark Edwards' boatyard in Hampton twice daily and cost just five pounds, and I had to admit that seemed a far more sensible idea.

That was two days before departure and Boogie was still without accommodation. I'd hoped the people at the Kohinoor Curry House might take him in since he spends most of his evenings round their dustbins. Or I thought the local Radio Rentals might put him up since he spends his days sitting outside their window watching the racing. Or perhaps the local police station since he frequently ends up in their cells. But everyone made impressively imaginative excuses, and so I turned first to the telephone and then finally to providence.

Crouch End in north London is a fine place to start a journey. It's on high ground, and as you walk out of your door you feel that wherever you're heading it's going to be downhill. A millennium or two ago, from the top of Crouch Hill you would have been able to look down over a forested valley to where the rivers Fleet and Tyburn joined the Thames and the Roman city of Londinium stood within its defensive walls. On the banks of such a strategically well-placed and piercing river the city flourished. It grew and then spread and ultimately sprawled, and now from the top of Crouch Hill you can see no further than the block of flats across the road.

I took a train to Tower Hill and sat there nervously, reading the adverts, rehearsing how I should break the news about Boogie to Jennifer: 'I didn't want him to come but what would you have done, let him starve? . . .' No, that wouldn't work, she'd say: 'Yes.' She's hard Jennifer is; fair but hard. 'Dogs are for life, you know? When you go away you can't just switch them off and take the plug out . . .' No, that was sarcastic. Jennifer has a strange sense of humour. 'I think you're being unfair to Boogie. You've just never taken the chance to get to know him.'

Maybe that was the way to handle it, be constructive. Boogie was a seasoned traveller after all. A river journey would be a good way for Jennifer and him to get to know each other. It would be a good way for us all to get to know each other.

It's not as if Boogie is a dependent sort of animal. I watched him as he sidled up the carriage to a man with a briefcase on his lap. Boogie put his head on the man's knee and looked him straight in the eye and within two stops the man had opened his case, taken out his packed lunch and fed it to Boogie piece by piece. Some people say it's wrong to let a dog beg. Maybe. The point is, begging has nothing to do with Boogie's performance – it isn't part of his repertoire and he wouldn't humiliate himself so. Middle age may have slowed Boogie down, in so far as he prefers to stay indoors now and watch a good documentary rather than go out and chase a cat, but it has also brought him experience and the realization that the best method of persuasion is not plaintive pleading but hypnotism.

The man with the briefcase didn't make the decision to give Boogie his lunch; he simply had no say in the matter. One look into Boogie's yellow, gas-filled eyes and he was in a trance. From him Boogie moved up the train as passengers rummaged through their pockets in an effort to find something to feed him. I sat back and watched the show. Seeing him perform like this I get the feeling Boogie is never more at home than he is on the London Underground system. It's his natural habitat. I quite expect to get off a train one day and find him busking. His only problem is escalators where he has to be carried. If ever you see a dog at the bottom of an escalator hitch-hiking, pick him up, it's Boogie.

I was at Tower Pier at eleven o'clock on the dot. Half an hour later there was still no sign of Jennifer. I strolled up the pier and watched the river roll: a fat, grey slob of a river with the tide slipping out, leaving a mark on the embankments like a ring around a bath. I followed a wave downstream and sensed an irresistible force. Any notion I had of this journey being an easy ride was forgotten here. I suddenly had the feeling this was going to be a far more demanding project than I'd imagined. My research had shown me that as far as Lechlade we could rely on a well-regulated waterway serviced by the Thames Water Authority, but from there on to Cricklade and beyond there were rumours of an untamed stripling river, and I knew that our chances of success would depend greatly on conditions. I looked in the water and tried to imagine the source in a field, and how somewhere among that flow was a drop that had come all the way from Gloucestershire.

With fifteen minutes to departure there was still no sign of Jennifer. The waterbus to Hampton sat looking bored, framed by the grey and blue twin towers of Tower Bridge. This was the last crossing before the sea, the grandest most famous bridge over the river, and it annoyed me the way it reminded me of a giant cruet. I sat down and counted the pigeons. With five minutes to go I went to telephone. I tried Jennifer's home, her health club and her car phone. Eventually I traced her to her office. Her personal assistant answered.

'Is Jennifer Conway there?' I said.

'Can I ask who's calling?'

'Mark Wallington.'

'Can I ask what company?'

'It's a personal call.'

'Can I ask what it's about?'

'No.'

'Jennifer Conway is engaged, can you call back tomorrow?'

'She was supposed to meet me at Tower Pier an hour ago.'

'It's not in her diary.'

'I want to speak to her.'

'She's just left the room. She'll be back on Friday.'

'Tell her I've smashed into her TVR. I've caused an estimated five thousand pounds' worth of damage, and I thought I'd give her my name and address. But if she's not there . . .'

Muzak came down the line, something from *West Side Story*. On the river a tug ploughed upstream and black-headed gulls circled overhead.

Jennifer came on the line. I said: 'Jennifer, what are you doing at work!?' and Boogie started barking as he always does when he hears her name.

Jennifer said: 'I'm sorry. I had to come in here on the way. Panic stations, I'm afraid. I'll be late. I'll have to meet you later in Hampton. What's that barking?'

'What barking?'

'That barking I can hear.'

'I don't hear any barking.'

'It's familiar barking.'

'It's the foghorn on the boat. It's leaving. I'll see you in Hampton.'

I ran on board and felt the turbulence push us away from the wharf. Boogie sat down next to me with an ice cream in his mouth. On the pier stood a confused eleven-year-old schoolboy. The kid didn't stand a chance.

John Hanning Speke and Richard Burton are the two names that most readily come to mind when one thinks of journeys to the sources of great rivers. I thought of these two great rivals as I headed upstream under London Bridge, how they departed from Zanzibar in 1856 and ventured into regions of Africa no white man had seen before, how they endured a year or more of privation in their obsessional quest for the source of the Nile, and how my journey had nothing whatsoever in common with theirs.

But I was beginning to relax now. In some ways I felt pleased to have this time to myself before Jennifer arrived. I'd felt tense. Now I sat back and watched the sun sparkle on the water. Boogie too decided to collect himself. He lay sprawled across the deck in typical fashion – i.e. in such a position as to cause the maximum inconvenience to everyone else on the boat. It's a rare gift he has. If you took him to a field he'd lie down so that he blocked the gate. Everyone took great pains to step over him and say: 'Aww', and feed him biscuits which of course just encouraged him.

A voice came over on the Tannoy: 'Hello, my name's Ken, any questions don't be frightened to ask. I know London better than the pigeons. I used to be a cab driver.' We passed Cleopatra's Needle and Ken said: 'Something to do with Egypt that is. Word of advice if you're driving along the Embankment here – you can't turn right at the lights going up to Charing Cross. I had a nasty accident there once. Blocked both lanes of traffic for three hours. Oxyacetylene job. Got a fine for that one.'

Most of the passengers were American and Spanish tourists. They listened to the commentary and looked at the view for a while but were far more interested in the Chelsea Pensioner on board. They kept buying him drinks. They lit his cigarettes and posed for pictures with him. He had the same sort of potential for attention as Boogie. People wanted to stroke him. An American woman said: 'Well, well, look at that coat, what do you wear underneath it?'

'I'm eighty-eight I am,' said the Chelsea Pensioner.

'Are you?'

'Course I am. I just said I was.'

We slipped under Westminster Bridge. A barge gave a blast on its siren and Ken took evasive action just in time. He said: 'Here's a building you'll all recognize: the Houses of Parliament. Particularly unpleasant roundabout behind there. I had three accidents in one afternoon there once. Got an endorsement.'

'Eighty-eight! Is that right?' said a Spanish woman to the Chelsea Pensioner.

'Eighty-eight, and I've only had one hip replacement.'

'I'm going to buy you a drink,' she said.

'Suit yourself,' he mumbled and took out his tobacco tin.

With the water so low and the Embankment so high we felt dwarfed by the city. We passed the Battersea Dogs' Home and Boogie hid under the seat. We passed Battersea Power Station and the Chelsea Pensioner said: 'I live there.'

Everyone took a step back.

'Not there, there!' he said, and pointed to Wren's Royal Hospital on the opposite bank. 'It's nice there; too many old people, though.' Someone handed him a can of lager and he said: 'It's not everyone can become a Chelsea Pensioner, you know. You have to have served your King and country for a kick-off. And have a clean record, military and otherwise. They wouldn't let you in if, say, you had a conviction for armed robbery. Forging bank notes would be right out as well. A parking fine and you might be okay, but arson and you wouldn't stand a chance. Treason and they'd show you the door immediately. Littering or not paying your television licence on time you might get away with.'

'Putney Bridge,' said Ken and a raspberry-flavoured Slush Puppy sailed over the parapet and landed on the boat's roof in an explosion of red ice. 'Of particular personal interest to me Putney Bridge is. It's the only bridge in London I've not had an accident on.'

The Chelsea Pensioner escaped from his fans and sat next to me. His coat had a few medals on it and lots of stains. His shoes were highly polished but his collar and cuffs were frayed. He leant over to pat Boogie.

'What sort is he?'

'Italian terrier.'

Actually, Boogie isn't an Italian terrier. In fact he's nothing like a terrier. He's nothing like a dalmatian either, or a beagle or a pekinese or a spaniel. He bears no resemblance whatsoever to a dachshund, and red setters and Boogie have nothing in common whatsoever. He couldn't be more unlike a Pyrenean mountain dog. No one could ever mistake him for a labrador and if you suggested he was descended from a husky you'd make yourself look foolish. The idea of confusing him with a bulldog is absurd and those who propose he has alsatian in him are talking nonsense. You could call him a mongrel but you'd be pushing your luck. Boogie is a dog – just.

'Italian terrier, eh?' said the Chelsea Pensioner.

At this point most people who try to guess Boogie's lineage realize the complexities of the family tree they are faced with, say: 'Thought so', and then try to change the subject.

'Thought so,' said the Chelsea Pensioner. 'I had a cat once,' and he puffed on his roll-up.

I said to him: 'I bet you've seen some changes in your time?' and he nodded and said: 'Everyone asks me that.'

We passed through Barnes and Chiswick and the river was now a place where people lived. Syon Park looked like a rain forest surrounded by property development. At Kew a number of people disembarked, and even more at Richmond where the Star and Garter Home stood high on the hill like a palace and the meadows below were full of buttercups. We passed islands and undergrowth and suddenly the city was gone. The Chelsea Pensioner said: 'By boat is the best way to see London, it's just that when the tide's out all you see is slime.' And then in the afternoon sunshine he nodded off, only waking once when we passed a strange collection of timber and plastic sheeting tied together on a raft and moored under a willow to make a sort of houseboat. A dirty little face poked through. A child waved, smiled and stuck its tongue out. 'Gypsies,' said the Pensioner, 'nothing wrong with gypsies.' He waved back and stuck his own tongue out and then fell asleep again.

It took us five hours to reach Hampton. 'Which may seem like a long time,' said Ken, 'but driving it can take two hours if the South Circular is chocker. Ah! Hampton Court, I know a lot about Hampton Court, or I should do – I hit it once. Got banned for that one.'

I walked down the towpath to Mark Edward's boatyard. It was early evening now and the river was on fire with reflections. Oarsmen and canoeists cut waves that lapped briefly at the bank but the river quickly reclaimed its inertia. Swan feathers floated on the water and there was a smell of diesel and old wood. There was no sign of Jennifer though.

I lugged my stuff into the boatyard and found Mark Edwards covered in wood shavings and smelling of preservative. He looked like the sort who, no matter when you called, would be covered in wood shavings and smelling of preservative. He smiled and said proudly: 'I'll show you *Maegan*.'

He led me down to where the skiffs were moored, and pointed to twenty-two feet of sparkling mahogany with the name *Maegan* inscribed in uncial on the backboard. She was broad-hipped and round-shouldered and looked more like a piece of furniture than a boat. She was exquisite. Mark said: 'Have you had a good look?'

'Not really . . .'

'Right, let's go to the pub.'

I pinned a note for Jennifer on the door and we went to a pub in Hampton village. The landlord said: 'it's always quiet on a Thursday.'

Boogie went round the pub and despite there being only three people in he managed to score a crab sandwich, a piece of quiche and some pâté and pickle. I asked Mark if he had any tips for me and he said: 'When you get to Pangbourne call in at the Swan, best pub on the Thames. And when you go past Vince Hill's house in Bray, wave, 'cos likely as not he'll wave back from his veranda.' I suggested he might have information of a more technical nature, perhaps pertaining to the stretch of river above Lechlade. 'Oh,' he said and leant over his glass: 'It's been a dry spring, lack of water is going to be your problem.' Then with the aid of two beer mats and some dry-roasted peanuts he demonstrated how I could build a makeshift flash-lock – an age-old locking system for hauling craft up river.

'That's the theory anyway,' he said, 'but it's a tricky trip to Cricklade.'

'How tricky?'

'Well, put it like this. I've never known anyone make it. Just you and the dog, is it?'

'No, a girlfriend's coming with me.'

'Sort of like *Three Men in a Boat*.'

'Well, sort of, except there are only two of us and one is a woman.'

'It's the centenary of *Three Men in a Boat*, you know? What you should do is dress up in a striped blazer and put on a boater and grow a Victorian moustache and re-create the trip. A number of people use my boats to do that. One a week this year. Bunch of prats if you ask me. Here, your glass is empty. We can't have that. Mine's a pint of Websters. Ta.'

Three Men in a Boat was the book synonymous with the Thames, and many people had made references to it when Jennifer and I had announced our intentions. I'd not been aware it was the centenary of Jerome's trip but now knowing only made me feel more uncomfortable. A re-creation was the last thing I wanted to do. I loved his story and to re-create it would be like seeing the film after reading the book and I knew I'd be disappointed.

I went back with the drinks and Mark said: 'But *Maegan*'s a good boat. My oldest. If anyone can get you there she can. She deserves a trip like this. I found her under a pile of rot in a Godalming boatyard. She had moss on her gunwales. Abandoned she'd been. She still bears the scars.'

I said: 'A bit like Boogie.'

He studied Boogie. 'Yes, I can imagine him with moss on his gunwales.' Boogie put his head on Mark's lap and Mark gave him his crisps.

'He likes you,' I said. 'You wouldn't like to look after him for three weeks, would you?'

'You take him with you. He'll be good company when your girlfriend leaves you.'

'What do you mean?'

'A camping skiff holiday can destroy any relationship. I never told you about Doreen and me did I? . . . Well, look at that, there's a dog hair in my beer.'

We were interrupted as a powerful motorbike pulled up outside, and the peace of the pub was broken as the door swung open and there stood a large leather-clad figure. He strode over to us. In one hand he had a crash helmet, in the other, a carrier bag. He looked at me through his moustache. 'Mark Wallington?'

'Yes.'

He handed me the bag. Inside was a pile of spare ribs, some barbecue sauce, some coleslaw, a baked potato, some strawberry cheesecake and a poem – 'Cars head down the rubble roads, travellers to far-off places. The darkness hides their dreams, their windscreens hide their faces, – Bon Appetit. Call me. Love from Jennifer.'

'That's a dreadful poem,' said Mark, leaning over my shoulder.

'It is, isn't it?' said the biker. 'It shows an inability to properly express herself at a time when she most wants to. If you ask me she's under stress and needs support.'

'Who are you?'

'I'm Michael, the courier for her firm. But most people say I'm too intuitive. Sign here please.'

Michael roared off and we walked back to the boatyard in the failing light. Mark showed me how to turn the skiff into a camper. What looked like an extremely complicated manoeuvre turned out to be very simple, involving a set of hoops inserted at intervals along the length of the boat to form a frame, and a canvas cover pulled over the lot. *Maegan* looked like a fairground caterpillar when all was finished.

Mark said: 'You'll be getting an early start I suppose, so I won't see you in the morning. Good luck. Make sure *Maegan* gets there. She can take anything you can give her. She's based on the design of the Viking longship, you know? See that curve on the gunwale? That's where you'd hang your axe if you were a pillaging Norseman.' He turned to go and then stopped and said: 'One more piece of advice. Watch out for your spoons – they go missing on trips of this nature.'

'Spoons?'

'Spoons.' As he spoke there were two sploshes. One was the sound of a dessert spoon falling in the river. The other was the sound of a three-stone mongrel doing just the same. I spun round and through the watery muck a little black head appeared in panic. I hauled him out and shouted to Mark: 'Run!'

'What!'

'Run!' But it was too late, and a gallon of turbid river water was sprayed over him and the rest of his boatyard as Boogie shook himself dry.

'Forget what I said about him being good company,' said Mark. 'He's going to be a bloody nuisance.' And he walked off home.

I sat on the river bank and had my spare ribs and made a mess of myself. Then later I found a phone box and tried to call Jennifer. I tried her home, her office and her health club, and finally reached her on her car phone. She was in Birmingham.

'Jennifer! What's happened?' I said, and Boogie started to bark.

Jennifer said: 'Listen. I'm sorry. Something big has come up. I can't make it tonight. You'll have to leave without me. I'll meet you at the weekend. I'm really sorry. I wish I was with you. Did you get the spare ribs? What did you think of the poem? I wrote it in a hurry. It's not finished. What's that barking?'

'Nothing.'

'I'm sure I heard barking.'

'The boatyard guard dog. I'll call you tomorrow.'

I took Boogie for a walk along the towpath.

'I suppose you think I'm wasting my time with her?'

Boogie went down to the bank and gargled with some river water.

'I suppose you think she's using me.'

Boogie shoved his nose into a rubbish bin and brought out an old running shoe which he started to chew.

'Well you're wrong; you just don't understand her.

She's got integrity, Jennifer has. And you'd be well advised to try to get on with her. She's good company.'

Boogie licked something off the path and started to foam at the mouth.

'Better company than you anyway.'

We strolled back to the boat. I lit the lamp and the shadows leapt across the water. A moth crashed into the glass and plunged into the bilges. A swan drifted past like a cloud. Somewhere a bicycle bell rang and an owl made a noise nothing like a hoot.

I looked round for Boogie and saw him watching from the bank, nonplussed. Then he saw me unpack my stuff and climb under the canvas and he started to chuckle. Oh how he chuckled. He grasped his sides and he began to roar. He held his stomach, lay down on the grass and rolled and giggled. He stood up, regained his composure then pointed at the boat and burst into a fit of hysterics.

Then I told him to get in.

I found him an hour later in the waiting room of Hampton station.

4. Be on Windsor Bridge at Seven – Prompt

The Thames is 216 miles long, an unimpressive length for a waterway of such stature. Diminutive, for instance, when compared to the Amazon. Insignificant when spoken of in the same breath as the Yangtze. A joke when placed side by side with the Mississippi. Nothing but a pathetic brook by the standards of the Zambezi.

The Thames is an undramatic river as well. In its meander to the sea it travels through water meadows for much of its length, falling only 350 feet from top to bottom. In that time it slips unmysteriously through places like Staines, Slough, Reading and Pangbourne, passing no waterfalls, no lakes and no swamps. The classic Thames animal is the duck. The classic plant, the geranium. The only tribe, the commuter. The Thames is a place where anything other than serenity is considered embarrassing. During my research it didn't take long to realize that to follow this river to its source had all the potential of one of the dullest journeys ever made.

And yet no river has influenced world history as much as the Thames, except for perhaps the Euphrates and the Rhine, and perhaps the Tiber, and then of course there's the Nile, and you can't rule out the Ganges. The reason for this is that the Thames refuses to compromise. It is a celebration of understatement. Its qualities are subtle in the extreme. In books about the Thames you rarely come across the adjectives awesome, stunning or spectacular. Peaceful you see quite often, and tranquil frequently, evocative is a favourite and ethereal crops up now and again, but breathtaking – never.

So I planned a departure from Hampton in keeping with the ambience of the river. I planned to rise at first light and get under way while the sun was a red button on the horizon and the mist still crawled on the water. I wanted to be the only boat on the river. I wanted to see the Thames without its wrinkles, without the sound of traffic. I wanted to be on it before the ducks even.

Instead I overslept, sleeping long after people who are about to set off to the source of a great river are supposed to sleep. This wasn't entirely my fault though, *Maegan* quickly established herself as a cosy and curvacious craft built for comfort not speed, and with the canvas overcoat stretched on top of her she cocooned all within in a tunnel of watertight sleep, so that it was still the dead of night inside the tent while on the outside buses were rolling past on the main road and newspapers were being rammed through letter boxes.

When I finally had the sense to lift up the tent flap and inspect the situation for myself, a laser-like beam of sunshine burst in and I was confronted with one of those yellow, green and blue days so perfect you feel envious of nature and the ease with which she can conjure up such beauty, and this makes you depressed and you want to go back to bed again.

I squinted at the reflections on the water. The river was still motionless; the same scum of wood chips and swan feathers surrounded the boat. In the workshop I could hear people building boats. I hurriedly dismantled the tent and dumped it in a bundle in the stern and arranged myself for departure. But I wasn't quick enough. A lad from the workshop came out with a cup of tea and said: 'Still here then?'

'Yes.'

'Huh.'

'Huh.'

'I bet you Robin Knox-Johnston never had a lie-in the morning he left Plymouth to become the first man to sail single-handed round the globe.'

'No I don't expect he did.'

Rowing – or rather sculling – isn't a particularly complicated activity, not on paper anyway. It's largely a question of rhythm, of getting both oars – or rather sculls – to do the same manoeuvre at the same time, then compensating for one's superior strength in one arm with an extra half stroke every five with the inferior arm, not forgetting to navigate a course in one direction while looking in the other, plus, in my case, coping with a hydrophobic dog trying his utmost to get out of the boat while at the same time trying his utmost to stay in it.

The result, that first morning, as I covered the stretch from Hampton through Sunbury and headed on to Weybridge, was a highly uncoordinated one. The onlooker on the bank would have seen a boat heading in the general direction of Gloucestershire but doing it the hard way, staggering from one side of the river to the other, ricocheting off islands and turning the occasional circle.

Fortunately there was little traffic about and, although my technique meant I was seeing rather more of places like the Molesey Reservoirs than I intended, it mattered little since the great thing about going to the source of a river is that it is very difficult to lose your bearings. As long as the channel gets progressively thinner and more shallow the traveller can assume that he or she is on

course. I calculated that all I had to do was keep heading
uphill and at any confluence follow the largest piece of
water, and sooner or later I would reach the inevitable
pool in a field.

Besides I was in no hurry. I had a couple of days to
familiarize myself with the river: to harden my hands, to
become au fait with the terms and techniques of the
activity, to victual the boat and learn how to manage life
afloat. That way all would be in order by the time Jennifer
arrived, and I could impress her with my waterman's
appeal. Boogie, too, would have time to acclimatize. The
truth is he's not really used to the outdoors. Scenic places
confuse him. He needed a little time to find his river legs,
and then scenes such as the one at the first lock we entered
would less likely be repeated.

This was Sunbury lock, and I arrived in a fashion befit-
ting *Meagan's* Viking heritage – full pelt, bow first,
straight into the doors. A jolly little man wearing a cap
and a shirt with epaulettes peered over the walls: 'Sorry,
I was putting in my bedding plants,' he said and proceeded
to operate the hydraulic gates. I paddled *Maegan* into the
lock. The gates swung shut, there was a tremor beneath
us and slowly we rose.

'What sort of dog's that?' said the lock-keeper.

'Argentinian ridgeback.'

'Thought it might be,' he said, then changed the subject:
'Going upstream?' I told him I was going to the source
and asked him if he had any advice to offer. He contemplated this for a while then said: 'Yes, make sure you call
in at the Swan in Staines, best pub on the river.'

He opened the upstream gates and that was when I
noticed Boogie had jumped from the boat and was standing on the bank. 'Stay!' I said with authority and he
immediately made a return leap. This time he didn't make
it though, or rather half of him didn't. He remained sus-

pended above the lock in a splits, two legs on land two on the boat, his attempts to reunite both sets pushing the boat further away.

I've never seen an animal's body elongate with such style. Boogie's back legs stretched until he was holding on to the bank with his claws. His front set did likewise, and when they failed him and he was falling towards the water, his teeth grabbed hold of *Maegan's* hundred-year-old mahogany. He resembled a canine gangplank for a while but ultimately he ended up where he was getting used to ending up. And if I'd thought the slick round Mark Edwards' boatyard was gruesome, it was spa water compared to the version found in locks. When Boogie surfaced and crawled up the steps to the lock-keeper's garden he looked like the Creature from the Black Lagoon, only less attractive. The lock-keeper took one look at him and dropped his trowel in fright.

'Run!' I shouted to the lock-keeper and ducked down in the boat, but it was too late and he and his house and half of Sunbury took a filthy shower.

At Shepperton I parked – or rather moored – on a rare piece of public bank among all the river frontages and No Mooring Strictly Private Stop Here And You're Asking For Trouble signs. I put the kettle on and lay back in the boat, the air so still, the water so calm that every noise was amplified: a man took his dustbins out in a house behind the trees; an expensive car door slammed beyond the next hedge; a hammer hit a piece of metal in an engineering works somewhere upstream and the noise carried over the river like birdsong. Above me jets from all nations circled looking for a parking space, or climbed and banked and quickly became a speck in the blue. At a lower altitude insects revved their motors, and on the water ducks flew in like seaplanes. It was a perfect spring day in suburbia; the ideal habitat for beasts such as *Midnight Rider II*.

At first all I was aware of was the growl of a powerful engine held on a leash. Then I was hit by a vast shadow and every creature in the vicinity dived for cover. A series of waves slapped against *Maegan* and leapt over her side and she bucked and smacked against the bank. The kettle fell off the stove, my hat fell in the water and I looked up to see a shining glass and plastic construction covered in antennae. It was the size of a cross-Channel car ferry and travelled through the water with its chin in the air. Along the bow was written the name *Midnight Rider II*.

I'd heard about these boats – the brochures called them cruisers, their critics called them Gin Palaces, a builder would have called them maisonettes. I'd imagined them to be as splendid as this, but never as sinister. *Midnight Rider II* was taller than she was long. She was fitted with radar and with lifeboats and everything attached to her sparkled to the extent that she dazzled oncoming traffic. On the deck in the conning tower were a woman in a swimsuit, and a man with mirror sunglasses. The boat was presumably on automatic pilot for no one was at the wheel, but then I couldn't see a wheel, just these two walking around the deck holding coils of rope and bumping into each other. They looked at me and waved and I sort of waved back and that was my mistake. *Midnight Rider II* slipped round the bend of the river and out of sight among the trees, but minutes later she returned and after much manoeuvring and general destruction of the environment and me – but mostly me – she moored next to me – but mostly on top of me.

'Sorry,' said the captain. 'Didn't disturb you did we? I wasn't too sure if this was public at first, but since you were here, well . . .'

From the saloon I could hear the television on.

'Funny-looking boat you've got there,' he went on. 'It's . . . it's not got a motor, has it?'

'It's a camping skiff. It's a hundred years old. It's got oars – I mean sculls.'

'Hmm,' he said. 'Mine was built in 1986. It's got all sorts of things. It's got a fire extinguisher for instance. Reception is lousy on the telly though. Where are you going?'

'The source.'

'Which way's that?'

I pointed towards Slough.

'I never go very far upstream. We live in Walton. We just got this to potter about in. TV reception gets bad upstream. The Crystal Palace signal gets weak round the Cotswolds, see. We had a booster put up in our area to reconvert the frequency. You need a different aerial but it's worth it.'

A funny-looking bird swam up to us. It was orange and white and smaller than a duck. It had the worst haircut of any bird I'd ever seen.

'I've seen a few of those over the years. You know what they are?' said the captain of *Midnight Rider II*.

'No,' I said.

'Neither do I. It's not a swan, that's for sure.'

'No, it's not a swan.'

'No.'

We looked at the bird for a while. There were probably no two less well-versed watermen on the river that morning. I dug out my bird book and identified the creature as a great crested grebe.

'It's a great crested grebe,' I said.

'Mmm.'

'With its legs situated under its tail the great crested grebe is ungainly and rarely seen on land, but supreme under water,' I read.

'Is it?'

'Its nest is usually a floating raft of vegetation. Both sexes incubate the eggs.'

'Mmm.'

A little black bird with a patch on its head appeared on the scene. I identified it as a coot or a moorhen. When the grebe saw it, it thumped its head in.

'That was unpleasant,' said the captain of *Midnight Rider II*. Then he looked at his watch and called out to his wife: 'Are those Yorkshires ready yet? The film's nearly started.'

She came to the hatch and said: 'Alan, come here a minute. There's a strange dog in our saloon watching television.'

I rowed – or rather sculled – on to Weybridge, a neat, smart, newly painted, traffic-light-controlled, streets-cleaned-every-night, bins-emptied-every-Thursday town with a W. H. Smith's, a Boots, a Peter Dominic and a Benetton.

This was my first riverside town and I was interested to see if, despite its suburban dormitory status, Weybridge had retained its former spirit as a commercial port. I walked up the high street looking for the one building where all travellers new to a town can go to hear the local news and meet the local folk – the supermarket.

I swung a trolley round the aisles, loaded it with provisions, then joined checkout two and stood amongst sun-tanned mothers with their teenage daughters. I was hemmed in by talk of time-share apartments and contraception.

We shuffled forward. Muzak from *Doctor Zhivago* filled every empty space. The man in front of me sneezed and his wife said: 'Did you know that the strongest sneeze ever recorded was over a hundred miles an hour and had the power of a force-seven gale?' At the front of the queue

a customer was paying by cheque, the next paid by Access
and the next by customer credit, for which forms were
filled out in triplicate. The next customer had a price
query, and the next was a friend of the checkout girl,
Lorraine, and they chatted about their friend Dave who
smashed up his dad's Ford Granada on Tuesday. I was
just getting the impression that Weybridge folk were a
civil and patient lot, with a rustic quality belying their
proximity to London, when suddenly the two nicely
dressed women behind me cracked and a battle for position began. 'I was here before you, you bitch!' 'Don't
call me a bitch, you slut!' Mr Davis the manager went
straight in and put up the Till Closed sign. We all
scrummed down and I joined checkout four. With two
people to go before me the till ran out of change and
checkout girl Rachael sat there with her arms folded looking out of the window thinking of Mike, the lad with the
long arms from dairy produce. The woman behind me
who only had a tin of tuna fish and a sliced loaf in her
basket said: 'You wouldn't mind if I go in front of you,
would you? I've only got two items,' but I didn't even
bother to turn round. I wasn't going to be taken advantage
of just because I was new in town. Besides, Mr Davis had
come over with a bag of change and there was just an
elderly man in front of me. But Rachael was giving him
a rough ride; 'You haven't weighed your tomatoes have
you?' she barked at him.

'What?'

'You haven't weighed your tomatoes!'

'What?'

'Go and weigh them!' And she threw the things at him
and sent him off. I moved into his space and smiled at her
and she snarled back and walked off for a tea break. Julie
took her place. She counted out her money, changed the
cash-roll and was about to pull the first item out of my

basket when she put her head in her hands and burst into
tears. Everyone at checkout four just stood there looking
at her. None of us' had any idea how to comfort a supermarket checkout person. I think someone might have said:
'There there!' but then one of us spotted checkout three
was open and we all scrummed down again. Mr Davis
moved in and led Julie away. 'I understand,' he was
saying. 'But it's like riding a horse. You've got to get
right back in the saddle.'

I had entered the supermarket a cool individual with
the swagger of a man about to journey to the source of a
great river. I walked back to the boat a seething, sweating
wreck with an in-depth knowledge of life in Weybridge
and a desire to kick innocent animals. Boogie, fortunately,
is very understanding in situations like this. When he sees
me in this state he gives me his 'it's all right; I know what
you're going through' look. 'You're all pent up and you
want to kick me, don't you? Well you go right ahead if
it makes you feel better. You relieve your stress on my
kidneys, that's what I'm here for. Go ahead, kick the dog,
I enjoy it really.' And I feel suddenly full of remorse and
think about people in the world less fortunate than myself,
and I bend down and stroke him and pat him on the head
and end up giving him a packet of biscuits.

We sculled through the afternoon. A policeman in a
patrol boat gave a 'good for you' wave. A work party on
a British Waterways Board launch whistled at me and held
up their cups of tea in an 'all the best' gesture. A man
sitting on his lawn in front of a bungalow by a sign
that said 'private' in italics, waved at me and probably
considered inviting me in for a glass of champagne but
then thought better of it.

My real friends though were the lock-keepers, and it
was clear after only a day on the river that they were all
friendly, helpful and good-humoured, and didn't mind

me smashing into their gates. They'd just nod knowingly and admire *Maegan*, and when I asked them if they thought I'd get as far upstream as Cricklade, some would say: 'Never! You'll get dragged down by weed and the boat will break her back on the rocks and your oars will snap in the narrows and the local farmers will shoot you; you'd be a fool to even think about it.' While others would say: 'Of course you'll make it, no trouble.' They all lived on islands in the most idyllic cottages and unlike most people in jobs where you get to wear a hat they weren't inclined to make comments like: 'You can't leave that here!' or 'That's what you think!' or 'Don't you under-stand plain English!?' If they wanted to make you aware of something they did it diplomatically, in just the way the keeper at Shepperton lock did to a blue-haired woman in a little cabin cruiser. She was busy at her stove as her boat rose up the chamber. The lock-keeper bent down and said: 'Just a word of friendly advice, Madam, but I wouldn't use the stove whilst you're in the lock as there can be a build-up of petrol fumes and there's a good chance that you and your little boat will be blown to bits.'

That evening I reached the village of Laleham. Racing sculls whizzed around me like wasps and I suddenly felt tired. I felt as though I'd travelled fifty miles, which is the feeling a beginner gets from having travelled only seven. A grassy bank in front of a riverside house was the ideal spot to moor for the night and I tied up and rolled out the canvas. Immediately a lawnmower of the kind popularized by cricket groundsmen came hurtling towards me. At the controls was a man with a frenzied look. Grass cuttings flew in all directions as he burned a trail in the lawn to my boat.

'Don't even think about mooring there!' he said.

'. . .'

'Can't you read?' And he pointed to a sign stuck in the ground a few yards away on which nothing was written.
'. . .'

'Public mooring stops there.'

On the other side of the signpost the words Public Mooring were indeed written. He wanted me to move *Maegan* six feet downstream, a manoeuvre which owing to my poor technique took fifteen minutes, and involved an inconvenience factor which Boogie and I made the most of with looks of absolute fatigue and despair. By the time I'd re-moored, the man on the lawnmower was ridden with guilt. 'Sorry about all this, old chap,' he said, 'but we can't be too careful, you know? Here, throw me your rope and I'll tie you up. Got water have you? How about dog food? We can let you have a can if you're out. There's a pub in the village by the way. Nice pub – does a good selection of baked potatoes with a variety of fillings, mushroom and sour cream, chilli and cheese, that sort of job. Peaceful sort of village, Laleham. Nothing of earth-shattering importance has ever happened here; it's never appeared on the *Nine O'clock News* or anything. Although there was a near miss between a British Caledonian 737 and a Cessna light aircraft once which would have focused world attention on us had they hit. Anyway . . .'

I went to call Jennifer. I tried her home, her office and her car and found her at her health club. She said: 'Where are you? You sound miles away.'

'I'm in Laleham.'

'Laleham! That's where Matthew Arnold came from! He's buried by the local church. "Life ran gaily as the sparkling Thames." '

'Listen, meet me in Windsor tomorrow evening, on the bridge at seven.'

'I'll be there. I should be back from Paris by then.'

'Paris!'

'Just for the day. It's business.'

'Jennifer! You can't behave like this.'

Boogie started barking at the phone box at this point.

'What's that barking?'

'I've got to go. The churchyard is closing. Be on the bridge tomorrow. I'll tell you all about Matthew Arnold's grave.'

I found the Arnold family plot near the church door. Children ran about between the mounds of earth. I was surrounded by screams and flintstone. The sun was setting and I was amazed. Amazed because I was standing in Laleham, a village I'd never heard of before and would never have had any reason to come to, and yet I was having a moment I knew I'd never forget. I felt giddy.

I went into a pub; it was almost empty. The barman said: 'It's always quiet on a Friday.' I bought some beer and before I'd got the glass to my lips I began to feel giddy again. Then the room began to sway. I bought some potato and mint flavoured crisps and went out into the garden, and the garden was swaying too.

Boogie went walkabout and managed to score a chilliburger, a piece of garlic bread, some scampi and some cold cuts. A woman with a steak sandwich gave him half, and her man said 'What are you doing? I'd have had that!'

'The dog's got that look about him,' she said.

'You gave a steak sandwich to a dog. I don't believe it! It's not even our dog!'

Then the table began to sway, then Laleham began to sway. I left my drink and returned to the boat and only then when I was back on water did I feel at ease. I diagnosed I had landsickness. The treatment? An evening with Delia Smith.

I sat in the lamplight with Delia Smith's *One is Fun!* cookbook in one hand and a pan full of piquant liver with a sherry sauce in the other. It tasted wonderful. Afterwards I lay in the dark in my sleeping bag as water lapped at *Maegan* and I felt I knew Delia Smith far better than I had before. It's an amazing thing, travel.

Next morning as I sat on the bank trying to untie the impossible knots I'd tied with such ease the night before, the driver of a canary-yellow cruiser called *Hesnotin* came to visit. He stood next to me and said nothing.

'What time is it?' I asked.

'Ten past nine. Breakfast telly has just finished.' He scrunched up his face, sniffed, scratched his stomach and made his eyebrows jump and said: 'That weatherman, that effeminate fella – not that I've anything against effeminate sorts – but anyway, that weatherman with the permed hair, he just said it's going to thunder and lightning. Glad I'm not in a rowing boat. Which way are you going?'

'Upstream.'

'River's moving faster today. Glad I'm not going upstream.'

I climbed back into my boat and set off and my cereal spoon dropped over the side. The river certainly didn't feel faster today, in fact it felt a lot easier. Maybe I was getting the hang of this sculling business. Maybe one day was all I needed to get fit. Maybe I felt like this because I was going the wrong way.

This was a bad mistake. For a brief moment I'd experienced how much easier it was going downstream.

For some folk Staines is the ideal holiday resort. For Boogie – who is content the minute he sees a pedestrian precinct or an NCP to play in, and who likes underpasses and bypasses and flyovers, and has a soft spot for No Entry Except For Access signs – it was the perfect spot. Likewise for a number of humans moored in their shiny launches outside the Swan. Launches were a step down from cruisers. They were all rather featureless, but this was probably because they were all hired from the company that monopolized the market. Some were dinky, others were modelled on the whale, but they were all uniformly painted in blue and white and their names all had the prefix Maid: *Maid Lucilla, Maid Yvonne, Maid Natasha*. They were like watertight caravans and were crewed by very friendly people in thick pullovers who all waved as I sculled past and called out greetings of the 'it's all right for the dog, eh?' and, 'it's a dog's life isn't it?' or 'get the dog to do some work, I should' or 'dog's got the right idea, hasn't he?' variety.

A number were moored by the London Stone, the point where, before the the river was locked, the reach of the tide ended. The date on the stone is 1285, although the real model was removed to a museum a number of years ago to protect it from vandals. A plastic replica now stands in its place, and that too is surrounded by bars. When that's smashed up they'll probably pin up a photograph of the monument and place an armed guard on it. The stone was the one-time marker of the western limit of the City of London on the Thames, an honour which now unofficially belongs to the M25 that crosses the river a few hundred yards upstream. A motorway is harder to vandalize than an historic monument but one lad was having a go at it as I passed. He was under the bridge scrawling some grafitti on the concrete slabs. He saw me coming and shoved his chalk in his pocket.

As we slipped into the shadow of the motorway the concrete rumbled, and the bridge created an echo like a cave. I could hear the drops of water drip from my sculls. The lad nodded at me and looked nervous and said: 'I'm sheltering, I am.'

'It's not raining.'

'That's what you think. Dog's got the right idea, eh?
How old is he?'

'Ten.'

'How old is that for a dog?'

'Er . . . ten.'

I was travelling slowly enough to have conversations
of this nature. In fact I was travelling ridiculously slowly
– a mile an hour was all I was managing. Even taking
into account my heading against the current this was dis-
appointing, and when a woman pushing a pram along the
towpath overtook me I slumped and said: 'I want to know
why you're pushing a pram and you're overtaking me?'
And she stopped, shook her head and said: 'Because you're
not leaning back, you're not feathering your blades, you're
not keeping out of the main current, your knees aren't
together and your boat's not balanced, that's why.'

For the rest of the morning I tried to correct these faults,
although the last of them I was unable to do anything
about, for the balance of the boat was dependent on the
items within it remaining still, and one of these items was
Boogie. As he grew to trust *Maegan* a little more he
experimented, leaning over the side until he caught his
reflection in the water. This so frightened him he'd lurch
to the other side and the boat would follow. He also did
a nice line in running from bow to stern whenever another
boat passed with a dog on it, and so for most of the time
Maegan, despite sitting on a flat calm of a river, was
behaving as though caught in her own Bermuda Triangle
of agitation.

'Please don't run up and down the boat, Boogie,' I'd
say very reasonably, and he'd give me his cute cow-eyed
expression which I knew from experience means 'don't
tell me what to do, sunbeam!' People often ask me why
Boogie is so disobedient. The reason is not, as they
imagine, because of his inability to understand commands

– he does that only too well – his contrariness is purely due to his demand to have the right to choose. He doesn't expect to be given orders; he expects simply to be consulted. Take stick-fetching for instance. To Boogie, stick-fetching is the most demeaning form of canine submissiveness and he insists I join him in his campaign to abolish such a mindless practice. At one point that afternoon, as we slipped into Berkshire, we met a woman throwing sticks into the river for her dog. She flung the things out into the middle and the dog sprang into the water and made for the other side, dodging motorboats. Having retrieved the stick, the dog would then return, exhausted, to the woman and drop it at her feet with a 'there, I've fetched it for you, now don't throw it away again' look. At which the woman immediately lobbed it straight back in the water and the dog sighed and gave her his 'all right, but this is definitely the last time' expression, and dived in again.

The woman looked up with a charming smile when we approached and said: 'Does your dog fetch sticks?' and I had to reply: 'No, my dog thinks fetching sticks is degrading to his species. He doesn't enjoy being treated like a circus animal, and before you throw that stick again for your dog he'd like you seriously to consider the implications of your action.'

'He enjoys it,' she said as the dog disappeared under a paddle steamer with a wedding party on board.

This campaign against stick-fetching was the first in a long line of anti-dogist stands that Boogie has made. His reasoning being that dogs shouldn't exist merely to play a role in the lives of human beings. After an initial protest, I have gradually come to understand and fully support him in his political career. People too easily dismiss Boogie as just an ugly little mongrel with a flatulence problem, but he's a sincere animal with a generosity of spirit, and, with regard to his position in the boat, I knew that if I were to put forward a reasonable case as to why he should cease his excursions from one end to the other, he would comply. Runnymede, I decided, would be a good place to address the problem. Runnymede would get him in a good mood. Runnymede, the Meadow of the Runes, the Council-field, the ancient site for the signing of treaties where in 1215 the earliest of constitutional documents, Magna Carta, was signed by the barons of the nation and their King John.

Quite why they had to do this in the middle of a field is not clear, although, the general theory is that the barons so distrusted their King and the King so distrusted his barons that neither party would go round to the other's place for fear of their lives. The occasion seems to have been a miserable affair from start to finish, with the charter itself showing all the bureaucratic flair of a local government report on a proposed leisure centre. It was the sort of document that created freedom by law in one clause, and abolished fishtraps in rivers, in the next.

Its boldest assertion though was to put the King in check by the creation of a parliamentary assembly, and although, initially, freedom was only granted to all as long as they did what they were told, the day it was signed was the day the nation first asserted the principle of constitutional government, which makes it probably the most important treaty ever signed in the history of the world and so it would have been nice if those involved could have been a bit less grim-faced about the whole thing.

Some say that the site of the actual signing is on Magna Carta island in mid-Thames, but I hope that isn't true since it would mean that the spot where civil liberty was created is now out of bounds to the general public. I'd much rather believe the other theory which claims the charter was signed in Runnymede meadows, an expanse of grass and woodland where a man and his dog are free to wander all they like.

It was by the Magna Carta Memorial that I put it to Boogie that on a journey of this nature one has to make sacrifices for the good of the expedition. The point being that running up and down the boat was undermining our chances of reaching the source of the river, whereas, sitting still in one position would in fact be contributory to the effort. The decision was, I stressed, entirely up to him, and if he chose to run up and down the boat creating havoc then he had every right as a dog to do so, but it would generally be more acceptable if he didn't.

In response he conveyed to me the opinion that he liked running up and down the boat creating havoc and couldn't give a toss about the expedition.

That evening I found a place to moor by the quaintly named Black Potts railway bridge from where there was a glorious view across the fields to Windsor. The castle stood thinly wrapped in a sepia shroud by the sunset. As darkness fell the walls were floodlit and I walked into town drawn by the glow.

The night air was sticky with a storm and the town was at boiling point, its bridge so crowded it seemed to sag with the heat and the stress. I waited outside a pub called the Donkey House where tables and chairs lined the riverside and there was a background of foreign languages and fairy-lights. A crowd were sitting on the quayside singing old Beatles numbers as from downstream a disco boat appeared – more lights and more Golden Oldies. It was the same paddle steamer as I'd seen earlier in the day. The wedding party had been put ashore and a few bulbs changed and the boat had quickly assumed a new role.

I was there on the bridge on the dot of seven. By eight

Jennifer hadn't showed. The pubs began to spill over. The castle glowered above as people without shirts leant against Wren's Guildhall clutching pint pots. There was going to be a storm or a fight, you couldn't tell which. It turned out to be a fight as from the George someone flew out on to the street. There were shouts and smashes of glass and a group of youths ran across the bridge.

I turned to get out of their way and bumped straight into a familiar figure in leathers wearing a crash helmet and clutching a carrier bag.

'Mark Wallington, right?'

'Yes.'

'Me again, Michael.' And he handed me the bag. 'She's got problems. She needs you. Remember that before you get angry. I've a feeling she has an unlocked trauma. Sign here, please.'

I signed and he nodded and said: 'I've been through it as well. It's not easy. If you want someone to talk to let me know.' Then he strode off.

Inside the bag was a note that read: ' "Is it so small a thing To have enjoyed the sun, To have liv'd light in the spring, To have lov'd, to have thought, to have done?" Enjoy the Bombay duck. Call me.'

Boogie and I sat on the bench next to a Japanese couple who smiled at us for twenty minutes as we ate crispy duck, plum sauce, pancakes, spring onions and mushrooms. Afterwards I found a phone box outside the castle gate.

Windsor Castle is attractive because each window you look through you can see some sort of life – you feel the laundry room is full of steam and the kitchen full of cooking smells and there's someone on the landing doing the Hoovering. You get the feeling someone really lives there, which is more than you can say about Jennifer's flat. The answering machine came on. 'Hello, this is Jennifer

Conway, I'm not able to take your call but if you'd like to leave a message I'll get back to you. And if that's Mark, I'm sorry but I've been delayed again, can't help it, something big. I'm really sorry. I should make it on Monday. Have an adventure planned for the afternoon. What do you think of the poem? It's not me – it's Matthew Arnold. But then of course you knew that.'

Concorde passed overhead and two large bats flew into the floodlights of the castle. An owl made a noise nothing like a hoot and I walked out of the town into the darkness and followed the towpath back to the boat. 'She's been delayed, that's all – can't be helped. I know you think her intentions are questionable but you're wrong, you'll see.' Boogie licked something horrible off the path and retched.

In the small hours of the night the storm broke. I awoke to a crack of thunder overhead and rain fired on to the canvas like shot. I lay there in a sweat, waiting for the first drop to pierce *Maegan's* skin, but she remained taut as a drum and took the battering without a protest. At one point during the night I lifted up the flap and saw the castle alive with lightning. The railway bridge hissed and steamed and the river swallowed and filled by the minute. At one point a flash illuminated a supermarket trolley poking out from the water like a skeleton. I lay there wondering what possessed people to throw supermarket trolleys into canals and rivers. There must be some strange thrill attached to it. I decided that at some time on this trip I would go to a supermarket and steal a trolley and push it into a secluded stretch of the river and discover the sensation for myself.

Next morning I was up at dawn, a time of the day which doesn't reach anyone sleeping in *Maegan* until eight thirty.

I breathed in a new day, felt the sun on my face. If you could ignore the goods trains rumbling over Black Potts

Bridge, the traffic on the Datchet road, the jet engines overhead and the blue and white bathtub that roared by crewed by Chelsea supporters chasing the ducks, it was a peaceful Sunday scene.

I sat in the boat during the morning and tried to make notes, but I kept being distracted. Water voles popped out of their holes to look at me, and swans came over and threatened me. So did a police launch. It cruised past and the officers eyed me suspiciously. I gave them my unsuspicious smile but they pulled over.

'Have you got a licence for that?' said one.

'For what?'

'That boat.'

'Er . . . well . . .'

'Right, you're nicked,' he said. Then his mate leant over and pointed to the pork pie sitting on my seat and said: 'What's that then?'

'My lunch. Want some?'

'Beneath it.'

Beneath it was a little blue sticker.

'That's my licence of course.'

I set off in the afternoon, sculling up through Windsor, catching a peek of the spires of Eton College through the trees. Some scholars loafed on the boathouse ramps but the river was too busy for them to take their fragile rowing boats out. All afternoon as the air thickened I picked my way through a milieu of boats: pedaloes, punts and cruisers, and ploughing a path through them all, a hotel boat with guests gazing down from the deck as if they were on a liner. The river was a playground and the splendid views of the castle supplied the classic backdrop. It grew smaller and smaller as I pulled my way westwards, then it was gone round a bend and instead a black cloud the size of a small European country filled the heavens, and suddenly all boats were running for cover. I wasn't really bothered. I just leant into the rain and felt the water refresh me. At one point a woman dressed in a coat and head scarf stuck her head out of a launch called *Maid Anita* and shouted: 'Are you enjoying yourself?'

'Yes thank you,' I shouted back.

'I should give up if I were you. We're going back to Datchet. Been a lousy trip all round. It's all right for him, he's been to sea. I haven't. We argue all the time. It all started in Marlow when I dropped the anchor over the side. Wasn't tied to the boat, see. People keep shouting at me.'

I reached Boveney lock as the rain intensified. The lock-keeper came out dressed in oilskins and sou'wester and, taking pity on the drenched duo that paddled into his chamber, he said I could moor for the night on his island. We sheltered in the gents' toilet. From the lock-keeper's cottage I could smell a roast dinner being cooked, which is a dreadful smell if you're not going to have any. I sat on the step and watched the vegetable patch fill with puddles. The cabbages had been gasping but now each leaf had a pond for the flies to dive in.

The rain stopped some time after dark but I spent a restless night as the weir stream roared. By the following morning the river had risen considerably.

As I packed up, the lock-keeper came and stood over me and shouted above the din: 'You should be all right. I'm not going to put the red flags up for the time being. Conditions aren't that dangerous, not yet anyway, not quite, almost though, could be by lunchtime. Travelling alone?'

'No, no. A girlfriend's joining me soon.'

'Dog's good company, I bet.'

'No, he farts too much.'

I cast off and felt the weir suck at me through its straw. And for the whole morning I battled against the wind and

the current. My hands were raw and blistered and to those
people who gave me waves of encouragement from the
bank I apologize now for not waving back, the reason
being that if I took my hands off the sculls for an instant
I lost all the ground I'd made in the previous half hour. I
particularly apologize if one of those waving to me was
Vince Hill.

It took me four hours to reach Maidenhead, and I was
rewarded with a town full of smooth edges that boasts a
Pizza Hut, a McDonald's, a Kentucky Fried Chicken,
and a Marks and Spencer's. It does have two fine bridges
though. The first is one of Brunel's greatest hits, a railway
bridge with two splendid arches incorporating the largest
and flattest brick span in the world. Such an engineering
feat was believed impossible when the bridge first opened,
and Brunel was persuaded to leave his wooden structure
in place to allay fears of collapse. Only when these supports were washed away in a flood a few years later was
the great man able to admit they never reached the brick-
work.

The second bridge is the town's, and is another graceful
construction on which I am now an authority since I've
been under it backwards, forwards, sideways and through
every aperture. Each time I neared one of the holes or
arches or whatever they're called, the current became so
strong it swept me either downstream or clean through
only to be picked up by another rush and thrown back
through a different hole.

After four attempts I took a break and tried to call
Jennifer. Her personal assistant answered.

'Jennifer Conway, please,' I said.

'Can I ask who's calling?'

'Personal call.'

'I'm sorry Ms Conway is busy.'

'It's Mark Wallington.'

'Oh, Ms Conway has gone to Brussels then.'

'What!?'

'That's the message she left.'

'Brussels! What the hell is she doing in Brussels?'

'She said she's sorry and that she would meet you later in the week. On Wednesday.'

'Wednesday?!'

'Hopefully. Personally I shouldn't think she'll make it.'

'Who are you?'

'Listen, you seem like a reasonable sort, you should steer clear of her, you know what she's like.'

I went back to the boat and thrashed my way under the bridge powered by raw aggression. I didn't need Jennifer's help or anyone else's to find the source of the Thames.

Not far upstream from Maidenhead I got lost. It was all the islands in the channel. They confused me.

5. Sonning. I'll Definitely Meet You in Sonning

Before Maidenhead the riverside had been tailored and well protected. It had been London's waterway and had had its edges clipped and every willow tree purposely placed. But as I headed up towards Cliveden, the east bank rose and grew into a cliff of beech and chestnut. Travelling backwards I hadn't noticed my approach, but now crags unfolded one after the other and the river was suddenly let loose. A mist crawled up into the woods so that the trees smoked and stood so still they appeared drugged. The river was a groove and I sculled slowly through the deep feeling heady, feeling for the first time the opiate of the river, and how it intoxicated all that it came into contact with.

At the top of the cliff among the trees stood the Italianate mansion Cliveden House. It was huge and loomed magnificently out of the mist and was impossible to look at without seeing a haze of scandal. For Cliveden had a reputation. If duels weren't being fought between dukes and jilted lovers in the gardens, then young women like Christine Keeler were being introduced to Ministers of War by the swimming pool, and it seemed to me to be more than mere coincidence when, passing the river frontage, I dipped my scull into the water and pulled out a sodden diary. I peeled the pages back in the hope I'd find material with which I could blackmail at the very least a member of the Cabinet, but the entries were clearly in code: 'Jan 1st. Dear diary. Got up late. Boring day. Anne Diamond is back on *Breakfast Time*. Arranged to meet Ben down the pub but the head gasket on his Toyota has blown. Started the jigsaw of the Matterhorn this afternoon. Think I'm getting a cold. Peter Snow chaired *Newsnight*.' At least I presumed the entries were in code. I didn't want to believe that someone's life could be so dull.

That night I sat in the boat in the lamplight and began my own diary. I wanted it to be an introspective and poetic account of the journey, but that didn't last very long. Instead I wrote about the wildlife I'd seen so far. My knowledge was scant but anyone who spent more than a few days on the river would soon have become intimate with all the creatures that lived on the banks, particularly the birds. I spent a long time each day just watching them paddle and scoot and swoop about their business.

Mallards, of course, were ubiquitous, but I'd never really noticed what beautiful birds they are, and how aerobatic. They left the water like jump jets and flew low and in formation, masters of their art. The males were recognizable by their beautiful blue-green iridescence, and their yellow grained beaks. The females, by the way they normally had three males on top of them. They were gregarious creatures but it was noticeable how they didn't get on with great crested grebes. I saw one have a fight with a grebe on one occasion and the grebe flattened it.

Canada geese were another common bird, although not so exciting to observe. They were awkward creatures that waddled everywhere with their noses in the air. They'd march along the banks or paddle on the water giving their young lessons in how to be supercilious. They mixed well with all the birds except the great crested grebes. I remember seeing a grebe mug one once.

Coots and moorhens were intriguing. They scurried about the riverbank and built their nests precariously among the reeds, or in empty burger boxes wherever the willows stroked the water. I liked coots and moorhens, I couldn't tell them apart but I felt we had a rapport. Great crested grebes didn't like them though. They picked on them and pecked them severely.

Herons were the most mysterious birds on the river. They were loners that stood for hours on logs at the water's edge, or by the weir streams. They were sad, silent fishermen, tall and sharp, skin and bone. Standing they reminded me of Fred Astaire in top hat and tails, and in flight their giant wingspan had a Wright brothers' design. Despite their size however they appeared timid birds – great crested grebes would beat them up regularly.

In fact great crested grebes were a generally violent bunch. They had a snarl on their beaks and a scar on their faces and they shuffled over the water with 'oi! are you looking at me?' expressions, shouldering everything else out of the way. Only one group of birds frightened them, the same one that frightened me – the swans.

In the short time I'd been on the river I'd already come to regard swans as remote and intimidating creatures. They knew their own strength and I always gave them a wide berth. Only occasionally would they try and charm, and then they'd paddle up to the boat, lean over the side and see what you had to offer. But their arrogance would prevail and they'd nudge you with an 'I'm beautiful aren't I? How about some of your lunch? Come to think of it, how about all of your lunch? Or the boat goes over, get it?'

But swans can afford to behave badly. Since the time of Richard I their population has been largely royal property and highly valued. When in the middle ages the king wanted to show his appreciation to the trading guilds and city companies for their part in the military rearmament, he ceded to them the privilege of keeping swans on the Thames. Two guilds – the vintners and the dyers – still exercise that privilege today, and join in the annual Swan-upping ceremony when the swans are counted and marked by the Queen's official Swan Keeper. Captain Turk of Cookham is the current incumbent of this position. I had an image of the swans with some sort of homing instinct that led them all to Cookham every July, but the truth is Captain Turk sets off from London Bridge in a ceremonial barge and heads upstream gathering the birds. It's a splendid and historic custom but of note primarily because the swan-keepers manage to do it at all. Pictures and engravings throughout history depict the swan-keeper of the time casually branding the birds with a brush or knife, while the swan just lies there like a dog having its belly tickled. My own experience of the birds was quite different. If I got anywhere near one, it came hurtling down the river, running on the water, wings wide, like wild white horses with hooves flying, and anything but mute. They could hiss like snakes, and the beat of their wings was a clamour. The idea of grabbing hold of one and writing on its beak with a felt-tip 'this bird belongs to the Queen' didn't seem like much of a job to me.

But Cookham is clearly proud of its role in the ritual. There's even a pub called the Swan-upper. I leant at the bar, and asked the barmaid what she knew about the ancient custom and she said: 'I don't really know anything about it. Stan does but he's not in tonight.'

Cookham looked lovely in the night time. Its moor was a spread of buttercups lit by the moon, and the floodlights from the parish church cast long shadows around the village.

And the next morning there was still a general yellowness. The village was lush and surrounded by rape fields and the buses were painted marigold. It was another beautiful day but you got the impression it was always a beautiful day in Cookham. It was such a reassuring sort of place: it had cottages covered in roses, there was a flintstone church by the river, and the local curry house had exposed timbers.

I'd stopped in the village to visit the Stanley Spencer Gallery. I liked his pictures for their irresistible wickedness, and for the way he never let the gravity of his subject matter smother his sense of humour. He painted the Last Supper with the apostles playing footsie under the table.

Throughout the first half of this century Spencer was a familiar figure in Cookham pushing the pram that contained his artist's tools through the streets. He incorporated many village scenes in his work including the Swan-upping ceremony and the Cookham Regatta. In his best known painting, *The Resurrection, Cookham*, he depicted a number of local villagers – himself and his wife among them – rising from their graves on Judgment Day, while the Thames slips by in the background. The gallery in the converted Methodist chapel where the painter used to worship houses a small but important collection of his work and I'd long wanted to visit it.

But it was shut. So I went to the churchyard to see if I could find Spencer's gravestone. I asked a woman if she'd seen it, and she said: 'Are you a visitor?'

'Yes.'

'So am I. Are you on the river?'

'Yes.'

'So am I. Who's Stanley Spencer?'

'A local artist.'

'No, I don't know him. We went to the Cookham Tandoori. George Harrison eats there and so does Vince Hill, or so I've heard. You know, him who sang "Edelweiss".'

The current had eased and the day warmed, I took my shirt off and sculled past the cliff edges of Cookham Dean Woods. The river began to meander, and the accents to thicken. At Bourne End I saw some cows in the river watering and heard some folk on the bank talking about tractors. There were hills in the background for the first time.

But I was entering a different phase of suburbia, that was all. The indiscreet chalets that had lined the bank downstream had now gone and been replaced by big houses in the pavilion style with windows thrust open to let in the spring. The residents sat in their garden furniture with their guard dogs at their feet, gazing at the water. I waved and said hello and they waved back to me with their teaspoons or celery sticks dunked in dip.

There was a sense of display here, though, that was unsettling. Because the trippers who passed in boats took photographs of these riparian owners the same way they would have of Dogon tribesmen in their mud-brick villages. If the locals were true natives, they would soon be forced to capitalize on the business potential here: 'We members of the Residents' Association have decided that each photograph takes away a little bit of our soul and so from now on, in line with the recent rate increases in the area, we've decided to charge a fee of 50p a snap. Cheques accepted with a banker's card only.'

As I passed one house I commented on the charm of the garden to the couple sitting in deckchairs on the lawn. In return they commented on the charm of *Maegan*. A rapport was established and their dog, an athletic-looking boxer, trotted down to the water front.

'He's been on TV, you know,' said his proud owner. 'He advertises a chain of hardware stores. He's the dog in the back seat of the station wagon that belongs to the chap who buys the loft insulation material. We're hoping to get him a role in the next series of *Juliet Bravo*. He was chosen for the glossiness of his coat.'

At this point Boogie appeared from under the covers and from then on relations went rapidly downhill. In my antique boat it was possible for me to melt into the scenery but Boogie stood out like a blot on the landscape. He has never been on TV, and he couldn't give a toss about a glossy coat – the more congealed the better as far as he's concerned. The couple in the garden took one look at him and called their TV star to heel – 'Come here, Bergerac.'

It was typical, really, of the culture shock Boogie was experiencing. Surrounded by all these pedigrees he felt insecure. For the rest of the morning he took his role as a passenger very seriously and lay on the back seat in protest. At the Marlow lock the keeper took a long look at him and said: 'Either that dog's dead or he's been doing all the rowing.'

His assimilation problems came to a head in Marlow, a pretty, neat, tidy, well-swept, parking-allowed-for-thirty-minutes-no-return-within-an-hour, thirty-five-minutes-from-Paddington, Georgian, brick and flintstone sort of place, with a Bejam, a Victoria Wine shop, a Waitrose, an Anglian Window Centre and an assortment of designer pedigree dogs, I tried out a few of the town benches, put some litter in the litter bins, sampled a zebra crossing and read some menus in restaurant windows, while Boogie made an effort and introduced himself to a red setter, a blue poodle, a labrador and, hardest of all, an afghan. They ignored him to a dog, wouldn't even point him to the local tandoori or the betting shop. He walked back to the river in disgust, only to find the boat surrounded by swans. Boogie doesn't know much about other animals except what he's picked up on *Wildlife on One*. When he sees something he's not familiar with, like a sheep, say, he doesn't chase it, he tries to nut it. I put him on his lead. I knew he wouldn't take to anything with a long neck and flat feet. Sure enough, with a 'red setters, afghans, swans, they're all a bunch of wankers,' shrug, he lunged at the birds. This moment of rashness coincided with the moment his lead snapped. He turned to me and gave me his 'I don't believe it, what sort of lead is that? I only lunged at these things because I knew you'd pull me back,' expression. I feared for the worst, but it only took a hiss, and a clout from a wing tip, and Boogie was cowering in the bottom of my shopping bag. Buses on the Wandsworth Bridge Road he could cope with, swans would take time and a complete rethink.

That afternoon I just dabbled slowly upstream, the river was in no hurry and neither was I. At Hurley lock the keeper, with an uncharacteristic display of officialdom, waited until I'd almost reached his gates, then looked at his watch, and hung up his Gone to Tea sign. The hydraulic locks on the Thames can be operated manually and the public are allowed to take charge when the keeper is off duty, but after an earlier attempt, when I left the river severely depleted and me severely exhausted, I elected to wait until the lock-keeper came back on duty. If the lock-keeper had a tea break, then so should I.

A few cruisers motored up to join the queue, I watched in horror as two adult coots or moorhens or whatever they were swam out of the reeds with their family of chicks, intent on giving them the hardest lesson of their lives – how to cross the river during rush hour. The adults headed off into mid stream, leading their family to what looked like a certain and very messy death as the brightly coloured hulls of the cruisers bore down on them like threshing machines. Used to the safety of the bank the chicks followed innocently, only to find themselves in heavy seas and having to paddle like riverboats just to keep their heads above the waves. They reached the other side somehow and had a roll call, but they would never have the same confidence in their parents again.

Presently, a beautifully decorated narrowboat pulled up. The man at the helm looked over at me and said: 'It's all right for the dog, isn't it?'

I smiled and he asked if I wanted a drink.

'I'll have a glass of champagne please.'

'I've got a cold beer,' he said and handed me a hot one.

'You know who you remind me of? *Three Men in a Boat.* My favourite bit is when they can't open the tin of pineapples. I'd love to do what you're doing and re-create their trip.'

'I'm not actually re-creating their trip, I'm just . . .'

'I mean the river's not really changed at all in a hundred years, has it?'

'I wouldn't be too sure . . .'

'I mean it may have motorboats on it and motorways over it, and the banks may be all privately owned, and most of the land developed, and all the commercial traffic may have gone, and the towns themselves changed unrecognizably, and of course all the mills disappeared, and there may be a fraction of the amount of wildlife there once was, and it might be impossible to find a mooring half the time, but it's not really changed.'

'Well, I think you'll find that . . .' But my point was lost as the lock-keeper opened the sluice gates and approximately eighty thousand gallons of water rushed off towards the North Sea.

The biggest Maid I'd seen joined us in the lock, *Maid Enormous* or something. It was like a bungalow. A man dressed in a suit leant out of the window and said: 'Tell us if we're going to squash you.'

They motored away and I was left to paddle out. The lock-keeper leaned on his gate, smoking, and I threw my eyes up in an 'honestly, the things that true watermen like you and me have to put up with, eh?' fashion, and he nodded and looked at my freshly sunbathed body and said: 'You're red, aren't you?'

Hurley was surrounded by chalk cliffs and dark islands where herons with beady eyes kept watch on the weirs. I paddled out of the lock cut to find I had the river all to myself. The flat calm returned and with it the acoustics lost on the winds of the previous two days: I could hear cuckoos everywhere. I leant back and thought about the most enjoyable thing I could think of. The truth was that when Jennifer did finally arrive it would be the first time we'd actually spend a night together, alone, in the same room as it were. It would have to be handled carefully. I couldn't be presumptuous. We were travelling companions, that was all. When she said she'd come on a journey with me nothing was implied. The important thing was to be reasonable. The river was good for being reasonable. It was soothing, and suitable for thinking things over. Since I'd made that phone call to Jennifer in Maidenhead, I'd realized my anger was simply directed at our different approaches to the journey. Mine was methodical, regimented. Hers was spontaneous, impulsive. But then Jennifer had always been an unpredictable sort. She'd made that clear from the start. We met by accident – a road accident that is. She knocked me off my bicycle. I was cycling to Italy, following the path of the first Roman legion to reach Britain in 55 BC, and I'd got as far as Blackheath and the start of the A2 when she reversed into me. I fell off and she insisted on buying me a drink. We went to a cocktail bar near the Blackwall Tunnel and she bought some champagne and said how she could easily fall for a man who cycled all the way to Italy. I explained to her that since my front forks were now bent beyond repair and my pedals made a noise that suggested a cracked bearing case, I would probably have to abandon the trip. But she said that such talk spoiled the romance of it all and she loaded my bike into the back of her TVR and took me to an Italian restaurant in Leytonstone where we had artichokes and garlic butter, and she got into a heated discussion with the waiter over the political role of the Catholic Church in Italy's social reform as a result of the unification. Over the zabaglione I said to her: 'Wouldn't it be funny if we got married because you knocked me off my bike?' And she laughed and said we must stay in touch. She gave me her phone numbers and we arranged to go out the following Wednesday, and that was the last I saw of her for six months.

'It's a contemplative thing the river is,' I said out loud, and I saw myself climbing up a slippery slope until it disappeared into the ground. 'A bit like life really,' I added, and a lone canoeist whistled past me.

'Pardon?' he said.

'Nothing. Nothing.'

A mile upstream I moored by the most beautiful house I'd seen on the river so far, Medmenham Abbey, a jumble of architecture, four hundred years old, standing in cool gardens. But its peaceful present disguised its decadent past, for here during the eighteenth century the Hell Fire Club met, that infamous, dissolute and ultimately rather silly band of men who under the aegis of Sir Francis Dashwood dressed up as monks and had get-togethers every Wednesday under the motto: *Fay ce que voudras* – do whatever you want.

To join the Hell Fire Club two qualifications were needed: 1) to have been drunk, 2) to have been to Italy. Meetings contained a variety of agenda, but virgins and satanic rites and the perverse things you could do with them seem to have been the most popular. Afterwards the gang would repair to the Dog and Badger in Medmenham village to unwind after a hard night's decadence. The pub has changed rather since those days. Now there are no cabals sitting in corners discussing whether or not to give the holy sacrament to an ape next week. Instead the pub is popular with RAF sorts sitting down to gammon steaks with pineapple rings. I sat at the empty bar. The barman said: 'It's always quiet on a Tuesday.'

I said: 'So what's all this about the Hell Fire Club?' and he said: 'I don't know anything about it.'

From somewhere Boogie came back with a half a fish-burger with garnish and tartare sauce. A man in a suit sat next to me and said: 'Huh, the dog's got the right idea.'

I recognized him from the big blue boat which shared the lock with me that afternoon. We sat in silence for a while then I said: 'Saw you on the river today.'

'What?'

'I saw you on the river today. We were in the lock together.'

'I haven't been on the river in twenty years.'

'You remember, you were in that big boat. I was in my camping skiff.'

'In fact, I haven't been on the river since Macmillan was Prime Minister.'

'And you said to me: "Let us know if we're going to squash you." '

'I can tell you an interesting fact about the river, though.'

'I'm sure it was you.'

'Herons eat ten thousand fish a year. Each.'

I found a phone box and left a message on Jennifer's answering machine for her to meet me in Sonning the following evening, then I took Boogie for a walk along the river towpath. A mist was down over the meadow. It swirled around my knees, and around his ears. It was a crisp cool night. I said: 'I'm glad in some ways Jennifer has given me a couple of days on my own.'

Boogie sniffed and clicked his tongue.

'And that's not to say I'm not missing her. I am. It's just that a trip like this is a time to be on one's own. That's the big difference between Jennifer and me. She doesn't like her own company. She doesn't like to be on her own for any long periods. I think that's why her poems are all so short.'

An owl coughed. Boogie turned and walked back to the boat. I spent the evening with Delia Smith. We cooked a delicious thick celery soup with smoked bacon. Afterwards I read her biographical notes and discovered that she lives in Suffolk and is married to the writer Michael Wynn-Jones. I also learnt her opinion on microwaves.

Next morning I planned to rise early, have a swim and get some sculling done before breakfast. Instead, I overslept. I pulled back the tent flap to see a fish jump out of the water and return with a plop. Above there was a vast sky crossed with the trails of aircraft. In the trees a rookery made a noise like a main-line station. The day had left without me again.

I made ready for departure as quickly as I could, but this process was taking longer and longer each day, not because of the tent dismantling, or any routine I had to go through, but simply because of my knots, a department of watermanship in which I had become particularly expert. I might even go so far as to say my knots were the most secure in the history of river navigation. Certainly they were the most original. The problem was they weren't the sort you'd find in any knot compendium and they could never be repeated or learnt. They were in fact different every time, and, rather than having any method, were simply the tightest jumble of rope I could manage. And so the measure backfired, because the disentangling of the trees, pillars, irons, stakes, gateposts, fences and cattle legs that the knot incorporated took hours the following morning. The strategy was successful in so far as I hadn't as yet drifted over any weir streams in the middle of the night, but it also meant that some mornings I wasn't on the water until midday.

The knot that secured me to Medmenham was a particular devil. I was keen to get moving but the knot was keener on me staying put. At one point I lost my temper with it and some walkers on the towpath made a detour around me. I didn't calm down until I reached Hambleden lock where the sun was shining off the lock-keeper's hat badge. He left his carrot patch to tend to me and say: 'Morning.'

'Morning.'

'All right for the dog, eh? Heading up towards Pangbourne?'

'Yes.'

'Make sure you call in at the Swan, best pub on the river.'

'Are all the pubs on the river called the Swan?'

'No, not all. There's the Trout at St John's Bridge. Then there's the Trout at Tadpole Bridge, and the Trout at Godstow. Not to mention the Perch at Binsey although I think they're going to rename that the Swan.'

This desire to conform was clearly part of the Thames ethic, and nowhere was it better expressed than in Henley, the town that lay just upstream from Hambleden at the end of the most famous mile on the river. My own performance along this the regatta course was unimpressive, hampered by my stopping halfway to feed some Winalot to the ducks. During the first week of July though, folk dressed in wellingtons are fenced off, and this part of the river is a rush of wood on water as very muscular people in very thin boats compete for silverware.

Of the many regattas held along the Thames, Henley's has always been the most popular, the rowers attracted by the long stretch of straight water, and the spectators by the town's facilities. As the halfway point by road and by water between Oxford and London, Henley was an important staging post long before the regatta was initiated and it could cope with the annual influx, one that increased greatly in 1851 when the regatta was given its royal cachet and became internationally renowned. Henley Week quickly grew to be the most popular date in the river's calendar with special trains from Paddington decanting spectators in the middle of the town from where it was a short distance to the riverbank and the lines of houseboats and barges. Elsewhere slipper launches, skiffs, punts and gigs fought for space and the river was a jam for a mile each side of the town. The whole affair was the biggest excuse for a picnic anyone had ever seen and somewhere among it all there was even time for some rowing.

For Henley was a place to be seen more than anything else. The crowds that fell off the train were nothing if not dressed in the latest river fashions. Men came in boaters and white flannels, blazers and canvas shoes; ladies, in laced hats, basqued bodices, serge skirts and mousquetaire gloves, all under a Japanese parasol. There is a feeling today that professionalism has crept into Henley's make-up, that the rowing has become too competitive and that the marquees are all public-relation tents for multinational companies. That may be so but nothing can change the image Henley acquired during the 1880s of the biggest annual festival of posing in the country.

I was almost two months early for the regatta but a grandstand and some marquees were already erected and the town was in a state of preparation. It was probably always so. There was a certain way of doing things in Henley – the regatta way – and everyone complied. Accordingly the town was a neat, well-organized, prosperous, meticulous, antiquified sort of place with a branch each of the Portman, Abbey National, Anglia, Halifax and Woolwich building societies, and a number of No Fishing, No Swimming, No Mooring, No Dogs, No Parking, No Ball Games signs.

Jennifer was arriving that night so I sacrificed half an hour of my life for her in Waitrose then lugged my groceries back to the boat and left town under the fine stone bridge which bore masks of the gods Thames and Isis. As I emerged I found an empty chocolate fingers packet had landed in my lap. And as Henley disappeared bit by bit behind willows, it occurred to me that most of the Thames towns and villages I'd stopped in had all been pretty and pleasant and historic, and yet despite – or maybe because of – their preservation societies they all looked strangely similar. I'd only been going a week but I was already having difficulty remembering one town from another.

'Backwaters!' said Mark Edwards, picking wood shavings out of his hair. 'They're great fun. You'll have a fine time exploring backwaters. Thanks very much, mine's a pint of Websters.'

Those were his very words as we sat in the pub in Hampton that first night. I remembered them well as I veered off the main channel a mile or two past Henley, and entered the darkness of Hennerton Backwater.

Although, it wasn't solely Mark Edwards who convinced me to take this diversion. A man I met just outside Henley helped as well. He was sitting on the bank on a stool, a duffel bag by his side. I said: 'Picnicking?'

'What's it to you?'

'I . . . I was just thinking what a nice day it was for a . . .'

'Ah shutup! Who cares? Clear off, you're disturbing the fish.'

'But . . .'

'But what?!'

'But you're not fishing.'

'Course I'm not! It's close-season, and it's a good job it is 'cos if it wasn't your boat would be just where my line would be.'

At other times of the year the banks of the Thames would have been lined with dark green and dour characters like this. The close-season had kept them indoors but this fellow was getting in a bit of practice at being abusive before the new season began. I said:

'What fish would you be fishing for it it wasn't close-season?'

'Chub! Now clear off.'

'Would you have had any luck? . . .'

'You're heading for trouble, you are, son.'

Fishermen were the most unpredictable creatures of the river and I knew they should never be underestimated. I'd heard stories of the most hardy oarsmen found in the bottom of weir streams or hung from willow branches by fishing line after they'd had the nerve to nod a greeting to a fisherman. But I took objection to this man's attitude and I said: 'On the contrary, I am heading for Cricklade.'

'Huh, not in that tub you're not.'

'Why not?'

'Too bleeding wide, you stupid git.'

'No she's not.'

'Listen, trout-face, you'd be lucky to get through Hennerton Backwater in that old pile of woodworm let alone Cricklade, now push off or I'll bombard you with maggots. And don't call in at the Swan in Pangbourne, 'cos, that's where I live and I don't want your sort there.'

So I thought I'd better test *Maegan* through Hennerton Backwater.

The opening was off the main channel through a veil of weeping willow. It was about fifty yards wide to begin with but very shortly tapered off to a slim cut. The water thickened and darkened to a slime and the vegetation formed a shroud so that only needles of sunlight pierced the foliage. There were no other boats. To begin with I was piloted through the undergrowth of fallen trees by a family of Canada geese, but after a way they disappeared and I was left with the nibbling insects. The birdsong sounded different here, and there were strange scuffling noises among the reeds. A couple of large water rats dived in the water with a sickly splosh.

After a few hundred yards the stream narrowed so badly I kept hitting the banks with the sculls and at each stroke I pulled a few pounds of weed out of the water. So in classic style, dressed barefoot and in shorts, I stepped up to *Maegan's* bow and began to paddle. I could have been travelling through the central American rain forest if it hadn't been for the sound of a lawnmower nearby.

Presently, I saw where the noise came from – a fine house set back a way through trees, with an extensive garden stretching down through orchards and coarse lawn to the water. All was peaceful until I saw the black head of a doberman peep through the willows.

Prior to this trip, if I'd been asked what the animal

synonymous with the Thames was, I'd probably have given the standard reply and said the swan or the duck. But my experience so far was steadily leading me to believe that these birds were heavily outnumbered by a different kind of wildlife – the alsatian or doberman guard dog.

On the river proper they weren't a problem. Boogie would sit in the boat posing like a pedigree, and stick his tongue out at the heavies, safe in the knowledge he was out of their range. The dogs could race through gardens to the water's edge and bark all they wanted – we were in mid stream and could pass with impunity. Down Hennerton Backwater though, the banks were a lot closer and this killer was striding alongside us just waiting for us to come that bit too close so he could leap aboard or even grab my paddle and pull us to the bank. I could see a low bridge ahead which would have provided safety but before I could reach it Boogie, in his typically tactful style, blew a raspberry at the beast and that did it – the thing was in the river and after us. And not for him any primitive stroke like the doggie paddle, this neanderthal was doing the crawl. He wanted Boogie badly.

There was a time in Boogie's life when he would have taken on the best of them. He was never particularly tough, not even in his youth, but he quickly learnt how to climb trees which was a distinct advantage. When he approached middle age and lost his speed he turned to diplomacy and learnt to negotiate his way out of trouble which is what he'd have done in this situation had his assailant not been so far beyond discussion. I had the feeling the doberman was a professional guard dog, partly because of its manner, but also because running through the trees after it was a security guard – a tubby breathless man who had one arm longer than the other. As he ran he shouted to us: 'He's not playing! he wants to tear your limbs off!'

Boogie was a model of composure. I'd like to say for a moment his hackles rose and he contemplated defence. But he knew the hopelessness of the situation, and so he turned to me and gave me his 'well, it's been a good life' look. 'Thanks for everything. I know I've not been easy to live with, but I want to tell you how I appreciate what you've done. And I'm truly sorry about that time I made a mess in the fruit bowl. One request, no pedigrees at my funeral. And if you want to have some sort of memorial for me, make it a seat on Crouch End Broadway outside Radio Rentals and have it inscribed: "To Boogie, who loved the view".'

We were almost at the bridge, five more strong paddles and I'd be under. But the guard was now shouting: 'Lie down and pretend you're a tree. The dog is a trained killer.' I turned and saw two paws on the back of the boat. I was standing right on the bow as far away from the stern as was possible and yet Boogie was behind me. The paws began to pull the rest of the dog up out of the water. I prepared myself for the first mauling of my life. Then suddenly, out of the reeds dived two great crested grebes, and like the cavalry, swam towards the dog. They didn't look as though they had any intention of intervening, but their effect was immediate. The doberman took one look at them turned and splashed back the way he had come, squealing. The grebes spat and swam slowly out of sight. The guard led the doberman away like a lamb. I turned and banged my head on the bridge.

Now gnats formed a cloud around us. From the woods on the bank came a noise half-human, half-double-decker bus. In the murk a supermarket trolley lay rusting, its wheels in the air. The vines curled themselves around my neck, the water bubbled and snapped and we reached another bridge, this one so low I had to lie down in the bottom of the boat to pass under. My nose scraped the roof; I tasted slime. But before I could stand up again there was a dull thud and I looked up to see we were back in civilization again. We were in a marina and we'd hit a cruiser named *Black Stockings*.

'Hello there?' said a man in a sunhat scrubbing his deck. 'Look, it's *Three Men in a Boat*. Dog's got the right idea.'

I imagined the upper reaches of the river would be like Hennerton Backwater only with less depth and ten times as long. It was a daunting prospect but I couldn't complain, so far this trip had hardly been an ordeal. It had been a sunny jaunt through a landscape that strained for perfection. Sonning, where I moored that evening, looked so perfect it had the feel of a working model. Even the telephone kiosks had preservation orders on them. Only the traffic lined up the road from the narrow bridge restored reality.

I'd told Jennifer to meet me in the Bull at eight. I was there on the dot, sitting in the corner, trying to look anonymous. It was the landlord's fiftieth anniversary and he was celebrating the occasion by embarrassing everyone. Boogie disappeared and returned with a salmon sandwich and some ardenne pâté on French bread. The landlord spotted him and staggered over. He said: 'What sort is he?'

'Albanian retriever.'

'I thought he was. Here, are you on your own? I'll have to get you fixed up.'

'It's all right; a friend is joining me any minute.'

'Tell you what, there's a PE student over there. She's got blond hair, like you; you'll get on fine. Hang on.' And he staggered off again.

'No, my girlfriend is joining me later, honestly.' Boogie

sighed and shook his head. 'She is!' I said. But he'd seen what I hadn't – a tall figure in black leather standing at the door holding his crash helmet in one hand and a carrier bag in the other.

'Hello,' he said.

'Oh no!'

'Me again.'

'I don't believe this!'

'Mexican tonight.' He handed me the bag.

I said: 'I'm angry now. I'm being taken for granted.'

The messenger nodded. 'I think you should be angry.'

The landlord staggered back over. 'Her name is Sandra. She's from Andover. Nice place Andover.'

The motorcyclist messenger looked at me, sincerely, and said: 'You shouldn't be afraid of your anger. If you really want this woman you've got to be constructive with your emotions . . .'

The landlord prodded him and said: 'Here, are you on your own? Can't have that; I'll get you fixed up.'

'That's all right thanks. I'm in a relationship. It's not perfect, but then every relationship is an exercise in compromise, isn't it?' He leant closer to me and said: 'I always say that you've got to fall out of love with someone before you can really learn to love them. Sign here, please.'

He strode out. The landlord said: 'Here, don't get depressed.'

'Who's depressed? I'm not depressed.'

'Go over and speak to Sandra. She's dying to meet you.'

Sandra was a pretty young woman in a Fred Perry shirt and track suit sitting with a friend also in a Fred Perry shirt and track suit. They both looked serious and cradled tennis rackets. I smiled at Sandra and gave her a little wave. She looked the other way, then said something to her friend and they left.

Boogie and I walked back to the boat along the tow-path, clutching the Mexican meal. Inside the bag was a card that read: ' "At least I have not made my heart a heart of stone, Nor starved my boyhood of its goodly feast, Nor walked where Beauty is a thing unknown." I've had to go to Bologna. I'm really sorry. But I won't be long.'

I said: 'You see, most men would have got tired of it all by now. But not me. I know Jennifer better than she thinks. She's frightened that she's getting close to me, it's unnerved her. She feels threatened so she's distanced herself, literally. Well if this is a challenge I'm ready for it. She can be as unreasonable as she wants. I'll show her. I'll not react. That's what I'll do.'

Boogie licked something horrible out of an old plastic bag and we strode purposefully back to the boat.

During the night the wind picked up. It rained hard and the current tugged at *Maegan*. Next morning, I sculled off with great effort. A man walking along the towpath, whistling tunelessly, stopped and screwed up his face and said: 'Strong current today.'

'Yep.'

'Strong wind too.'

'Yep.'

'No motor, eh?'

'Nope.'

He weighed up the facts.

'Going the wrong way, really, aren't you?'

'Yep.'

6. Sorry About That. Give Me a Ring From Pangbourne

For two thousand years the Thames had no equal as a trading route and communication link. With all but ten miles of its length navigable it was an artery leading straight to the country's heart, and the Romans, the Saxons, the Vikings and the Normans all quickly realized that control over the river was a prerequisite to control over the nation.

They also realized that to keep this vital channel open, strict regulation was essential, otherwise the river would flood in the winter and be reduced to shallows in the summer. The millers and the fishermen had by Saxon times found a solution to the problem with crude versions of the weir. These provided pressure for the millers' wheels, and a trap for the fish, but they also provided a dead end for the boatmen, since they were little more than barricades across the stream. So flash-locks were introduced i.e. weirs with removable slats which provided a 'flash' of water on which a boat could be ridden downstream or winched up. These kept the boatmen happy, who now, on a good day, could ride the same flash all the way downstream – although on a bad day they would

probably drown – and they kept the fishermen happy
since the fish were channelled as before. But now the
millers had grievances because the flashes of water undermined their waterpower. They made extortionate charges
for boatmen to ride a flash; or frequently, if water levels
were low, they'd simply refuse to open their gates. The
result was huge delays for the boatmen who took to ram-
ming weirs for their entertainment.

Fortunately, in Italy, where the Renaissance was well
under way, Leonardo da Vinci was working on the problem. While our boatman and millers were standing on
weirs squabbling, Leonardo was taking a far more system-
atic approach to the far greater problems facing Italy's
waterway network. This had to cope with rivers that fell
three hundred metres in as many miles and da Vinci knew
that the only device of any use would be one that operated
independently of the weir stream and yet used a compara-
tively small amount of water. His solution was the pound
lock. Two hundred years later in the middle of the seventeenth century, the British got to hear of it and started to
convert.

This was a costly and slow process. The first pound
lock on the Thames was introduced at Iffley in 1633 but
not till 1938 was the last flash-lock replaced. By then all
parties concerned were largely grievance free, but this was
because they were all largely redundant. The country's
rivers and canals had declined as commercial routes in
place of the railways; the fish were victims of pollution
or people brought them in frozen boxes anyway; and
watermills had been a joke for a long time. But the locking
of the river did see the creation of one role: that of the
lock-keeper.

I think it was at Sonning lock that I realized my vocation
in life was to be a lock-keeper. The keeper there didn't
speak to me as far as I remember, but that morning as I

rose up the granite walls a further five foot four inches towards the source, and surfaced into a world of trees, flowers and mist to see the lock-keeper bent over his gate, nodding and smoking his pipe, I knew that his was the job I'd always wanted. It was clear to me that a lock-keeper was a man who woke up in the morning and stood on his front porch scratching his belly, surveying his vegetable patch and thinking to himself: Life is good when you're a lock-keeper. Then he would dedicate the day to being helpful to people, chatting to them, advising them, forgiving them when they gouged chunks out of his newly painted lock doors. He'd spend his spare time weeding his herbaceous borders, oiling his hinges, patting his dog and painting everything diamond white and gloss black. Then at lunchtime he'd take a break in his cottage which would be a hundred-and-fifty-year-old flintstone building with bright curtains and a crammed larder. In the afternoon he'd potter in his fruit cage and shine the plaques that commemorated the flood of 1847 and the year when he won Best Kept Lock of the Year Award. Then he'd bottle some jam for sale to passing boaters and go and sit under his sycamores for his tea break. After that he'd check the flow of the weir stream and as the sun went down he'd top up the hydraulic fluid levels and count the boats that had gone through his chamber that day, then close his register and go in for his supper. In the evening with the weir rushing under the moonlight he'd read Arthur Conan Doyle stories until he fell asleep in his armchair, the world a better place for the day he'd spent.

And so at the Caversham lock where the keeper had freshly painted bollards, manicured flowerbeds and permed hair, I said: 'You've got the best job of the world.' And as luck would have it he replied: 'There's a vacancy if you want.' But then he added: Long hours and lousy money and you don't meet as many girls as you'd think.'

'Oh.'

'It's boring as well.'

'Oh. Garden looks nice though,' I said.

'I hate gardening. It's boring. Do you know your boat smells of roast dinners?'

As it happened I had noticed a faint smell of roast dinners all morning but I couldn't understand where it was coming from. In fact I couldn't understand a lot of things that morning. The most odd was Boogie's desire to help me out with the sculling. I should have guessed his behaviour and the smell were connected. His lassitude of the previous few days forgotten, he spent the morning trying to push me off the sculls and take over my position in the boat. He even started to lick the scull-chocks and that was when I made the connection. I'd greased the sculls before I set out from a tin I'd found in the bottom of the boat. The grease had come straight from a roasting tray, and now the sculls were like beef lollies.

We were approaching Reading. Gathering on the horizon were the gasworks, pylons, scaffolding and railway cuttings of the biggest city since London.

Some swans escorted us in, or rather made sure we kept to a certain lane. There were a large number of them on the approach. They'd found a refuge in a house on the bank where a man stood by his open back door and threw bread and vegetables for the birds and they clamoured around him. I'd seen similar scenes on a number of occasions since London. The houses were surrounded by swan dung and feathers, and the people who fed the birds had long necks and noses and walked with flat feet. When they died they'd have their ashes sprinkled over the river and for years afterwards the swans would come and expect to be fed.

We passed the river Kennet and the entrance to the

Kennet and Avon Canal. And for the first time I felt the
river narrow noticeably. In London it had been an old
and worn corrugated slab of water looking as though it
expected to find the sea round the next corner. Here it
was young and gritty and needed big gulps to swallow a
river like the Kennet.

Reading was a town with a charm all of its own. As
we slipped under the town bridge an empty Toblerone
packet landed in the boat thrown by a lad who leant over
the parapet with his tongue stuck out. I said: 'What's your
name?!' And he shouted back: 'Nigel Leyton, aged twelve,
what of it, Mister?'

And then by Caversham Bridge a gang of skinheads sat
all over a bench, smoking and shouting and throwing
things. I asked them what Reading was like and they were
surprised to find someone addressing them. They were
suddenly quiet as they tried to work out who was to be
their spokesman. Finally, one said: 'It's got an inner ring
road and an outer ring road.' And then another said: 'It's
got a biscuit factory.'

I stopped in Reading briefly just to fill up with water,
but Boogie saw a Pelican Crossing and had to have a go
on it. Then he saw a car park and he wanted a run in that,
and then we had to have a walk down the pedestrian
precinct and have a look at the bus depot. Finally he
wanted to lick some parking meters and visit the railway
station redevelopment, and in the end it was a couple of
hours before we could get away.

But, like all the towns it passed through, the Thames
left Reading by a back door and within ten minutes I'd
found an island in the stream and was sat on a branch of
a low-slung willow, brewing up.

A coot paddled past me; a moorhen followed. I fancied
I was finally able to tell the difference between them. It
wasn't their paddle motion or the size or shape of their

nests. And it wasn't their cry or their mating ritual, nor the size of their brood nor their defense tactics. The difference was that coots had a bright white head while moorhens had a bright red and yellow one. Birdwatching isn't easy but you get the hang of it after a while.

I snuggled into the tree sheltering from the warm drizzle. I liked these islands in the river. They'd been a feature all the way since Kew. The Saxon word for them was eyot and there was something dark and disturbing about them, except for when they had executive hotels and landscaped lawns such as on Monkey Island near Maidenhead, or when they had housing estates like one near Shepperton.

This particular one was just an overgrown lump of vegetation and didn't look as though anyone had set foot on it for years. Hardly had the thought left my head than a cloud of diesel called *Maid Ugly* appeared. Its wash climbed my boat. The coots and moorhens dived for cover and bits of bank fell in the water as the driver leapt out and tied up: 'Good place you've found here,' he said. 'Look, there's even a supermarket trolley.'

Sure enough a supermarket trolley was sticking through the mud on the bank; only an experienced eye would have spotted it. I said: 'I can't understand why people throw supermarket trolleys into rivers.'

'That's because you've never done it, have you?'

'Have you?'

'Yes, I have as a matter of fact.'

'What's it like?'

'Well, put it like this: now I think the world is divided into two sorts of people – those who have thrown supermarket trolleys into rivers and those who haven't.'

I greased the sculls again and Boogie licked them dry again and we headed up to Mapledurham. The sun came out and the river was a mirror. The reflections of Mapledurham House and the old mill were a shimmering water-colour, a pool of life that looked as though one could walk on it. I threw a stone and a shock of ripples hurried over the surface with a shiver then the water quickly returned to its mirage-like state. The river was made up of many things, but it was the reflections that gave it its extra dimension. It was easy to forget about them at times, to take them for granted and not notice them for long periods. But every now and again I'd see a special display such as this and then I could see the whole earth and sky in the water. The reflections were sharper at some times of the day than others but they were always there some-where, and in the evening as the dusk seeped into the edges of the landscape and the sun set, the reflections were left behind in the water for a short time, until the last of the daylight dragged them off into the woods.

The stretch from Mapledurham to Pangbourne was glo-rious, the sort of scene I'd pictured when, before I set off, I'd closed my eyes and tried to imagine the journey. On the bank stood old sycamores so colourful you could taste their sweet blossom. Insects skated on the breathless surface; fish shoved their faces through a ring of water; some horses came down to the bank to look at me; and there in the most splendid setting was Hardwick House, standing back from the water, its gardens sloping grandly down through vivid meadows. By the landing stage two herons stood motionless on a log, like guards, grinning and waiting.

The evening had become calm and warm. The only sound was *Maegan* breaking the water. I had the reach to myself and I spent hours exploring every creek. The river was a box of tricks and I crept about, frightened to move too suddenly in case I broke something.

At length I got to within sight of Whitchurch Bridge and I moored to watch some canoeists playing water polo.

I made camp and then walked along the towpath towards Pangbourne, preparing myself for a frank telephone conversation with Jennifer. Her behaviour was putting the expedition into jeopardy. It was time to be firm. Well, firmish.

Some other boats were moored for the night, but there was little activity from them. I'd hoped there might be some sort of boatman's camaraderie on these mooring sites. I'd thought there might be campfires at night and folk gathered together singing songs of the Thames, roasting fish on the fire and telling tales of ghost barges and house prices in Chertsey. Instead, most crews threw their slops out of the window, then pulled the blinds and switched on the television, and that was that.

As I neared the bridge though, I saw a different kind of boat. It was moored away from the others and looked put together out of orange boxes and rope. Its blue and white paint was peeling and faded. Washing hung from bow to stern. The windows were coated in grime and condensation, and lashed to the deck was an impressive display of paraphernalia: a bicycle, a fishing net, fenders, petrol cans, a mattress, a standard lamp, a Hoover. It looked like a tramp's steamer. But the most unnerving part of it all was the dog bowl on the bank outside. It was the size of a bucket and had the name Ralph written on it. Where Ralph was I didn't know but I didn't want to meet him, that was for sure, and I passed on tiptoe. Boogie, on the other hand, who is either fearless or stupid, but probably stupid, went over to the bowl and started to lick it out, tripping over a mooring line in the process. Like a spider sensing a touch on its web, a man came dashing out of the cabin. He had a tattoo on his arm and a snarl on his face, and he said: 'Get lost.'

'Sorry.'

'What's your dog doing?'

'Nothing.'

'Clear off.'

'Yes, we're going.'

'You were pulling up my moorings.'

'It was an accident.'

'Push off.'

Then he eyed my wellingtons. 'You've got wellingtons on,' he said.

'Yes.'

'You don't see many wellingtons on the river these days.'

'No?'

'You've got a stupid hat on as well.'

'Yes.'

'You don't see many stupid hats on the river these days.'

He eyed me meanly, then reached behind him and put his own hat on. It was really stupid.

'Where are you heading?' he asked.

'The source.'

'What sort of boat?'

'Camping skiff.'

'Like *Three Men in . . .*'

'I promised myself I'd hit the next person who said that.'

He sniggered. 'You can come in if you want.'

'What about Ralph?'

'Ralph? That's me.'

'You've written your name on this bowl?'

'It's my bowl isn't it? I write my name on everything that's mine.'

He had indeed. As I climbed down the steps into the cabin I found myself in a room that resembled a loaded removals lorry, only more tightly packed. You could pick something up to sit down but then there was nowhere to put down the thing you'd just picked up. Ralph had got round that problem by sitting down on the thing he would have picked up. In the end I held on to the thing I picked up – a picture in a broken frame – and I sat on a box that contained another box. Ralph handed me a cup of something. The cup had Ralph written on it. So did Ralph's cup.

'Where are you headed?' I asked.

'I'm not headed anywhere. I live here. Lived on the river for thirty years.'

'Bet you've seen it change?'

'Everyone asks me that.'

'What do you tell them?'

'I tell them it's changed.'

He gave me whisky with dust in it. I wanted to ask him so much but he liked silences. He'd asked me on board and now wanted to share a silence with me. I looked at the picture I had in my hands. It was of a medieval bridge across the river. The bridge was on piers and there were buildings and turrets and a chapel on it. Underneath, the caption read: Old London Bridge. Ralph looked at me and said: 'Do you believe in time travel?'

'. . .'

'If you could choose one period and place in history to go back to where would it be?'

'. . .'

'If, say, you could go on your holidays to the period of your choice; if you could just walk into a time-travel agent and flick through a brochure of periods in world history and pick the one you wanted to visit most, where would you choose?'

'Ancient Greece.'

'Good choice. You know where I'd go? I'd go back to London when that bridge was there.'

I looked at the picture again – stalls and carts and horses, grand houses several storeys high jutting out over the water, boats and mist and flags. All life seemed to be going on.

'Lasted over six hundred years that bridge did. The city was a skyline of spires and belfries in those days, and as cosmopolitan a place as you could find in Europe. Traders from all over settled in London, and the bridge was its pulse. Ravens flew among the turrets, and decapitated heads hot from the Tower were stuck on poles at the bridge gates. Here, hold this a minute.' He handed me a box, then another box, then a typewriter and then a sewing machine and he burrowed down into his belongings. With surprising speed he was at the bottom of the pile, emerging with another picture, an engraving this time. It showed a frozen river and in the background the same bridge.

'The bridge used to slow the river down, see, and it would freeze, and then everyone would take to the ice and great frost fairs were held. Winter celebrations with oxen roasting on the ice. There were bear fights, bull-baiting, games and market stalls of all sorts. You could drive a coach and four over the river.'

I could recall the Thames freezing over in my lifetime but never in London, always upstream. I said: 'When was the last frost fair?'

'Beginning of the nineteenth century, just before they knocked the old bridge down. The new one hadn't the number and thickness of supports and the water wasn't dammed like it had been. They built embankments as well and so the river was narrower and faster and couldn't freeze.'

He seemed sad. He filled his glass and said: 'But what a sight it must have been. I've lived and worked on the river for years and I miss that bridge even though I never saw it.'

'You worked on the river?'

'Yes.'

'Doing what?'

'All sorts.' He didn't want to talk about it, but he was the first waterman I'd met; someone who could actually tell me something about the old commercial river.

'What sort of work?' I asked.

'Towing. We towed barges down from Lechlade to Reading.'

He was silent again.

I said: 'I bet you've seen it change?'

'Everyone asks me that. In fact you've just asked that.'

'Ever been further upstream than Lechlade?'

'Once. Wish I hadn't.'

'Why?'

'Let's talk about London Bridge some more.'

'Have you ever found the source?'

'No. But I met someone who did.'

'Where is it?'

'It's by a tree.'

'Any particular tree?'

'Can't remember. But the tree had TH written on it, or so I was told.'

'TH?'

'TH.'

'What does TH mean.'

'I don't know, maybe Thomas Hardy went there and carved his initials, how should I know. I'm going to bed now. You be careful going to the source. You'll lose all your spoons.'

I left Ralph and walked round Pangbourne looking for a telephone. They were all broken so I went into a hotel and put mud on the carpet and asked to use a phone. As Jennifer's number rang I rehearsed my speech: 'This is getting ridiculous. You're being unreasonable. I'm not prepared to take any more of this. If you're not here by the weekend . . .' The answering machine came on: 'This is Jennifer Conway. I'm sorry I'm not able to take your call but leave a message and I'll get back to you. And if that's Mark, I know what you're thinking. You're thinking: this is getting ridiculous. She's being unreasonable. You're not prepared to take any more of this. If she's not there by the weekend . . . Well, I've got good news and bad news. The bad news is I've got to go to Oslo. The good news is I'll be back by Tuesday. Promise. Did you visit Reading Gaol? Of course you did. It's where Oscar Wilde was imprisoned. That's why I sent you that Oscar Wilde quote. I would have sent you lines from the *Ballad of Reading Gaol* but I discovered he wrote that in Paris not Reading but then I'm sure you know that. Leave a message at the office where you'll be on Tuesday. I can't wait.'

I walked back to the boat, lit the lamp and began to prepare chicken in a paprika sauce. Tonight it would be me and Delia again. I looked at her picture on the cover of her book. How pleasant she appeared, standing there with her hands under her chin. She looked like a wholesome sort, good to travel with. Not the sort to let you down on an expedition to the source of a great river. She'd be there by your side doing her share of the paddling, no matter what. I sat in the shadows on the border of Berkshire and Oxfordshire and prepared chicken in paprika sauce and tried to imagine what it would be like to travel with Delia Smith. A journey across the Sahara would be more her forte. I could imagine her trading with the nomads for juniper berries to give her pepper steak piquancy. I could just see her bartering in the medinas of Tamanrasset for root ginger to give her stir-fried mange-tout that essential zest. She looked like a resilient woman, not the sort to be discouraged just because her brown kidney soup got full of sand. She knew the meaning of the word commitment – you only had to read her opinion on packeted Parmesan cheese to recognize that. By the same token though, you only had to read her section on tinned tomatoes to realize she wasn't the sort of woman who couldn't improvise if needs be. If we got caught short of food, for instance, she could probably rustle up something very nourishing from Boogie's Winalot. These things are important when you're considering a travelling companion.

Inside the tent, the paprika sauce simmered. Outside, the water lapped on *Maegan*'s mahogany, and the shrill song of the night birds pierced the dark. The noises of the night were so sharp I could even hear fish; I was sure I could. They made a faint pop when enough of them got together and broke the surface. Only the river was quiet. For such a large mass travelling such a distance at such speed it was a remarkably silent work of nature.

The chicken was wonderful. Tomorrow I would write a postcard to Delia and let her know. I lay back and made animal shadows on the ceiling. The lamplight shone on the Winalot packet. There was an offer on the back: fifteen tokens for a plastic dog bowl. Thirty tokens for a feeding mat. A hundred and twenty-five tokens for a giant wool-and-mixed-fibre blanket. On the side there was a chart recommending the size of meal to give each size of dog. It turned out that Boogie, who should have been eating the same amount as a corgi or a standard dachshund or a fox terrier, was putting away the recommended diet of a doberman. I cut out the coupons. At the rate he was going we'd have the mixed-fibre blanket before we reached Oxford.

Outside, an owl cleared its sinuses. Inside, Boogie came over and lay by me; he seemed to sense my solitude. He tried to climb in my sleeping bag; I seemed to sense his foul breath.

He looked at me sorrowfully. 'Don't look at me sorrowfully,' I said. 'She'll turn up. I know she will. You'll see.'

I turned the light off then turned it back on again and made a note on my mental state. I was concerned by the way I had taken it for granted that Boogie would be with me when I travelled trans-Sahara with Delia Smith.

The rains came again that night and the river rose and was far too fast for me to get up early and have a swim so instead I had a lie-in. But I was there at the gates of Whitchurch lock as the keeper came on duty. He looked at me with great concern as I rose up to his level, then said: 'What day is it?'

'Friday.'

'Bugger,' he said, then went back to his flowerbed.

The current was a struggle again, but I was better able to cope with the vagaries of the river now. I'd learnt how to feather my sculls, and I bent my knees and pulled with my body, and I never took my wellingtons off unless I had to. I had the vernacular as well. I used expressions like 'astern' rather than 'the back end', 'amidships' rather than 'that bit there'. I called the depth of *Maegan*'s water displacement 'the draught'; the extreme front of her the 'stem'; and the people who motored up the river at fifty miles an hour and disturbed the coots 'bastards'.

I pulled steadily away from the lock. The river felt thicker after the rain, and the sensation of being in the control of something powerful and inevitable grew stronger with each mile. The elixir-like flow drew all life to its banks. And not just wildlife – churches loved to hide in its recesses; the fine country houses that I passed were all possessive of their river views; the land and the farm stock all lurched towards the water for sustenance.

And I began to find something significant and something personal attached to each meander, nowhere more sad than at Basildon where I arrived mid morning. I'd stopped to see Basildon Park, a splendid Georgian mansion with, so I'd been told, an Ionic portico and strange octagonal-shaped rooms. I understood it to house a unique collection of Anglo-Indian objets d'art, as well as some fine frescoes and a garden of great design. Unfortunately it was closed, so I rested for a while in the local churchyard. I'd pulled against the strong current for three hours and wanted to rest in some shade, and here was a haven of trees, long grass and wild flowers, a miniature wilderness, untouched by Black and Decker edgers, where butterflies flourished and grass grew to four foot in places. Boogie had three different species of spider crawling over him.

I strolled around reading the gravestones. It's normally easy to distance oneself from these brief biographies, but there was one here that brought a lump to my throat and illustrated what a taker as well as a giver of life the river is. It was a memorial, a stone sculpture to two young boys, erected by their parents. An inscription told how the boys had drowned in a backwater nearby in 1886. The family had lived at the church farm at the time. The river had flowed past only a few hundred yards from their door and was an integral part of the local life, but it shouldered no responsibility. It couldn't be trusted. It acted imperviously and hurried on its way without a thought.

There was no one about in Basildon. The village and the fields were deserted. Only the rooks and the aircraft caught the eye; the only noise came from the hammers of the British Rail workers on the bridge downstream. I left feeling like a voyeur – my biggest fear when travelling. And in this case particularly unsettling, because with the ease of changing channels on a television, I went from the saddest part of the day to the most exciting.

For if Basildon was sad and silent the Goring Gap, a mile upstream, had the air of a celebration. This gorge is

the place where the post ice-age Thames burst through
the ridgeway formed by the Berkshire Downs and the
Chilterns, then swallowed the river Kennet and continued
east through its new valley. Before I'd set out everyone
had told me this was the most impressive stretch on the
river and I remember feeling a tension that was strange
because it was so unlike the Thames. As the banks tightened and rose into cliffs I could sense the land choke so
that approaching the gap was like being poured out of a
bottle.

I entered the gorge and came upon the village. The
postcards in the local shops were all pictures of the gap
and of the lock, and Goring was undoubtedly a picturesque place, a fine example of what nature can do given
beech trees and chalk cliffs. But the most compelling part
of this village is something that could never be photographed – not unless Ralph's idea for time travel got off
the ground – for above all else the village is an historic
junction, the place where the two ancient trade, military
and stock routes, the Ridgeway and the Icknield Way,
linked up. Since stone age times news from the east met
news from the west here, and as I walked round the
village and its neighbour, Streatley, I had the feeling I was
treading on a very worn and smooth pavement. I must
have been looking very intense because as I towed *Maegan*
into the lock a man with a briefcase saw me and said:
'Cheer up.'

'Sorry, I was ruminating on stone age man and the ice
age, and thinking how insignificant in general we all are,'
I said.

Then he saw *Maegan*: 'Of course, *Three Men in a Boat*.
You realize, of course, that it was in Goring they stopped
to get their clothes washed? They got a woman to do it
in that pub over the bridge. I suppose you're re-creating

the trip. It's a hundred years ago that Jerome wrote the book, you know?'

I asked him if he lived in Goring. He said he did and it was pleasant enough. He'd played for a pub darts team a number of years ago. But he was too tired most evenings now. He said: 'The best thing about Goring though, is it's handy for Junction 6 on the M4 and only thirty-five minutes from Paddington.'

It was a casual remark, but as I pulled away from the lock I realized he'd perfectly described the commuter-land ethos. To me Goring felt a long way from London. It had grown because of its role as a crossroads and was independent of the capital. That is to say it had a heritage. But now, like everywhere else the river had led me through, Goring had been revalued on the strength of its proximity with Paddington and the motorway, and I was sure the circling Boeings of Heathrow were a comfort to most folk rather than a disturbance.

There was, of course, a price to pay for this convenience. Commuter towns and villages had such a high desirability status that everyone wanted to live there, but by the time the commuters had purchased their property they had nothing left to spend, so the communities were dead. Not only did folk spend all day in London, they then came home and spent each night indoors. Something fundamental to the village had been lost. The community spirit was reduced to a Neighbourhood Watch sticker in every front window.

I sculled away through a sea of dandelion seeds. The gap soon disappeared and the river retained its composure after its brief fling. Ahead was Moulsford Bridge, a grand and angular span of red brick skewed across the water. I could see its elegant form from a distance, and yellow-nosed 125s flashing over. And I smiled when I thought that there was a man who could be held responsible for the creation of the commuter belt, our old friend Brunel, the man who never saw a hill without seeing a tunnel, never saw a river without seeing a bridge. His railway line had given all the Thames' towns and villages their high-speed link with the capital, and ultimately their convenience rating.

At yet, unlike the roads which crossed the river, the railway line seemed woven indelibly into its fabric. Part of this was nostalgia, but part of it was because the railways seemed under control whereas the roads were an impossible strain on the land. I waved to the passengers on the trains and they all waved back and I knew that, if anything, I found the railway lines reassuring. I remember them especially in the dark. I'd peer out of the tent some nights and see carriage lights tracing their way through the dark countryside and I'd feel a strange comfort.

Now I stopped under Moulsford Bridge and waited for an Intercity. I could feel the vibrations a long way off: the river began to crease as the train came over the adjacent field, pushing the air before it. The bricks began to roar, the whole bridge to groan, then the train screamed overhead and the river rattled.

I sculled long and hard that evening, almost reaching Wallingford. In the dusk I tied up under a high bank with the mist crawling over the fields towards me. A grebe paddled into a clump of reeds. There was a thump and a scream and an oof! and a duck limped out, winded.

I pulled out the canvas and struggled to tie the ropes which had shrunk in the rain of the previous night. Boogie was lying languidly in the long grass and I said to him: 'It's your decision of course, but I'd be really grateful if you could hold this end of the rope in your teeth because it would aid me considerably in securing the canvas. I'm not saying you have to, it's your right as a dog to refuse, you might for example prefer to be up in the village in the local pub right now, but if you could assist . . . Come back here!'

I decided to cook outside. I set the stove up and suddenly there was a greyhound standing next to me, eyes ablaze. It was a shock that made my heart jump. The thing pinned me to the boat, its face not two inches from mine. Out of the half-light its owner approached, a man whistling a tune tunelessly. He said: 'People are always terrified by my dog, can't understand it, myself.' It was the second most stupid comment I heard all night.

The most stupid came from the same gentleman but a little while later when it was dark and the railway was a distant flash and clatter. I was washing my dishes in the river. A spoon fell in the water never to be seen again – I was down to my last one. I sat there watching the ripples slowly iron themselves out when suddenly the greyhound was sitting next to me again. It was uncanny, like turning a light on and off. One minute he wasn't there the next he was. I called out for help to my faithful travelling companion who had come back from the pub now and was having his meal, but Boogie's a lousy guard dog at the best of times and with his nose in a bowl of Chum he's stone deaf. 'I've saved your life three times on this trip!' I screamed, but he put his paw over his eyes and continued eating.

The owner turned up again, whistling a different tune, although just as tunelessly. He called his dog away: 'He likes you,' he said. Then he looked at Boogie and said: 'How old is he?'

'Dunno.'

'He's getting on.'

'Yes.'

Then he looked stuck and he smacked his lips and said: 'They get old, dogs, don't they?'

And that was the most stupid thing I heard all night.

But it could well have been a crucial point in the journey as far as my mental state was concerned. Because the next day when I reached Wallingford a strange thing happened to me which left me rather unsure of the effect the river was having on my general condition. A woman walking along the towpath saw Boogie and said: 'What sort of dog is that?'

'Maltese spaniel.'

'Thought so,' she said, then skilfully changed the subject by giving me some indispensable piece of knowledge concerning *Maegan* and Victorian rowing boats in general, finishing with a lovely story of her grandparents who had gone on a camping skiff holiday on their honeymoon from Wallingford to Oxford and back.

Had I been fresh on the river I'd have joined in conversation with this delightful person on the whimsical joys and contemplative pleasures of the Thames. But it was as if having been on the water for a while I badly needed the bilges in my brain pumped out. I could feel myself becoming more the sort of person who walks up and down the towpath at nightfall, whistling tunelessly, and so I said: 'Huh; it's all right for a dog, isn't it? The dog's got the right idea.'

And she looked strangely at me and said: 'Travelling on your own?' And I thought of Jennifer for the first time that day and hurriedly said: 'No, no, a girlfriend's joining me on Tuesday. She was supposed to be starting the trip with me in London, but . . . well, she's a busy woman, and then she got delayed when I was in Hampton, and then in Windsor and then in Sonning, and then she had to go to Oslo or somewhere, but she's coming on Tuesday for sure.'

The woman nodded but looked as though she'd meant to shake her head, and said: 'Well, I hope so.'

7. I'll Wait for You outside Boots in Oxford

Next day I called Jennifer's office. Her PA answered.

'I'd like to leave a message for Jennifer Conway,' I said.

'Ms Conway is in Os . . .'

'I know she's in Oslo.'

'It's you again, isn't it?'

'Tell her to meet me in Oxford on Tuesday.'

'She won't be there.'

'That's her decision.'

'You really expect Jennifer Conway to go with you in your silly little boat up the Thames?'

'Yes.'

'You're nuts.'

'Just give her the message.'

'Listen. You must be meeting all sorts of nice girls, why don't . . .'

'Just tell her to meet me outside Boots at two o'clock.'

One thing this trip had taught me was that every town has a Boots.

It was Saturday, and the cruisers were out in numbers, I had a couple of near misses but generally other boats cleared a passage for me – it was an advantage of travelling backwards.

Near Benson though I collided with a very expensive-looking vessel and since it was stationary I had to take the blame. But the owners were very understanding. They leaned over the side, saw Boogie asleep on the back seat and said: 'Ah! poor dog. We didn't wake him did we?'

They asked me on board for a drink. I sat there on the hot plastic of the driver's seat before an array of levers and switches. Basically all these boats were very similar, but the owners always managed to express themselves in some way or another, usually in the choice of name. This is the most difficult decision a boat owner on the Thames ever has to make, needing the ability to sum up your past, your future, your bank balance, your politics, your sexuality, your marital status, your creativity, your childhood traumas and whether or not you've read *The Lord of the Rings*, all in one word.

The most popular nomenclature was the bucolic – names like *Burwood* and *Skylark II*. Then there was the naval – *Pompey Boy*, *Jolly Roger*; and the cute – *Dollydrop*, *Pretty Penelope*. Some were poetic – *Windrush*, *Zephyr*; and some were enigmatic – *Zagala*. Then there was the macho – *Hesoutonisownagain*. And the unashamedly sexist – *L'autre femme II*. The cost of these beautiful boats would, I'd have thought, made them the craft of the few, but that wasn't the case at all. Some of the most unlikely sorts were at the helm. I got the impression some boats were the spoils of crime, they should have had names like *Dunmuggin*, or *Brinxmat Job '84*.

The boat I'd collided with was called *Betibob*, a member of the domestic set, simply a combination of the couple's names, a symbol of their happy retirement. And they'd created that atmosphere perfectly. There was Bob on the deck with his arms folded, grinning, and there was Betty at the table putting hard-boiled eggs through the slicer.

I said: 'I saw an old Victorian houseboat downriver a

few miles back,' which was a complete lie but I was lost for conversation and so I thought I'd make something up. I had seen pictures of old Victorian houseboats though, and they looked the most splendid constructions, luxurious and stylish display cabinets in a fanciful game of oneupmanship played by the wealthy. I told Betty and Bob this, but they took it as a challenge to their own observation skills. Bob said: 'Mmm, I saw a hovercraft just below Wallingford Bridge.'

'Mmm,' I said. 'I found a supermarket trolley with six traffic cones in it in the backwater up by Shiplake.'

'We found a dead donkey in the weir by Boulter's Lock,' said Betty.

'Really,' I said. 'I found a frozen chicken in Pangbourne Reach.'

'We met someone who said they'd found a World War II mine in the marina in Reading,' said Bob.

'Yes,' said Betty. 'And they'd met someone who said they'd seen Lord Lucan in a narrowboat just past the Goring Gap.'

I sat back. I couldn't match that. The plastic seat stuck to the back of my legs and from the saloon came the smell of a hot television. Betty peered over at Boogie who was still asleep on *Maegan*'s back seat. She said: 'Doesn't the dog have a life jacket?'

'No,' I replied. 'The truth is he finds them more of a hindrance than a help. You see, he's highly trained as a life saver. Don't let that calm, dozy exterior fool you for a moment. He's constantly on guard. If any child, or any person for that matter, was to fall in the river now he would instantly dive in and haul them back to shore, administering kiss of life on the way if necessary. A life jacket would only slow him through the water, losing valuable seconds that could mean the difference between life and death.'

'Oh,' said Betty, and Boogie yawned, stretched, licked his lips, rolled over, farted and went back to sleep again.

The day grew hot then humid, gripped in a sweaty hand. As I sculled under the elegant Shillingford Bridge some sandwich crusts floated past me. I pulled my way through the sticky afternoon and into the evening until I reached the mouth of the river Thame. A low bridge prohibited larger craft access but I was able to scull up it to a sandbank and I moored there under a willow among the reeds.

Later I walked through the meadows into Dorchester, a pretty Oxfordshire village crammed with cottages, coloured with wisteria, and all wrapped around its abbey.

And there was a concert in the abbey that night – concertos and cantatas by Bach and Albinoni. I sat in the audience as the sun moved slowly down the stained-glass windows and the whole nave was caught in a prism. As the soloist lifted her head her voice hit the corners and alcoves, and in the sunbeams you could see dust fly and cobwebs vibrate. The musicians played selections from the *Brandenburg Concertos* and the audience sat there stiffly, all in evening dress, except for one sort who wore a T-shirt and wellingtons and had no one sitting next to him.

At the interval there were refreshments. A woman in a long purple dress came up to me and said: 'So what brings you to our lovely village?'

'I'm on the river. I've got a skiff. I'm travelling to the source.'

And she nodded her head and said: 'What star sign are you?'

'Star sign!? Er . . . Taurus.'

Then she shook her head and said: 'Oh no you're not,' and went back to her seat.

There was something cryptic about Dorchester. Afterwards, I walked through the village and it was if the place were under some sort of spell. A face with a long nose poked out of a hedge. A toby jug sat on a window sill and its eyes followed me as I walked past. There was a chill in the air and everyone had a grin.

And then the next morning when I climbed the Sinodun Hills, that rose above the trees on the opposite bank, I suspected that by coming to Dorchester I had walked through the looking glass. I crossed the river by the lock and climbed to a hilltop where some ancient earthworks lay smoothed by time, remnants of the earliest settlement on the Thames. The view was superb: ahead the river wriggled like a silver fish and the valley stretched away miles into the distance, while behind stood Didcot Power Station, a designated Site of Outstanding Natural Ugliness dominating the countryside the way only a power station knows how.

There was an adjacent peak topped with trees like a tuft of hair on a bald head. As I walked over to it I heard a lone voice singing sweetly. It grew louder the nearer I got to the trees but when I reached them it stopped and I found no one. It suddenly felt like winter. Boogie stuck his nose in the air and sniffed. I sniffed and smelt burning leaves. A man and a dog approached through the trees. He stopped and said: 'Was that you singing?'

'No.'

'Probably a transistor. They bring them up here at the weekend. My boy came up here for his birthday one year, at midnight. He's got some strange friends. I think one of them's a Druid. It's a nice spot though. Shame about the eyesore down there. Is that a Swedish bulldog?'

'Yes.'

'Thought so.'

I turned round to look at Boogie. From somewhere he'd got a french bread and honey-glazed ham open sandwich.

I didn't mean to spend long in Dorchester that day, but

I was distracted and ended up staying until the afternoon.
I lost a mooring iron and I was hunting round the bank
for it when a man passed in his dinghy and asked me the
problem. I explained my loss and he offered to give me a
stake he had. 'Let me pay you something for it,' I said. It
was only a bent bit of metal but it looked as though it
was an important part of his boat.

'Oh I couldn't take any money,' he said. 'You're in the
country now; folk help each other out. You'll do the same
for me one day.'

'Are you sure I can't give you something for it?' I said.

'Oh, okay then, give us ten quid and we'll call it quits.'

He asked me where I was going and when I said the
source, he said: 'Well, you're here.'

'Pardon?'

'Do you know anything about this Thames and Isis
business?'

'Not much.'

'Right, good. This is the start of the Thames here.'

I looked over the bank to where the Thames was visibly
continuing in a westerly direction and was about to protest
when he said: 'That's not the Thames, that river up there.
The Thames ends here. That's the Isis up there. And that's
the truth.'

I'd heard this story before: how, above Dorchester, the
Thames becomes the Isis. Other theories claim it becomes
the Isis as far back as Henley. Another theory claims it is
the Thames all the way to the source except for a brief
interlude in Oxford where it becomes the Isis. Then again,
others say it is the Isis in Oxford and Henley, but the
Thames above Oxford and below Henley and between
Moulsford Bridge and the third stile along past the caravan
site just downstream from the Beetle and Wedge.

But my friend had proof: 'Do you know anything about
the Romans and the Thames?'

'Not much . . .'

'Right, good. You see Thame is the old English word for river. So when the Romans arrived and asked the ancient Britons what the name of the river was they got the answer: 'It's called the river.' But the Romans couldn't cope with that. They liked giving rivers flowery names like the Tiber and so on, and so they decided to call the river the Isis after the Egyptian god. So it became known as Thame Isis, which in time became Thamesis and eventually Thames. And that's the truth.'

What he said was either a fascinating piece of etymology or absolute gibberish, but you can't say that to someone when they've just supplied you with a boat hook and so I nodded and said: 'I see. Listen, thanks for the boat hook. I've got to go.'

'Go where?'

'To the source of the . . .'

'I've just told you. You don't listen, do you?'

'Mmm.'

'So, you can come to the pub. I've got loads of interesting things about the Thames to tell you. My name's Jeff. Did you know, for instance, that Thames salmon frequently mistake Barn Elms Reservoirs for the North Sea?'

The pub had a beautiful garden with many people balancing veal and ham pie on their laps. I bought two pints of beer and some mackerel-flavoured crisps. Boogie had some cold tongue with piccalilli and a gherkin. Jeff spoke with his mouth full: 'Do you know anything about the Thames Barrier?'

'Not much . . .'

'Good, because in twenty years' time the thing will be useless. It's true. The polar icecaps are melting. By the turn of the century London will be underwater.'

'Who told you that?'

'Doesn't matter who told me. What matters is that the

Bank of England, Buckingham Palace, Wembley Stadium, the M25, all of them will be underwater.'

'Buckingham Palace underwater?' said an American voice behind me.

'You bet,' said Jeff, and introduced himself to the four American women sat at a table eating veal and ham pie. There was a great grandmother, a grandmother, a granddaughter and a great granddaughter. Boogie introduced himself as well, scoring off the great granddaughter, the granddaughter and the grandmother. The great grandmother though was harder to crack. She ate slowly and meticulously, never taking her eyes off her food. The grandmother said: 'She likes to eat.' Boogie gave his 'we've got something in common' expression, and moved in on her.

The women told me they had a hire car and were just driving. 'We've been to London, Bath, Stonehenge, York and Stafford,' said the great granddaughter.

'Why Stafford?' I asked.

'Because we thought it was Stratford,' said the granddaughter.

The pub closed. Everyone else had finished their meals a long time ago but the great grandmother still had a plate of blackcurrant and apple crumble and some cheese to go. Boogie was resting his head on her lap, giving her all his best faces, just waiting for her to look once into his eyes so as he could hook her, but she never looked away from her plate. He lay on the ground showing her his protruding ribs. Then he sat up and gave her his 'you could make me one really happy little dog, old lady' expression. But nothing. She spooned the food methodically to her mouth, scraped the bowl and sat back. Boogie hung his head in disbelief. I was shocked. The woman had had a three-course meal and Boogie didn't get so much as a crust. I'd never known him fail so badly. Fortunately, Jeff offered a reprieve. He said: 'Let's go for a walk along the towpath, and then go to the Abbey Tea Room. A real treat.'

'Did someone mention afternoon tea?' said great grandmother.

'She likes to eat,' said the granddaughter.

I wanted to get moving, but I couldn't deny Boogie this re-match, so I joined them all on a walk along the river. Boogie lagged behind. Like a gambler whose system has failed him he was frantically checking and rechecking his mathematics.

A swan came nuzzling up to us. 'If only we had some bread,' said the great granddaughter.

'I've got some bread,' said Jeff, and from his pocket he pulled out a packet of sandwiches.

'Oh, we can't take your sandwiches,' said the grandmother.

'Course you can,' said Jeff. 'You're in the country now. Everyone shares everything.'

'We must repay you somehow.'

'Oh, all right, give us a fiver and we'll call it quits.'

The sandwiches were fed to the swan who was partial to corned beef and tomato.

We found the Abbey Tea Room in the old cloisters that ran up the driveway to the abbey. Jeff led us to where the proprietress stood on the front step. He nodded to her and she completely ignored him. There was a Morris 1000 parked outside and I knew it was hers.

In keeping with the Dorchester allure there was an element of surrealism about the Abbey Tea Rooms. We were sat at a big round table in the middle of the room. On the wall a sign said: 'The taking of too much jam and butter will render the management violent.'

The proprietress spoke with assertion. She said: 'Your first time?'

'I've been here before,' said Jeff and she ignored him.

'If it's your first time I'd better explain. My ladies and I run this tea room to raise funds for the church. The system we operate is as follows: we supply the cakes and biscuits. You eat them and then tell us what you've had and we charge you a price slightly in excess of what it costs us to bake them, thus reaping a profit. It's a system that works quite well, we find.'

Then she turned and walked into the kitchen and immediately a troop of women bound in aprons descended upon us. They ran round with teapots saying: 'The first cup of tea is twenty pence, the next ten, the rest five.' Then they pointed their spouts of each of us in turn and said: 'Strong, weak or normal?'

Cakes, biscuits and scones were dispersed. At our table sat four generations of Americans all eating cake and shortbread and cream teas. Boogie positioned himself by the great grandmother. With cream tea at stake I knew his performance would be exceptional.

He began with basic clinical hypnotism. His pupils small, but rotating in opposite directions. This achieved no response whatsoever. Next he moved on to auto-suggestion – masticating, swallowing and licking his lips; he even belched for effect, but his opponent didn't blink. She finished her cake and licked her fingers and moved on to the shortbread. Boogie looked at me in despair.

The tea room filled up, but nothing was too much trouble for this noble collection of tea-ladies, they glided around the room as though they were on casters: 'Party of twenty-nine? Certainly, how many with milk and how many without?'

The great granddaughter said: 'England's just the way you expect it to be, isn't it?' And the granddaughter said: 'It's just like the films and the Agatha Christie books.'

'More cake anyone?' said a little lady in a cardigan with leather patches.

'Did someone mention more cake?' said the great grandmother.

'She likes to eat,' said the great granddaughter.

Boogie sat down by her again. This would be his last chance. But I didn't realize how desperate he'd become. As the great grandmother lifted a brandy snap to her mouth, Boogie nudged her chair. A cheap trick, but the brandy snap fell and Boogie opened his mouth in antici-pation. Like a lizard the great grandmother flicked out a hand and caught the brandy snap, then dunked it in the cream and popped it in her mouth in one fluid movement. This was the knockout blow. Boogie started to watch the food rather than the face – a beginner's mistake. I knew he was in big trouble when he started to drool. Boogie never drools unless he's worried. The great grandmother ate the last piece of coffee cake and that was that. To rub it in she wiped her hands on him.

We all walked back to the boat, Boogie trailing, looking suicidal. 'Are you travelling alone?' said the granddaughter.

'A girlfriend's joining him in Oxford,' said Jeff.

As I climbed back into the boat the great grandmother gave me a paper napkin in which was wrapped a brandy snap stuffed with cream. She said: 'Give this to your little dog, will you? He looks fed up.'

They all stood on the bank and waved to me as I sculled away, and the granddaughter called out: 'We must meet for dinner when you get back.'

'Did someone mention dinner?' said the great grandmother.

'She likes to eat, doesn't she?' said Jeff.

I sculled away into the evening past a house where a bust of the Duke of Marlborough peeped over the hedge.

Then on through Clifton Hamden and under its pretty bridge. As it grew dark I camped by what looked like an abandoned swan's nest, made up of reeds and moss and plastic bags, not to mention a car radio, a Lucozade bottle and an old deckchair. I noted all this in my wildlife diary under the swans' section.

The night was warm and I sat out on the old deckchair – just me, the willows, the water and the breeze, and the electrical glow, concrete, steam and wires of Didcot Power Station that sat in the distance like a city. Inside the tent Boogie lay severely depressed, confidence shattered, racked with self-doubt. I said to him: 'Hey, don't worry, champ, you've still got it. The woman was probably a witch.' But he wouldn't be consoled.

Later, when I was eating my kedgeree with kippers – Delia has a way with kippers – he glanced at me and I pretended to be hypnotized by him, and spooned a great dollop of rice in his bowl. This cheered him up marginally, but I didn't give him the brandy snap, that would have been cruel. It would also have been impossible since I'd eaten it myself.

Power stations were to feature heavily the next day. I use the plural because although on the map you will only see one identified, there are at least five. They all look alike, I agree, and people will argue that there is only one, but if that's the case it moves around a lot. That morning Didcot Power Station was round every bend in the river and peeping through every hedge. I sculled away from it and suddenly there it was behind me. I sculled towards it and it sneaked up on my port side. It was confusing for a while but then I realized that the river was hopelessly lost and was doubling back on itself as it wandered about trying to find Oxford.

And after a while I have to admit I grew a certain

affection for the power station. The sun beamed on its
grey cooling towers, and the silver pylons that surrounded
it were all embedded in fields of dazzling rape. It had a
symmetry and a brilliance, and clearly the longer one lived
with it, the more an integral part of one's life it became.
The lock-keeper at Culham lock was a great fan. 'I love
that power station,' he said. 'I dream about it. Sometimes
on a nice Sunday I'll go and drive round it with the wife
and our Peter and Lucy and we'll have a picnic by the
perimeter fence.' I nodded sympathetically, and slowly
rose to his level as ninety thousand gallons of water burrowed beneath me.

'I mean,' he went on, 'I'd much rather have that power
station there than a scenic beauty spot. You know, an oak
forest or an example of glacial drift, or a windmill or
something poncey like that. Give me the hum and the
glow of Didcot any day.'

He seemed like a sage, so I asked him if he had any
ideas on where the source was, and he said:

'In Gloucestershire somewhere.'

'Could you be more specific?'

'Yes. It might be in Wiltshire.'

He went back into his cottage and I moved off. Then
after I'd gone about a hundred yards he ran out again,
waved his arms at me and shouted something. I hurriedly
sculled back to him and he said: 'I almost forgot. You
must call in at the Swan in Radcot. It's the best pub on
the river.'

I made good time to Abingdon, a neat, double-yellow-
lined, hanging-basketed town with friendly policemen.
There was a great abbey here as long ago as the seventh
century, but none of the original building remains. Instead
there's a beautiful County Hall and around that there's a
Halford's, a Dixon's, a Woolworth's and a Curry's, and

a shopping precinct with ornamental tubs similar to the ones in Basingstoke, Exeter and Hull.

I spent my half hour in the town in Budgen. From the conversation in the queue I learnt that the one-way system was not what it should be, that the Nugent's boy was getting married (again), and that mature English cheddar was much cheaper in the market in Aylesbury. When I went in to the supermarket it was a peaceful spring day and I was cheerful. When I came out a gale was blowing and I was in a bad mood.

Litter blew down the medieval streets and fresh green leaves were ripped from their boughs and whistled hard down the river. Sculling was hopeless. It hadn't taken me long to get fit on this journey, just for my hands to get hard, but no amount of preparation could have equipped me for the battle with the wind. I'd be pulling away for all I was worth, and I'd look at the water and see the stream rushing past me, giving me the impression I was travelling at speed, then I'd look at the bank and realize I wasn't moving.

That evening, never in the history of sculling has there been so much mental effort devoted to the invention of a contraption that would enable a dog to row. I began to get frustrated, then angry. On the towpath a man with a poodle waved and said: 'It's all right for the dog, eh?' and I swore at him. 'Pardon?' he said. And I swore at him again.

Before long I made camp by the entrance to a backwater called the Swift Ditch. There's a theory that this was once the true course of the river, and that the monks at Abingdon diverted it to drive their mills. I took Boogie for a walk down the channel to see if I could find any trace of a navigation but it was all overgrown. I lost the path and emerged in a field where I sat in the shelter of a hedge until it grew dark, just watching a whole rape crop

sway in the wind. I was feeling chatty. I said to Boogie:
'I bought another packet of Winalot today. Five more
tokens. Only a hundred and fifteen more for the giant
wool-and-mixed-fibre blanket measuring sixty by one
twenty-five inches.'

Boogie sniffed a rabbit hole and gave me his 'what do
you want me to do jump up and down and do a cartwheel
and bark at the moon?' expression.

We walked on. An owl made a noise that resembled
the end of a factory shift. I said: 'So, Jennifer arrives
tomorrow. I bet that makes you feel happy. I mean, I'm
happy to an extent. Although I'm not really bothered one
way or the other. It would be nice to have her here, that's
for sure. But I'm not going to let it worry me.'

In the distance electricity cables were slung across the
land and the pylons strode towards Didcot.

Next morning I had breakfast with my shirt off sitting in
the sunshine on the quay at Sandford lock, and I decided
I'm at my best when I'm having breakfast with my shirt
off sitting in the sun on a quayside.

Then a large woman in sunglasses said with glee: 'It's
not going to last, you know. There's a low coming in.'

She said she lived in Oxford. She said she had a house
by Folly Bridge. She said if I saw people waving at me
from a red-brick house by Folly Bridge with a cheeseplant
in the window, it would be her and her grandchildren.

I said: 'I'll come in for a glass of champagne shall I? . . .
Ha.'

'No, I shouldn't do that,' she said.

Sandford had some pretty horses in its meadows and
some rotting, sinking barges on its riverside. These were
old college barges, the craft on which the Oxford colleges
would gather to watch their fraternity rowing teams in

action. Once they were lavish and exquisite queens of the
river but now they were full of weeds and old newspapers.

But they were the first sign of what was to come – a
stretch of the river dominated by the university, and, in
particular, the university eights. I'd seen a few of these
rowing teams in action before. One had flashed past me
in the Pangbourne Reach, and then near Wallingford I
remember being woken early one morning by a mega-
phone. There was a huge inhale and exhale of breath, a
coordinated grunt and then a wave had hit *Maegan* harder
than anything from a cruiser had ever managed. I whipped
back the canvas and saw nothing but a ruffled river. But
a few minutes later the thing returned. It resembled an
animal more than anything. An octopod slicing through
the surface like a glasscutter. The eight bodies balanced in
the boat were glistening and steaming, all shoulders, and
anything that got in their way wasn't struck so much as
cut cleanly in two.

One boat I could cope with. I could cower in the willows till it passed. But above Iffley lock was something
quite different. Here was a school of them waiting in the
pound above the lock like sharks, blind with sharp edges.
The crews were less impressive than the one at Wallingford, varying from gangling skinny youths to whom this
activity was clearly compulsory, to squat chubby sorts
stuffed into their seats, to whom the activity was also
compulsory. They all had a freshman's innocence, but at
the stern of each boat, wedged into position, sat the cox,
and there was lodged the jaws of the vessel.

I watched for a while as the boats basked in the sunlight.
Then I left them and set off upstream, imagining that they
practised in that little corner of the river only. I did find
it hard to imagine how they produced teams to win the
Boat Race with that sort of training, but television is
deceptive, and besides, I thought, if they used the whole

river there'd be no room left for other craft like me, would there?

Suddenly there was a draw of water and a scream of sweat being forced through pores and round the bend it came, oars flapping in a fury, heading right for me, sharp end first. And from those little heads on the back of the boat came a string of abuse reserved traditionally for the rowers, but on this occasion redirected at me: 'Take the pressure, row, row, row, feel for the stroke . . . what the? . . . Get out of the bloody way! You! Yes you, you cretin! You with the ugly dog and the stupid hat. Clear off!'

I splashed wildly for the bank only to find myself in the path of another boat skimming along the water from the other direction, blades drawn. 'You're dead!' came a voice from somewhere and as the boat passed me I had the feeling I'd just been run through with a sword. Somehow I managed to weave a path as far as the boathouses and there I decided to wait until the rowers took their lunch break.

Inside the boathouses, the boats were carefully stacked. I snooped around, went up close to them and carefully touched one with my finger as if it might bite. Out of the water they'd lost none of their grace or their venom. They sparkled with gloss and varnish. They seemed as fragile as insects.

Above the boathouse were the grandstands that had taken over the role of the barges. A woman in a bright blue rowing shirt was sunbathing and drinking Pimms. She'd seen me moor *Maegan* and she laughed at Boogie and said: 'It's all right for the dog, isn't it?' which disappointed me, I'd have expected something more original from an Oxford undergraduate. She had a book open on her lap and I said: 'What are you studying?'

'Nothing,' she said. 'I'm a buyer for John Menzies. I'm a friend of Dave's. How about you?'

'I'm not studying anything either. I'm just passing through. I don't even know Dave.'

'Doesn't matter, no one here goes to the university. At least Mike, Clive and Tina don't. We just hang around.'

She explained the activity on the river. The boats were training for the Summer Eights, an important social and athletic occasion. The races were called Bumps because the river wasn't wide enough to enable the boats to race in line and so they competed a length behind each other, the aim being to bump the boat in front. A successful team ascended a position the following year.

We were interrupted by a commotion in the water up by Folly Bridge where the eights turned. A couple of drunk skinheads had hired a dinghy and were in the middle of the river behaving like pirates, trying to disrupt the college crews. The row boats came flying for them and the skinheads laughed and jumped up and down and then fell in the river. The eights' coaches, patrolling the towpath on bicycles, asked them politely if they'd mind behaving less obstructively, and the skinheads' response was to drop their trousers.

Oxford had its fair share of drunk skinheads on this balmy lunchtime. While the undergraduates were all rowing on the Thames or punting up the River Cherwell clutching strawberries and cream, behaving just as they were supposed to, the skinheads were outside the Head of the River with their shirts off, drinking Swan extra-strong lager, behaving just as they were supposed to. One big egg-headed lad was standing on the balustrade of Folly Bridge shouting to his mates: 'Watch this, watch this!' then he'd leap in the river with all his clothes on and climb out giggling, and repeat the stunt. It was harmless and mildly entertaining until *Maid Unexpected* appeared from upstream heading for the bridge. The skinhead, oblivious to the approach of the boat, climbed up on the bridge and prepared to launch himself once more. His mates could envisage just what I could – *Maid Unexpected* emerging from under the bridge to twelve stones of closely shaven and vividly tattooed youth smashing through her roof. This isn't the sort of thing you see every day and I was tempted to stand by and watch the performance, so indeed were his mates who were suddenly paying far more attention than they had before. Fortunately, someone warned him just in time and *Maid Unexpected* motored under the bridge with the occupants sitting at the dining table eating salads. They smiled and waved at the skinheads who responded with the bare bum treatment again.

I had some time before I met Jennifer but I'd planned it this way because I wanted to visit Merton College, one of the earliest Oxford colleges, dating from 1264, and a fine example of the Decorative and Perpendicular period. The fourteenth-century library had a rare collection of old books and manuscripts and it was these I particularly wanted to see.

But it was shut, so I bought some strawberries off a couple of undergraduates pedalling a strawberry and cream wagon about town and then lay down in Christchurch Meadows until two o'clock when I was standing outside Boots as prearranged. By three Jennifer hadn't shown and the staff in Boots were giving me funny looks. I closed my eyes when I heard the familiar roar of a powerful motorbike from round the corner, hoping it would pass by, but it stopped of course, and Michael the motorcycle messenger strode towards me.

'Hello.'

'Hello.'

'Me again.'

'Yes.'

He handed me the familiar carrier bag, 'Indonesian today. Satay with peanut sauce and coconut pieces.' I took the bag and put it straight in a bin marked Keep Oxford Tidy. Michael then gave me an envelope. I tore it open; it read: 'Call me as soon as you get this. I've got bad news.'

I screwed it up and threw that in the bin as well. Michael said: 'You're angry now, aren't you?'

'Yes, I am.'

'I think that's good. Now you've got to show her you're angry. It's all very well coping with it but if you really care for her, you'll risk everything and express your anger directly. Anger is a positive emotion. You must always remember that.'

'Oh fuck off!'

I found a phone box and called her. Her PA answered.

'Hello, it's me. I want to speak to Jennifer Conway, now!' Boogie started barking. Passers-by peered at me through the broken glass of the kiosk.

'She's not here,' said the PA with an unfamiliar urgency. 'But I'll give you a number where you can reach her.'

I dialled the new number. I'd be angry with her all right. I'd tell her to forget it. I'd announce that Boogie was here. I'd say: 'Boogie's here, and he's good company . . . well, he's not bad company . . . well at least he's here.'

Jennifer came on the line. She said: 'Mark, I'm so glad you've called. Thank you for worrying about me. I suppose you thought something had happened to me. Well it has. I'm in hospital. I've had a car accident. I was on my way, I really was.'

'What!?'

'Nothing serious. They want to keep me in for a couple of days for observation. The firm have insisted. I smashed the car up. I've bought another one though. Another TVR. A blue one. I hope you're not angry.'

'No, no, of course not.'

'I mean I suppose I could discharge myself but . . .'

'No you mustn't. You must stay there. This is terrible.'

'It wasn't my fault even. A taxi driver hit me on Putney Bridge. He'd just got his licence back, he said. Did you get the satay?'

'Yes. Thank you. Listen are you sure you're all right?'

'Yes. I'll be with you on Thursday, promise. I can't wait. I've got my bag with me now, all packed. I'll come straight from hospital. What's that barking? I can hear barking again.'

'I'm calling you from outside a pet shop. Oops, my phone card is running out. See you Thursday.'

I stayed in Oxford a while and peered in at some under-graduates sitting in big rooms swotting, but the city was choked with traffic, and the heat was getting to everyone. I felt I should stay longer and look round, but I felt happier out of urban areas. I also felt happier on the river and it seemed to ignore Oxford once it passed Folly Bridge. In most towns the Thames attracted parklands and salubrious housing and was a desired area. But in Oxford, after the splendour of Christchurch Meadows, it took on the appeal of a canal and snaked through the back yard of the city past terraces, under railway bridges and round the back of factories and allotments.

'Not putting your spinach in now are you?' said a voice from behind a hedge.

'Course I'm putting my spinach in now,' said another.

'Too early.'

'I always plant my spinach two days after the full moon in May.'

'Rot!'

That was the sort of talk I wanted to hear, and I gave an extra tug on the sculls.

The only other event to mark my exit from the city was an episode at Osney Bridge. As I emerged there was no empty yoghurt tub in the back of the boat, no newspaper, no drink container and no fresh fruit cores, instead there was a ten-year-old lad, dripping wet.

And suddenly I was under attack as a group of his mates swung from the trees on ropes and splashed into the water round *Maegan* and tried to clamber over her gunwales. Boogie sat up at this point which caused the pirates to stop and reconsider. One said: 'What sort of dog is that?' and I replied: 'he's a doberman alsatian, and he's in a bad mood so I should clear off.'

Boogie's problem is that he doesn't quite have what it takes to be a ferocious guard dog. His natural disposition is to smile at intruders and say: 'Hi there! C'mon in.' He's about as aggressive as a welcome mat. His only weapon is his tongue, although on this occasion that did the trick. As the kids started to grab my sculls and anything else they could lay their hands on, Boogie leant over the boat and licked the leader.

'Eagh, he licked me. He licked me,' screamed the kid. 'I'll get Aids.' And that did it.

Osney Bridge was low, just how low I didn't realize until the other side where I saw a sign proclaiming 7'6". This prohibited many cruisers from continuing upstream and one could sense the river beginning to enter another new phase. Past the entrance to the Oxford Canal the land flattened and stretched. On one bank was a shady blaze of sycamore and hawthorn, while on the other, water meadows stretched for miles, and horses, cattle, swans and geese all stood together in the heat haze, drinking at the water's edge.

Gone now were the No Mooring signs. No longer were

the spires of the towns and villages and the metallic flash of motor cars drawn to the water. The river was suddenly wilder and more exposed. I put my hat on for the sun and set off for Gloucestershire. A grebe swam across my path and disappeared into a clump of weeds. There were a few thumps, some gasps and some squeals and a moment later a couple of bruised ducks, a limping magpie and a Canada goose with most of its feathers missing crawled out.

8. See You on Tadpole Bridge. And That's a Promise

Tadpole Bridge was just twenty-five miles upstream from Oxford but it took me three days to reach there. The pace of the journey changed, so did my lifestyle. I emerged as a waterman with crusty hands and a dirty neck. I began to degenerate. *Maegan* began to look messy. Only the blossom that tumbled from the hawthorn and chestnut trees kept her fresh. She looked as though Boogie and I had just got married in her.

The breeze was with me for a change and I sat easily in the saddle of the boat. I lost the sensation of travelling. I was just following a rail and had no control over my destination. The rain came as everyone had predicted and so I travelled with the tent half unfurled to form a canopy. It acted as a sail and I was blown westwards. Then whenever a shower came I'd roll down the sides and be watertight in minutes. I'd sit there wrapped up out of the damp as the warm rain made the river steam, and I'd watch the dragonflies land on the water and disappear into the pink gob of a chub.

I liked to watch the rain. It felt reassuring to see the land drink it up. It was like a transfusion, and there was a reverence about the whole process. There was a silence just before the first drop and then the reflections would begin to disintegrate as the river surface grew agitated. The grey cloud merged with the grey water. The songbirds were quiet, and Boogie would sit on the end of the boat with his mouth open.

I'd never realized how noisy rain is in the country. The leaves cracked and the grass shivered, and the meadows and woods were dented as the rain and wind pelted them. The showers were never long but they were a display and everything stopped until they were over. And then there was a sense of celebration. The river sparkled anew. Cuckoos, pigeons and magpies poked their heads out from trees. There was an irresistible smell of wet grass. The ducks came out and started squabbling. The gnats gathered in clouds and did whatever gnats like to do. The pylons began to hiss. A train shuddered in the distance over wet rails. Somewhere upstream a lorry splashed through the puddles over a five-hundred-year-old bridge. The cracks in the mud were filled. The river was a millimetre higher, the grass a shade greener, the earth watered. And then there'd be a blue crack in the sky and shafts of sunlight that made my hat steam. The reflections returned as bright as before and I'd look around and make a note of how well I had got to know cow parsley on this trip.

After almost two weeks on the water I was easily pleased and my days were gloriously indulgent affairs. Boogie too seemed settled. He was aware of the change in our surroundings in so far as he was totally confused now whereas he'd been only moderately so before. I remember him one afternoon standing on the bow, ears pricked, a daisy chain around his neck, sniffing the air in that intense way he does, giving the impression he is sorting out every smell and every sound and identifying them as only an animal of instinct can, whereas the truth is he hasn't got a clue what any of them are. As soon as we lost the diesel smells of Oxford he was baffled.

And now the wildlife became more prolific and less shy. I got to know the water rat population well. I saw my first curlew – a humorous creature if ever there was one. And I watched the herons for hours. One landed very close to me one evening and I watched it fish as darkness fell. It stood motionless, staring into the murk, and then every so often its head would dart into the stream and emerge with a grin all over its face and a struggling silver fish in its beak. The bird would swallow visibly and then resume its stern posture.

If I wanted supplies I'd walk to a village. They all had little supermarkets, and all the little supermarkets had little queues. But for some reason these no longer bothered me. In one I turned to the woman behind me and said: 'Would you like to go in front of me since you've only got three items?' And she eyed me suspiciously, but edged her way slowly to the front, then paid her bill and ran out.

My only other link with humanity was the lock-keepers. They were my source of information and I relied on them. At Eynsham the keeper was planting his annuals for the coming bank holiday weekend. He said: 'It's much quieter on the river now. You should have seen it twenty years ago. It was busy then but I liked it. I liked it when you had to collect money and there were really long queues.' And he recalled how before boats were licensed each vessel had to pay a toll to pass through the lock. 'Your skiff would have cost ninepence,' he said.

I told him I was looking for the source and asked him if he had any knowledge on the matter and he said: 'All things considered, if you were to ask me that question what with me being a lock-keeper and having a working knowledge of the river, particularly so above Oxford, I'd have to say I don't know a thing about it. My! will you

look at the size of that?!' A perch had come to the surface.
I knew it was a perch because the lock-keeper said: 'That's
about the biggest perch I've ever seen. Fifteen years ago,
before they cleaned the river up, they had all but
disappeared.'

The weir streams were less frantic now, and the locks
smaller and all manual. In place of hydraulics the keepers
had long poles and big muscles. They were mostly local
people and their lifestyle more reclusive. At Shifford lock
I even managed to have a look inside a keeper's cottage.
He came flying out when he saw me approach and began
to wind up his gates for all he was worth. He said: 'You're
not trying to break any records are you? 'Cos if you are
I've got bad news. One of my sluice gates is stuck.'

I'd heard stories of teams of rowers heading downstream as fast as they could trying to break records, but
the very idea seemed appalling. Over the last few days I'd
become convinced of what I'd always suspected to be true,
the Thames can be anything you want except a rush. So
I said to the lock-keeper: 'Yes, I'm trying to break the
record for the slowest time between London and Lechlade.
I've taken nearly two weeks so far, what are my chances?'

'Pretty good, I'd say.'

I asked him if he had a toilet I could use, and he said I
could use his own. I regarded this as a privilege and
thanked him graciously, then walked up his path to the
house imagining rooms full of flowers and river memorabilia, a boiler, a tiled fireplace, the smell of soup and
smoked willow. But it was a dump. It wasn't even lived
in. The only furniture was a microwave and a table with
a half-completed Airfix kit scattered around it.

I pulled *Maegan* up the river, keeping a steady rhythm,
taking time to think about what I saw. How, for example,
did that pair of checked trousers end up in that hawthorn
bush? It was a mystery probably very few people could

explain. Placenames began to interest me as well. We'd passed Moulsford, Oxford and Swinford, and I'd satisfied myself they were all places where it was possible to herd mules, ox and swine across the river. This theory rather faltered though when we reached Duxford.

I was also confused by the bunkers on the river's north bank. I asked the lock-keeper at Pinkhill what their history was, and the answer, although straightforward, was interesting because it illustrated what a barrier the Thames has always been, from the time when man first began to walk the Ridgeway, through the Roman and the Norman occupations, right up to the Second World War. It was during that war, when the threat of a German invasion was real, that the Thames was designated the line of defence behind which the country would retreat should the Channel coast be taken. Provision was made to blast every bridge over the river, and bunkers were built every mile. The lock-keeper said: 'Bunker's a good name for them, I reckon. That's all they're used for now – bunk ups. Huhuh.'

In the evening I'd find a pub if one was near, or I'd pull the canvas over and sit in the lamplight, and try to write poetry. These were unproductive evenings though. I only ever wrote one poem and that was to Delia Smith. She was beginning to play an intrinsic role in the expedition, far more intrinsic than Boogie, anyway. He spent his evenings lying in the bottom of the boat, dreaming, making strange noises as he re-enacted the television programmes he was missing.

He and I were becoming better company though. I remember on the Tuesday night I camped in a wild spot. I don't know the name, I just remember there wasn't a house or road or light to be seen, just the distant pylons. We'll call it Dogford because Boogie, in an effort to get a drink of water, dived into the river, or rather he leant over the side of the boat too far and fell in. Why he should even have attempted this I don't know since his water bowl was always full of fresh water and sat wedged in the bottom of the boat. And yet ever since his first taste of river water he'd regarded it as vintage and would drink no other.

I pulled him out, saving his life for the fourth time. We sat on the grass. Boogie looked at me and gave me his 'stupid dog eh? falling in the river' look. It occurred to me that the river had cast its spell over him as well, and might be helping him to find the inner animal. Later when we went for a walk along the towpath, I whistled tunelessly and said: 'The thing is, see, Boogie, the thing we've got to understand is that if someone's behaviour seems unreasonable the chances are it's indicative of something more deeply rooted. Just as the real reason Jennifer has kept me waiting for two weeks is locked away within her, your tendency to fall in the river is probably a result of your traumatic upbringing and being orphaned at an early age and suffering the ignominy of being beaten up by cats all the time. You could be a depressed dog, but don't worry, I know a very good vet.'

Boogie licked something horrible off a stile and we walked back to the boat.

I was just about to crawl inside the tent when I could see a figure in the fading light about a half mile away. It was a man striding across the field towards us. I watched as he approached, his hat at an angle, his baggy trousers bulging at the pockets. He walked straight up to me and invaded the space one doesn't normally invade when you're meeting someone for the first time, particularly if it's in a lonely field at dusk. I thought he might be about to ask me back to his house for champagne but he looked at me from eye to eye and said: 'Evening!'

'Evening.'

'One pound fifty, please.'

'What?'

'One pound fifty.'

'What is?'

'The cost.'

'Cost of what?'

'You camping on my property. It costs one pound fifty.'

'What?'

'You're camping. This is a farm camp site. I'm the farmer. It's simple enough. One pound fifty.'

I looked behind me. I looked in the distance. I looked to either side. There was nothing but fields and woods and mist I said: 'This is a camp site?'

'That's right.'

'You're joking.'

But he wasn't joking.

I thought: Okay, if he wants to be like that, and I said: 'But I'm not actually on your property am I? I'm on the water.'

'You're on my bank. Your mooring irons are on my bank. It's seventy-five pence a mooring iron. If you had an anchor it would be all right, but you haven't so that's one pound fifty.

The pylons hissed. An owl made a noise like Roy Orbison. This was about the quietest, least spoilt spot I'd seen on the river, and this man must have walked miles to charge me for standing on it. I said: 'If this is a camp site where are the toilets and the showers and the camp shop selling Camping Gaz refills, and where's the ping pong room?'

'Three miles away in the village. It's a big camp site.'

I was having such a pleasant evening until he arrived. I paid him to get rid of him and said: 'What's your VAT number then?'

'Same as yours. Goodnight.' And as he walked off into the mist he called out: 'If you're going to Lechlade try the Swan. Best pub on the river. My nephew works there.'

Back in the tent I undressed and grumbled and searched for my sleeping bag. 'All right, Boogie! I'm in no mood for games. Get off it!' But he wasn't on it. I looked everywhere a sleeping bag could sensibly have got to: in the luggage, under the seats, in the lockers. Then I looked in silly places where a sleeping bag could never have got to: in the Winalot bag, in the bilges. But the thing had disappeared.

Then I looked outside. It was a beautiful, misty blue night. The moon on the wane. The water the colour of a Milk of Magnesia bottle and very still. The only clue that there was a current at all was the cylindrical silhouette of my sleeping bag floating slowly back towards London.

There are many ways a dog can show his loyalty to a human being but there can be none more altruistic than sharing his blanket in a time of crisis. And Boogie took no persuading at all that night, I'm proud to say. All I had to do was inform him of the soaking wet sleeping bag situation, and that my sleeping bag falling overboard was in effect similar to his blanket falling overboard since we were a travelling team, and that I wouldn't hesitate in letting him share my sleeping bag if the needs were reversed, and he understood completely. I gave him the decision, of course. I told him it was up to him. He had every right to say: 'Get lost! Get your own blanket.' But his response was typical. He did shriek as I whipped the blanket from under him, and then bared his teeth and made primitive wolf-like noises, and his eyes turned red, but I knew this was merely a playful performance to try to draw maximum humour out of the situation, to keep spirits up.

And apart from the occasional strange smell and him

grinding his teeth in his sleep, it was a perfectly comfortable night. I dreamt that Jennifer was lying next to me. Her shoulders were bare just above the blanket. I was attracted to the smooth curve between her collar bone and upper arm. I put my hand out to touch her. She looked beautiful but she had a cold nose.

Then I was woken by birdsong. It was eight o'clock, I felt a touch of dejection. I'd travelled up a hundred miles of river and I still hadn't got up in time to see the sunrise. What sort of explorer is it that never gets up before eight o'clock? I asked myself, and I steeled myself for a swim. I lifted up the tent flap and saw the water laced with a thin cold mist. The idea of immersing myself battled with the idea of going back to sleep and to Jennifer. I turned over, and there, staring at me, was Boogie. He licked me and grinned. I know I don't look my best in the morning but I don't look anywhere near as bad as he does.

The river continued to narrow. The willows hung their boughs in the water. I began to see faces in the gnarled trunks, grotesque faces. In some places the trees had been blown over in the storms of the previous winter and now they lay on the land, the bank beneath them pulled up like a curled lip. I didn't see many people during those days. The river was secretive now and it crept up on villages. It may only have been a half mile from a main road but it had become a master of disguise, lurking beneath its banks and willows like a nervous animal.

But the few people I did meet were sympathetic characters who seemed in touch with the spirit of the river. One afternoon I saw a woman walking along the bank. She called out: 'I never thought I'd ever see one of those again, not this far up.'

She was referring to *Maegan* and so I paddled over to her. 'We used to have a skiff like that when I was a child,' she said. 'My father would row us up from Oxford to our bungalow. That was in the twenties. I've not been in a boat for years now.'

I asked her if she wanted a ride upstream and her eyes lit up like a child's. She must have been seventy years old but she jumped in the back seat and said: 'It's all right for the dog, isn't it?'

She was a farmer. She and her husband had retired and bought some land near Northmoor but they weren't doing well. 'We keep cows but as soon as you reach your quota that's it. It's not enough to live on. We should move into sheep; there's money in sheep.'

A magpie flew overhead and made a noise like an owl. 'Noisy buggers magpies,' she said. Then she lay back and used Boogie as a pillow and said: 'It's so nice to be back on the river again. We had a boat once but a pig trod on it.' A B52 flew overhead and the river shook. 'Noisy buggers, B52s,' she said. 'Can I have a row?'

She climbed in beside me and we sculled up to Bablock Hythe. There had been a ferry across the river here for almost a thousand years, but it had recently ceased operation. The woman said: 'No one looked after it. Not even the Thames people. They didn't take an interest and it got too bad to repair.' The same thing seemed to have happened to the pub. The Ferry Inn it was called and it had weeds in the car park and smashed windows. 'The landlord didn't pay his electricity bill and they cut him off. He should have looked after that ferry. But the river's changed now. The motorboats have changed everything. They've driven all the wildlife away. You don't see any kingfishers any more. Sorry, I've dropped a spoon of yours overboard.'

We pottered about the river up to Northmoor where she climbed out. I told her I was heading to the source and asked her if she knew anything about it and she said: 'No. But Kelvin will.'

'Kelvin?'

'You'll find him in the Dun Cow in Northmoor. You'll like the Dun Cow. It's full of life. All the youngsters go into the Dun Cow.'

I moored by Northmoor lock and that evening walked the two miles to the Dun Cow. Northmoor seemed to be the most remote village I'd come across, but arriving in villages on a footpath from the river gave me a different perspective from arriving by car. I normally surfaced through the back yard of a village, through the churchyard or a housing estate, rather than in the traditional way on a road, over roundabouts and past a Welcome To sign. The locals always looked surprised to see a stranger appear in their midst in this way. I felt like an alien and since I didn't have a map with me all I knew of my location was that it was somewhere west of Oxford.

Many eyes watched me as I walked through Northmoor. I could see movement behind net curtains. I went into the Dun Cow leaving Boogie lying down outside in front of a pot of geraniums. I was the only person in the pub. Presently one of the many doors opened and a woman came out tying up her apron: 'Always quiet on a Wednesday,' she said. The room was a sitting room with armchairs and pot plants, prints and books, and no bar, just a doorway with barrels. I was pulled a drink and told to make myself at home.

The barmaid sat down with me as if I'd just walked into her house and needed to be entertained. I asked if the animal in the field by the side of the pub was a donkey and she said: 'It's a hinney.'

'A hinney?'

'A hinney.'

'What's a hinney?'

'A cross between a stallion and a female ass. You're not from round here are you?'

'No.'

'You've got a boat on the river haven't you?'

'Yes.'

'A rowing boat?'

'Yes.'

'Rowed from London haven't you?'

'Yes.'

'Thought so. I go to London sometimes. The Tower. Hampton Court. Vince Hill's house. I don't like it much.'

'I'm looking for the source of the river. I want to speak to Kelvin.'

'He'll be in later.'

A couple of elderly regulars came in and sat down. 'Put my spinach in today, I did,' said one.

'Too early,' said the other.

'Too early be buggered.'

'Too early. Don't put spinach in till third weekend of May,' and he laughed and put his head back to show off his hairy nostrils.

'Ha, you'll be laughing when you've no greens.'

'You have to have greens,' said the barmaid. 'A meal's not a meal without greens.'

'Too early for spinach.'

I chipped in with my newly acquired knowledge on the subject: 'It's best to plant spinach two days after the full moon in May, I've always said.'

'He's waiting for Kelvin,' said the barmaid.

Everyone looked out of the window. They seemed like people who had come to the pub every single night for the last forty years, and yet they could still amaze each other with a conversation about rhubarb. But, it was more than just a conversation. It was a celebratory recounting of the day. They sat in silence now but silence was a very

important part of the process. And I was so obviously
the stranger because the silence made me fidget. I felt
responsible, I could hear the clock tick. I smiled a few
times; smacked my lips a few times. Then looked round
the room, pretending I was fascinated by a picture or an
ornament.

The eldest man brought out a coach timetable and
flicked through it. 'Taking my girlfriend on an outing, I
am,' he said.

'She won't go with you,' said his mate.

'She will. I'll make her.'

'Where're you going anyway?'

'Romsey. They've a good brewery there.'

'I used to go to Romsey to buy cattle.'

'Don't see so many cattle about now. I was just thinking
tonight as I walked here and saw the empty field. You
don't see many cattle like you used to.'

I bit my lip then said: 'There's more money in sheep,
isn't there?'

'Kelvin will be here soon,' said the barmaid.

Everyone looked out of the window again. There was
another silence. A car pulled up.

'There's Dave,' said the barmaid.

'That's never Dave. Since when has Dave had a green
car?'

'It's his sister's.'

'It's his mum's,' said the barmaid.

Dave came and sat down. He said: 'Whose dog is that?'

'Mine,' I said.

Everyone in the pub looked out of the window at
Boogie. He was eating a leg of chicken with rice and
pepper salad and garnish. I said: 'He's getting old. But
they get old, don't they, dogs?'

'He's waiting for Kelvin,' said the barmaid.

'Kelvin's on holiday on the Algarve,' said Dave.

'Oh yes,' said the barmaid. 'Kelvin's gone on holiday to the Algarve. I forgot.'

'Yes, he's gone to the Algarve,' said the other two.

I walked back to *Maegan* across the fields and under the pylons. A handful of swallows darted in and out of the wires. We reached the towpath and walked back towards the sound of the weir stream. It would take time to become a local in Northmoor, I decided.

I said to Boogie: 'I've been thinking. It might be an idea to live together when we get back.'

He licked some cuckoo spit off a thistle.

'Not you. I don't mean live with you. I do live with you. Unfortunately. I mean live with Jennifer. I feel as though I've somehow got to know her better on this trip. Even though she's not arrived yet. How would you fancy living with Jennifer?'

Boogie looked up at me, he had a dead fish in his mouth.

Back in the boat I lay down surrounded by the sound of the weir stream but it was as murmurous as a lullaby now.

Then it was Thursday afternoon and I was on a telephone at Tadpole Bridge speaking to Jennifer's PA.

'Is Jennifer Conway there?' I said.

'Is that you?'

'Yes.'

'Well, she says she's coming this afternoon, although I don't believe it myself.'

'I'd like to speak to her please.'

'Yes, yes.'

The Muzak was *Chariots of Fire*. Jennifer came on: 'Where are you?'

'Tadpole Bridge.'

'I'm on my way. I'm coming tonight. I can't wait.'

'. . .'

'Hello?'

'You're joking?'

'No, I'm not joking. Meet me on the bridge at six.'

'You're really coming?'

'Yes.'

'. . .'

'Hello?'

'There's something I've got to tell you.'

'What?'

'There's something you should know . . .'

'Yes?'

'I've been meaning to tell you this for some time . . . I've got . . . I've got a shortage of spoons, can you bring some?'

'Spoons?'

'Yes.'

'Right.'

There was a pub by the bridge. I went to the gents' and looked at my reflection. I was filthy, knotted and hairy. I looked at Boogie. He was filthy knotted and horrible. I walked back to *Maegan*. She was filthy and littered, full of willow and hawthorn, duck feathers, crisp packets, soft drink containers, sweet wrappers, colour magazines and apple cores all lobbed at me from countless bridges.

First I turned to *Maegan*. I swept her out, scrubbed her gunwales, coiled her ropes, tidied her cabinets and aired her canvas top. Then I turned to myself. I stepped into the shallow river, shaved in my reflection, dried out my sleeping bag, washed my clothes, and laid them out over the canvas. I combed my hair back, scrubbed my nails, and put talcum powder into my wellingtons. Lastly I turned to Boogie. After which I had to turn back to myself and the boat again. On the dot of six o'clock I was sitting on the handsome parapet of Tadpole Bridge wearing

damp underwear. Boogie was at my side sitting to attention, hair parted, not a scrap of muck on him. How could
anyone resist him?

The first hour passed quite quickly and pleasantly.
When the sun set it cast a magnificent one-eyed reflection
of the bridge on the water downstream. The second hour
passed more slowly and was more boring. I counted the
radio masts in the fields to the north and I squinted at the
military aircraft just a few thousand feet up. Presently a
local character with slippers on his feet sat down next to
me and told me his name was Ivor.

'That your dog?' he asked.

'Yes.'

'Messy, isn't he? What sort?'

'Nicaraguan dachshund.'

'Thought so.'

Before he could change the subject a car had stopped
and a woman wound down her window and said: 'Can
you tell me where Bampton is?'

Ivor stroked his chin, looked both ways and said: 'Two
miles that way, turn left and it's on your right. This is a
Nicaraguan dachshund, by the way.'

The woman looked at Boogie and smiled and said: 'I
once had a dachshund. It was called Roman. We bought
it off a family who were going to have it put down because
its leg was damaged at birth. But we nursed it and looked
after it and it grew healthy and was a marvellous pet for
years, wonderful with the children. It even won prizes.
Then it squeezed under the garden fence one day and ran
across the road and a car hit it.'

We sat in silence. I could hear rooks down by the river.
The woman looked very sad. Ivor said: 'What sort of car?'

She drove away. I said to Ivor: 'Waiting for the pub to
open?'

'No. I don't go in there. It's got a stuffed fish on the

wall. I often come and sit on the bridge, though. I direct the traffic. I live in Bampton.'

Another car pulled up. The driver wound down the window and said: 'Is Hinton Waldrist round here?'

'Two miles that way, turn left and it's on your right,' said Ivor.

The car drove off. Ivor said: 'They need directing, see. People in cars are always lost. They depend on people like me.'

We sat there in silence. I was getting to understand the timing of these silences now though, growing more comfortable with them. As Ivor mused I imagined Jennifer and me lying in separate sleeping bags at either end of the boat. Then I imagined us in a double sleeping bag in the centre of the boat. Then I imagined Boogie lodged in between us. Ivor said: 'I've been sitting on this bridge looking at the river for years.'

'I bet you've seen it change?'

'Everyone asks me that. He's ugly, your dog, isn't he?'

The woman who had stopped earlier drove past and stopped again. I asked her if she'd found Bampton. She said she had, eventually, and added: 'When I was a young woman I walked up from Oxford to Lechlade along the river towpath. I remember there was a wonderful village square at Bampton; tonight I was just passing and wondered if it would be how I remembered. I seem to recall having my sandwiches under a big tree and a woman came up and gave me a bag of raspberries and I ate them all the way to Lechlade. I imagined the square would be much smaller than I remembered, but strangely it was bigger.'

There was a silence. The woman looked sad once more. The rooks were quietening down as the light faded. A low-flying aircraft roared overhead polluting the moment. When peace returned Ivor said: 'What sort of sandwiches?'

The woman smiled and said: 'Can you tell me how I can get back on the Oxford road?' And Ivor stood up and said: 'Two miles that way, turn left and it's on your right.'

I waited two hours exactly and then went into the pub. It was called the Trout. Boogie had a half gammon steak, some grilled tomatoes, and some creme caramel, then he came and sat down under the table. I patted him. 'I'm through with that woman,' I said.

Boogie belched.

'If she turned up now I'd tell her to go home again.'

There were a few people at the bar. I made comments about the stuffed fish on the wall, about the beautiful reflection of the bridge in the water at sunset and about the assortment of military aircraft in the sky. This earned little response, so then I asked the barmaid how she cut her finger. She looked at me and said: 'It's always quiet on a Thursday. Only gets busy when we get a nice day, and we never seem to have those on a Thursday. Is your dog hungry?'

'No, he's not.'

I sat down. People were looking at me strangely. I wanted to get back to my boat and get sculling. A stool squeaked on the stone floor. A man with his shirt outside his pants turned to me to speak but before he could say anything a blaze of light hit the pub as outside four headlights spun through the car park. There was the crunch of tyres that cost £97 each on the gravel. A car door slammed.

'Hello,' said a man looking out of the window, 'a TVR,' and into the Trout walked Jennifer.

Behind her came Ivor.

Ivor was the first to speak. He said: 'This young lady has asked me out for a drink.'

Jennifer stood there in a green jump suit and baseball cap. She looked at me hard for a moment, and took in my new waterman's appearance. Then I strode towards her and kissed her and I remember the rim of her hat dug into my forehead. The local characters watched silently with drinks poised. One man had hiccoughs. Jennifer took her hat off and I expected to see her hair fall. But she'd had it cut, cut short. At first I didn't like it then very quickly I decided it looked lovely. She said: 'I'm here.'

I said: 'Yes.'

She said: 'I'm late but I'm here. I've got luggage. Where's the boat? It's a beautiful night. I've got luggage.' And I think she may have been about to kiss me again when there was a shuffle below the table and Boogie struggled out from under a chair. He had a baked potato skin in his mouth. Jennifer looked at him. Boogie looked at her. Her face fell. So did his. Her body stiffened. His tail went between his legs. She said: 'What's he doing here!?'

I panicked and said: 'I don't know . . . he must have followed me.' But she didn't see the funny side of that remark, so I said: 'Listen: whilst you were in Paris, Oslo and Bologna, Boogie has been my faithful companion for a hundred miles of river and . . .'

'Well, introduce me to your friends,' she said, but she was already introducing herself. 'That's a fine fish,' she said, indicating the stuffed job in the glass case.

'Chub,' said the local character with his shirt hanging out of his trousers. 'Interesting fish the chubb, shy, likes cover, tricky to coax out. Got to be up early to get a chub.'

'Do you want a drink?' said Jennifer to Ivor.

'If you insist I'll have three pints of bitter, please.'

Jennifer moved to the bar. She said to the landlady: 'Is it always this quiet on a Thursday?' And the landlady said: 'It livens up later.'

We all played darts. We all bought rounds. As the night

progressed the pub filled and we all made friends. Ivor followed Jennifer around all night. The chub fisherman offered to take her fishing if she'd like to meet him on the bridge at five thirty. It was the best night of the trip so far. Then I said to her: 'Are you hungry?'

'Starving!'

We walked back to the boat along the towpath. Boogie lagged behind. We carried armfuls of luggage. She'd brought her tennis racket. She'd brought bathroom scales. She'd brought six pairs of shoes. She'd brought the collected works of W. B. Yeats, Wilfred Owen and John Donne. She'd brought spoons.

'You've brought spoons,' I said, excitedly. 'Great. Spoons.'

She looked at me and smirked and said: 'Have you been all right on your own?'

'Yes. Of course. Fine. I've had a great time. Boogie has been a good friend and . . .' As I spoke I could have sworn I heard a telephone ring.

'Can you hear a telephone ringing very close to us?' I said, but she was already digging into her bag. 'It'll be for me,' she said and produced a white Vodaphone. I looked on aghast as she composed herself for a moment – ran her fingers through where her hair used to be – and then answered the instrument: 'Jennifer Conway . . . Why? . . . Why? . . . No . . . Why? . . . No.' Then she put the phone away, smiled and walked on.

As we approached *Maegan* I could see a cruiser had moored next to her. A big fat chrome-and-Formica job with a lifeboat and a deep freeze. It was named *How's your Father*. It dwarfed *Maegan*, made her look like a broken branch off a tree. Sharp lights pierced the blinds and I could see the flicker of a TV.

Jennifer said: 'Oh she's splendid. She's magnificent.

She's everything I ever thought she'd be. She's even got a lifeboat.'

'Er . . . No, this is *Maegan* over here,' I said, pulling back the damp moth-eaten flap.

Jennifer is used to not showing her emotions. That's why she's such a good businesswoman. That's why she's good at poker. That's why touching her you often get an electric shock.

She said: 'She's splendid! She's magnificent. She's everything I ever thought she'd be.'

I climbed in and lit the lamp. Jennifer followed and immediately the boat was full. Boogie decided to sit outside. I fed him his daily tin but he hardly touched it.

'I'm going to cook you fried mozzarella with a Provencale sauce,' I said and I took out Delia Smith. 'This is Delia Smith.'

Jennifer looked askance and said: 'Are you sure you've been all right while I've been away?'

'I've been fine. I've had lots of adventures,' and as I added the garlic, chopped tomatoes and basil to the onion and pepper I told her about the wild supermarket of Weybridge, the mad dog of Hennerton Backwater and the deadly rowing eights in Oxford. She sat there entranced, and then as I sliced the mozzarella in quarter-inch strips and coated them with seasoned flour, then dipped them in the egg mixture, Jennifer told me about Paris, Oslo, Bologna and Lisbon and her lunch date with Tiny Rowland.

'Lisbon?! I didn't know you went to Lisbon!'

'Just for the day. Waste of time. I did write a poem though: "Cabo di Roca I'm standing on your tip, like a rocking stone I'm trapped, with just a tumble or a trip, what voyage of discovery I would map . . ." It's awful, isn't it?'

'It needs just a touch more basil, and it's ready.'

We toasted each other with a bottle of claret and she said: 'I'm glad I'm here at last. I've always wanted to come away with you.'

And I said: 'I always knew you'd come.' From outside the boat came the sound of a dog being sick.

The meal was a disaster. It tasted strange. We struggled to eat it. The most memorable moment of the meal came when Jennifer dropped a mouthful from her fork on to her lap. She went to pick it up but there was suddenly a black flash as Boogie dived into the boat and grabbed it. Jennifer, playfully, went for him with her fork, but I held her back and explained that Boogie considered anything fallen on the floor as his. She protested. She said it had landed on her lap. I explained that since she was sitting on the floor Boogie had been confused. She said in that case Boogie had better watch his Kennomeat from now on because if he dropped any she'd have it in a sandwich out of spite. I told her not to worry: Boogie had never in his entire life dropped a morsel of food.

But this didn't spoil the evening. Jennifer quickly calmed down and we talked about the journey. She asked me if I'd visited Oscar Wilde's cell in Reading Gaol. I admitted I hadn't. She asked if I'd visited Mapledurham House where Alexander Pope was inspired, not to mention Galsworthy. I told her no. She asked me if I'd visited the meadows between Eynsham and Godstow of which Matthew Arnold wrote: 'Through the Wytham flats, Red loosestrife and blond meadow-sweet among, And darting swallows, and light water gnats, We track'd the shy Thames shore.' And I said I must have passed it but I couldn't exactly remember that bit.

I suggested instead we discuss the expedition. I said: 'The information I have is all rather based on hearsay but it appears a large piece of water does leave the main river just after Cricklade. Some call it the Swill Brook, some the River Churn. We'll find barbed wire across the river and we might have to carry the boat a couple of miles, but I've heard there's a tree . . .' And then Jennifer started to yawn. She said: 'I want to go to bed. Where does the dog sleep?'

'In the boat, of course.'

'What! Doesn't he sleep outside?'

'Boogie is my constant companion. He's been at my side throughout this journey. He's a member of the crew.'

'You've been watching too many Lassie films. He's a dog. He'd probably prefer to sleep outside.'

'We'll let him make the decision,' I said and took Boogie for a walk along the towpath.

It was a longer walk than usual. The moon was a marble. I could see veins running through its face. A chub plopped. Boogie stopped, sat down and scratched his ear more aggressively than I've ever seen him do before.

'She's a character, you've got to admit that. It'll take her a while to settle into the river's routine, of course. But don't worry about her. We're a good team, Jennifer and me. We work well together. Anyone can see that. It's good to have a woman on board as well, isn't it?

We walked on. The water slapped against the bank. My wellingtons glistened in the moonlight. 'It's a lovely night. The sort of night to sleep outside under the stars, to really get back to nature. I would do myself but I've got company. I don't know why you don't, though? You being a dog and all that. I mean it's your decision of course. You can sleep where you want. But I just thought it might be nice for you to sleep outside.'

Boogie stopped and banged his head on a gatepost. I thought it was an accident but then he did it a second time. When we got back to *Maegan* I paused on the bank and patted him: 'Listen, Boogie, I wouldn't normally ask you to do this. But . . . it's our first night together. You don't want to play gooseberry, do you?'

I pulled back the flap and he dived in and ran over the pile of dishes and bedclothes to the stern where he lay down and started to snore.

'He's made his decision. He wants to sleep in the boat,' I said.

Jennifer was lying in her sleeping bag. She had a vest on and the gas light made her shoulders flare as they had in my dream.

I went through my going-to-bed routine. I placed all the breakables in the stern, all the foodstuffs at the bow. I put the milk outside to keep cool. I arranged the kettle and the stove for the morning so I could just lean out of bed and turn it all on. And I made sure my torch, matches and notebook were handy. Then I brushed my teeth and watched the white trail of Signal drift down towards Oxford. I was so excited I dropped my toothbrush over the side. 'The river has a gentle, soothing effect,' I said. 'It wraps itself around you. I've never felt so calm as I have the last two weeks. I feel as though I'm having little say in where the boat is taking me. I'm just following a groove that I've no control over. The river has, I think, more than anything else, made me feel insignificant. It's made me . . .'

'Are you going to sleep with me tonight?' said Jennifer. She was leaning on her elbow and the light illuminated the little black hairs on her forearms.

'Yes,' I said.

'Good.' she said, and then she zipped the sleeping bags together.

Later that night an owl hooted at last.

9. What? Lechlade Already?

Jennifer and Boogie have never got on, not since the time they first met and Boogie made a mess in her handbag.

They're such uncompromising characters. Boogie dismisses Jennifer the way he does pedigree dogs. He thinks she's pompous, discriminatory, opportunist, whereas none of this is true. I've tried to communicate to him that Jennifer is simply a perfectionist. She likes things to be without blemish. Boogie's problem is he isn't satisfied with something unless it's covered with blemishes. The more blemishes the better is Boogie's motto. That night on the boat was the first time they'd seen each other for years, but it hadn't been long enough as far as Boogie was concerned. He was outraged at the idea of Jennifer joining the expedition. Over the last two weeks he'd established certain parts of *Maegan* as his territory, and now it had been invaded. He felt usurped.

The next morning I woke early. Light was streaming in through the canvas. At the end of the boat Boogie lay with his eyes open, but next to me was an empty space. I looked at my watch: it was seven o'clock and something was splashing about in the river. Then two hands grabbed the side of the boat and there was Jennifer.

'I suppose you've been for a swim every morning?' she said. She took her wet T-shirt off and threw it into the boat. It landed on top of Boogie who leapt up as if someone had plugged him into the mains. Jennifer laughed. Boogie shook himself and covered her with wet hairs.

It was a lovely day. 'Breakfast?' I said.

'In a little while,' she replied, and then she put on her running shoes and set off along the towpath. She ran for four miles she said, then, when she came back, Boogie and I lay in the sun surrounded by buttercups and watched as she did aerobics for twenty minutes. Then she dived in the river again. When she finally climbed out, she said: 'I suppose you do that every day as well.' I shrugged and scratched my hat. Boogie licked his bits and went back to sleep.

For breakfast we had croissants, figs and yoghurt, orange juice and herbal tea. Jennifer breathed in deeply and said: 'You're the only person I know who would take me to somewhere like this.' Then she went back to the car and returned with more luggage. She was well equipped for the trip, there was no doubt about that. To her already sizable pile she added a guitar, a wok and a selection of pot plants. 'I couldn't trust anyone to water them for me,' she explained, securing a philodendron to the bows.

So I explained that that was the very reason I had brought Boogie along, and she turned sharply and said that she hoped that me bringing Boogie wasn't deliberate after she'd expressly asked me not to. She said she hoped she couldn't sense a power struggle. I said that a power struggle was exactly what I had no choice in sensing, considering her behaviour and the amount of time she'd kept me waiting. She said if she'd known Boogie was here I'd have been waiting a lot longer and that it seemed ridiculous that a grown man couldn't go anywhere without his stupid dog. I said how thoughtless she was and that if she respected me she should respect my dog as well. And then she said who said anything about respect?

I was only a travelling companion. I backed off here and said that if we went on like this any more we'd have an argument. She suggested we were already having an argument and if we needed one to clear the air then we should have one. It was at that precise moment that Boogie, who had wandered off at the start of this altercation, came charging back to the boat hotly pursued by a herd of Jerseys. He jumped into the middle of breakfast with his dung-covered feet while the cattle screeched to a halt on the bank. Then the ones at the back started pushing the ones at the front going: 'Go on! Get in there and get the little bugger, you saw what he did to Margaret,' until one of the front rank lost her footing and her two front legs landed in the boat. Staring into the face of a cow I did what I considered to be the most noble thing – I clapped my hands loudly and threw a croissant at it. Jennifer, who clearly wanted to release some aggression anyway, hit the creature over the head with her wok. It was then I remembered my plan was not to react to her but to be reasonable, and so when the cow had got out of the boat I said: 'Anyway, the whole business doesn't really bother me'. And I think she may have been about to raise the wok to me when the phone rang.

She ran her fingers through her hair, composed herself momentarily as before and then spoke into the instrument: 'Jennifer Conway . . . Why? . . . Why? . . . No . . . No.' Then she put the phone away carefully and looked at me so as I could see the whites of her teeth. I decided it was time I took charge.

'Time we were heading out,' I said as authoritatively as I could. 'We've got some sculling to get done,' and I went to untie the moorings. But I'd tied a half-hitch sheepshank with a bowline reef the previous evening and the dramatic effect I'd hoped for was lost while I spent the next twenty minutes unravelling the tangle.

The problem with two people sculling together is that they have to keep in time. A missed beat results initially in much crunching of sculls and ultimately in a trail of zig-zags. Jennifer, who was in the stroke position, was powered by aggression and from the pace she was setting she clearly had a lot of it to work off. I looked at the bow wave we were creating and estimated our speed at about 20 knots. Having just got the coots to trust me I was now sending tidal waves to terrorize them.

We passed Rushey lock, where the beautiful garden was made even more colourful by two peacocks. The lock-keeper said: 'I used to have more, but they don't get on with the plants.' He leant on his shovel and smiled at us, time on his hands. 'You know something,' he went on. 'You're the only people I've had through here this morning.' And Jennifer said: 'Well get a bloody move on then. We're in a hurry.'

'Right,' said the lock-keeper, taken aback. As we rose up he saw Boogie and said: 'It's all right for the dog, isn't it?' and Jennifer said: 'Just open the gates, will you?'

'Right,' said the lock-keeper and he wound up the sluice gates as fast as he could. As we paddled out he said: 'If you're going up to Lechlade call in at the Swan, it's the best . . .'

'Where's your toilet?' said Jennifer.

'We haven't got one,' said the lock-keeper. 'We've got a wastepaper bin but no toilet.'

'You must have a toilet. Where do you go?'

'I've got my own. It's an unofficial one.'

'Where is it? Or I'll go on your petunias.'

'Er . . . First door on the left down the hall.'

Jennifer leapt out of the boat. I turned to the lock-keeper and said: 'Sorry. Her first day on the river.'

'Most of them are like her,' said the lock-keeper. 'My problem is I bottle it up.'

'Mmm.'

We licked up the river through meadowland, and flashed under Radcot Bridge, the oldest on the upper river. Someone threw a piece of orange peel at us but it fell in the water behind the boat. We were too fast for it.

The wind picked up. But half the time it was a head-wind and half the time a tailwind, so erratic was the river's course. Jennifer said: 'Why does the river meander so?' And I replied: 'It's a very simple and natural process following inescapable laws of physics. If a river finds an obstruction in its path, say, sediment or a tributary stream or even fallen debris, the river course diverts. The deflected current hits the opposite bank where it carves the land away, and the underflow carries the resulting sediment, depositing it on the inner curve. As the surface current ricochets back to the other bank another meander is created, and the process is repeated until the river becomes a series of curves, changing the shape of the flood plain constantly. The longer it runs the bigger the curves become, thus in the case of the Thames, by the time it reaches Essex, the meanders are miles apart.'

Jennifer stopped sculling and my oars crashed into hers. She turned round and said: 'Who told you that?'

'A lock-keeper.'

Then she tensed and said: 'Quick, hand me a piece of paper; you've inspired me.' I tore a piece out of my note-book and handed it to her and she was silent for a while as she wrote in snatches. Then she punctured the paper with a full stop and said: 'Thank you, you made me write that. I knew this trip would be like this. It's wonderful. You must have written lots of stuff. Poetry is so therapeutic. Listen. About this morning. I'm sorry about our disagreement.'

'So am I.'

'I'm glad I'm here.'

'So am I.'

'Want to hear my poem?'

'Sure.'

'It's not finished yet. But the ideas are there. It's about reflections and how you forget they're there and then suddenly you see them again and realize they're always there. Everything on the river happens twice.'

'That's my idea.'

'What do you mean?'

'I noticed that almost as soon as I started on the trip.'

'So what?'

'Well, nothing, I was just pointing out that I was struck by all the reflections as well. I wrote it down myself. About how the reflections give the river its extra dimension, how it's easy to forget about them and not notice them for long periods, but then suddenly you can see the whole earth and sky in the water.'

'So you're saying I've stolen your idea?'

'No . . . I'm just . . . let's hear it.'

'No, I don't want to read it to you now.'

'Go on.'

'No.' And she leant into the sculls again.

In the afternoon we reached Kelmscott. I felt tired. I lay on the grass while Jennifer went for a jog to 'warm down'. When she came back she said: 'William Morris used to live in Kelmscott. I'd like to go round his house.'

William Morris's house is a beautiful sixteenth-century Cotswold stone manor house that just peeks over the trees to catch the river. Morris moved here from London to escape the pressures of his public life but he made the mistake of leasing the property with a fellow artist, Dante Gabriel Rossetti, who shared Morris's life rather more than Morris would have wished, falling in love with Morris's wife, Jane. Rossetti painted her again and again, in a way you wouldn't normally paint the wife of the man you've just leased a house with. Morris, depressed by the whole business – although unable it seems to do much about it – buried himself in his work, producing unrivalled designs for ceramics and fabrics, many of which are still kept at Kelmscott House. The house is open to the public only a handful of days during the year. Fortunately the day we were there was one of them.

We left Boogie guarding the boat and walked out of the heat into the cool, panelled house. It was a treasure of tapestries and furniture. We looked at each other and knew we were in a precious place.

A small number of people were quietly walking around, speaking in whispers. The couple in front were gazing at a tapestry. The woman said: 'It's just like Eileen's, only more complicated.'

I put my arm through Jennifer's and we controlled our laughter. I said: 'Shall we get a place like this?'

'You're not serious?'

And I wasn't but she looked at me in a way that made me think she'd be disappointed if I was joking. So I said: 'Yes.'

Then she looked disappointed so I said: 'Well . . .'

'You and me, live together?'

'We get on okay.'

'No we don't.'

'We do.'

'We argue all the time.'

'We don't.'

A woman was showing the visitors round. We were attracting attention. I stopped beneath a tapestry and put my arm through Jennifer's again. She said: 'No one has ever wanted to live with me. I'm selfish. I'm a loner. I use people.'

'No, that's just the image you give. I know it's a veneer.'

'No it isn't.'

'It is.'

'Listen, I'm telling you it isn't.'

'C'mon. It must be.'

A man with dark glasses was looking at us. He turned his head away but I knew his eyes were still focused on us.

'Besides,' said Jennifer. 'I couldn't live with that dog.'

We walked through the village. It was the most beautiful I'd seen on the river. There was a stone fence around a meadow. There were dovecots in walls, pigs in back yards, vegetables in the gardens and Volvos in driveways. The spring had laundered everything in inimitable fashion. The foliage was unblemished and unravaged. The blossom on the chestnut trees was a perm fresh from the salon. Nothing was fat, flaccid or pale; all was small tight and vivid, and I remember that day in particular for the irresistible sense of optimism to be felt when the first warm spell of the year arrives and you know that summer is finally here, and the best part is it's all still to come.

Eventually we found ourselves in the churchyard standing over Morris's grave. ' "Love is enough; though the world be a-waning, And the woods have no voice but the voice of complaining." He was a refreshing poet,' said Jennifer.

'It would really please me if you'd just try to get on with Boogie.'

'I will on one condition.'

'What's that.'

'He doesn't moult, breathe, or fart in my direction ever again.'

'Listen, he's not as unpleasant as all that. He's not a puppy; he's an adult now, responsible and mature. Treat him with respect and he'll repay you in the only currency he has: loyalty.'

Jennifer sighed and smiled and we walked back to the boat. As we crossed the field to the river Boogie was lying in the stern snapping at a dragonfly and Jennifer said: 'All right. What does he like to eat best of all?'

'Curry,' I replied.

'Tonight we shall have curry. Where's the nearest takeaway?'

'Probably in Oxford.'

'I'll call Michael my motorcyclist to . . .'

'No! Delia and I can make a curry.' And although we were still a hundred yards from the boat, as soon as that wonderful word was uttered, I saw Boogie sit bolt upright on the back seat and look around wearing his 'okay, who said curry?' expression.

Outside, the day lay dying. The water meadows of Oxfordshire slipped into a mist. The sun went down behind the electricity lines and melted. On Radcot Bridge a great crested grebe knocked an old-age pensioner off his bicycle. *Maegan* sat very still on the water.

Inside, we were wrapped in the thick and heady aroma of a Sri Lankan egg curry. I sat at one end with Delia Smith in one hand, a wooden spoon in the other. Jennifer sat opposite, chopping up onions. Boogie sat behind her, his eyes full of tears.

As I added the garlic and ginger to the chopped vegetables, I told Jennifer of my desire to be a lock-keeper. As I blended in the turmeric, flour and curry powder just as Delia instructed, and stirred it to soak up the juice, I said: 'We could get a lock-keeper's cottage – something like the one at Sonning. I could be the lock-keeper and you could be the lock-keeper's wife.'

'I want to be the lock-keeper, you can be the lock-keeper's wife.'

'I don't think there are any female lock-keepers.'

'Well, we'll soon see about that, won't we?'

As I mixed in the creamed coconut and added a tiny bit of lemon juice to sharpen the flavour and then poured the sauce over the eggs and rice and chutney, Jennifer asked me how much lock-keepers earned. I told her I imagined about eight thousand pounds a year but that included electricity and the house came rent free. She told me she'd earned eight thousand pounds in the time I'd been on the river.

The curry tasted dreadful. It was a disaster. Boogie loved it but that meant nothing. We ate what we could then piled the rest into his bowl and he ate it the way he always eats curry – quickly. Afterwards, I washed the plates in the river and watched the orange slick drift off towards London. Then Jennifer said: 'It's Friday. I want a night out on the town.'

We walked up the lane to the village pub, arm in arm, Boogie at our side. 'See, he's cute once you get used to him,' I said. Jennifer patted him and something brown came off on her hand.

'It's only curry,' I said, but I wasn't sure.

The pub was empty but for a few men sitting round the bar. The landlord said: 'It's always quiet on a Friday.' Jennifer ordered the drinks. She said: 'Pint of bitter and . . .' She was interrupted by one of the wits at the bar. He said: 'And what's your fella having, a Slimline tonic?' He laughed and all his mates laughed with him. I cringed. Jennifer calmly continued: '. . . And another pint of bitter and a Castella.' Then she lit the cigar and swigged back half a pint, and said: 'Okay, who wants a game of arm wrestling?'

The men weren't local. They came from Yorkshire. They were itinerant barn erectors. They travelled the country putting up barns wherever they were asked. 'We even went to France to put one up once,' said a lad with shaving cuts on his face. 'Have you ever been to France? Great place, France.'

I remember him because he was the first to take up Jennifer's challenge.

'Arm wrestling with a woman?' he said. 'Don't be daft.'

'For a fiver,' said Jennifer.

'I wouldn't take your money,' said the lad.

'A tenner,' said Jennifer.

'I wouldn't rob you.'

His mates were gibing him. 'Fifty quid,' said Jennifer.

There was a hush. 'Put your money away,' said the lad, feeling uneasy now.

Jennifer leant over him and said: 'Beat me and you can sleep with me.'

His mates yelled and pushed him off his seat.

'Er . . . okay,' said the lad, and blushed.

They sat at a table in the middle of the room. The lad put fifty quid on the table. They held hands; their grips tightened. The lad's hand hit the table so hard it caused the ashtray to leap on to the floor.

'Next,' said Jennifer and a big lad from Featherstone got up and sat at the table. He put his fifty quid down in front of him and said: 'Can I sleep with you as well?'

'Sure,' said Jennifer, and she nearly broke his wrist.

The next challenger was a man in a T-shirt with the word Rams on the back. He said: 'I once built a barn on the Glasgow Ring Road all on my own.'

He sat down and fixed his upper lip into a snarl. Then he grabbed Jennifer's hand, and for a moment it seemed as though she had a match. But she was only playing with him. Suddenly she lunged, bringing his arm down to the wood with such force he nearly fell off his stool.

She pocketed a hundred and fifty pounds, then walked back to the bar and ordered another round and said: 'Anyone else fancy a go?'

'I'll have a go,' I said.

'Okay sucker,' she said and we sat down at the table. I took her hand and she let it go limp and I slapped it down.

'You win,' she said. 'Your place or mine?'

'Mine.'

'Let's go.'

We walked back through the village, laughing. The night was so bright it was blue. Jennifer's shorn hair sparkled. I felt very close to her at that moment. I was about to tell her so when the phone rang.

She stood there in the icy grey reflection of the Kelmscott stone. She breathed in heavily and exhaled slowly, then she picked up the receiver. 'Jennifer Conway . . . No!' Then she replaced it in her bag again and we walked back to the boat through a field of cows.

Maegan looked more of a home now she had two people living in her and pot plants dispersed around her deck. But as we climbed inside and settled down, an appalling smell threaded itself through her. The air had taken on a different consistency and I knew instantly that Boogie had farted horribly.

Jennifer looked at Boogie and grimaced. I said: 'That's not Boogie. It's the cows. I'll go and frighten them off.'

I took Boogie for a walk along the towpath, a longer walk than usual.

'Now look! I know what you're trying to do. You're trying to antagonize her, aren't you? You're trying to show what disgusting company I keep. Well let me give you a word of advice: she's trying to get on with you. And I think the least you can do is try and do the same. Now, I know you've just had a curry, and I know what an impressive farter you are, and I know you're merely exercising your right to fart, but I'm warning you – you are living on a knife edge, boy. One more word out of your bum tonight and you are going home Red Star.'

When we got back to the boat Jennifer was in the sleeping bag. I ordered Boogie to the stern and crawled in beside her. She said: 'Do you really think my aggressive image is just a veneer? Do you think that beneath this selfish and cynical exterior there's a woman you could live with?'

'Yes.'

'I don't.'

'You're not trying.'

'It's always the same. The people I like don't stay around me long and the people I dislike stay around even less. I've a self-destructive streak in me. Anyone who gets close to me I hurt. It's because of what happened as a child.'

I had a feeling I was about to hear something she told very few people. I remember thinking to myself: The river has got to her already. I said: 'Yes?'

'I've never told this to anyone . . . My mother deserted me shortly after I was born. I was left on a doorstep. The nurses called me Jennifer after the policewoman who found me. I was brought up in a variety of foster homes around the Docklands. Once, when I was six, I was locked in a darkened bedroom for three days. I've always had to look after myself. And now it's instinctive for me to think of no one but myself. I'm full of resentment.'

The water lapped on the mahogany. Outside an owl made a noise like a washing machine. I suddenly realized how alike Boogie and Jennifer were. I felt elated. I said: 'Of course! You're just like Boogie. He was . . .'

'What!!' And she was up and out of the bag and staring at me with tears in her eyes. 'I've just told you the most private thing I can, and you say I'm like your dog. You're sick . . .'

'No, the point I was trying to make was that I'm used to the problem of . . .'

'You're weird. I've heard you talking to that animal as well. I don't know what you've been up to on this trip but it doesn't seem very healthy to me. I don't know how much more of this I can stand.'

'No, listen to me . . .'

'I don't listen to people. That's the first thing all the people I know, know about me. I'm unreasonable.'

'We can work on it. I'm just the opposite. I'm incredibly reasonable.'

But she'd turned away.

I lay there feeling the chill in the air. I felt helpless. I leant over to touch her but as I did so I plunged my head into a cloud so vile it made my nose run. At the back of the tent I could see Boogie's eyes green with mischief, his teeth starry in a grin.

'Not now, Boogie, please. This is a very insensitive time to fart,' I whispered.

Jennifer stirred and sniffed. 'What's going on? What on earth is that smell? It can't be . . . Oh my God! Get that dog out of here. Get him out!!'

I thought quickly: 'Er . . . actually, that was me.'

'What?'

'That was me. I did that. I'm responsible for that rather distasteful smell. Sorry.'

In the half light I could see a look of disbelief on her face. She shook her head and settled down again. I glared at Boogie. He glared back and lifted his rump and trumped again. The canvas around us sagged.

'You'll pay for this, you will. I promise you, you will pay for this.'

Like a marsh slick, the fetid cloud slipped from beneath him and drifted towards me. I furiously wafted my hand at it but it was too powerful. Jennifer stirred again. She looked at me, her face creased in pain. 'That can't be you?'

'Yep. Sorry. That was me again. The curry, I'm afraid. Huh.'

At the back of the tent Boogie released another. It curled its way towards us. 'Oh no!' said Jennifer as she inhaled the fresh blast. 'That's the most foul . . .'

'Sorry. Me again,' and I tried to grin. 'These little idiosyncrasies are what you learn to get used to when you live with someone. You know, the Real Me, and all that.'

'If that's the real you, you can sleep on your own!' she said, then climbed out of the boat and went and slept under a willow.

The river was becoming more shallow. In the past few days we'd passed the confluences of sizable rivers like the Evenlode and the Windrush and their contribution to the stream was missed. I began to grow concerned about the water level. If it was this low here what would it be like past Lechlade? Jennifer's arrival had distracted me and I felt it was time we re-established our commitment to the river. I decided we should hold an expedition meeting.

I was roused the next morning by a flash of light as the tent was ripped off the boat and there stood Jennifer panting and dripping. She'd been for another run and swim. She had little white socks on that just covered her ankles. She threw her arms out and said: 'Happy birthday!' and then she dived on top of me and kissed me like a vacuum cleaner. 'How did you know it was my birthday?' I asked.

'I never forget birthdays. C'mon, breakfast is ready. Today is your day. I'm doing all the cooking.'

We had scrambled eggs and crispy bacon with garlic mushrooms, followed by pancakes and maple syrup and espresso coffee. The day was dazzling and the ducks flew in and gathered round the boat. The sun shone on their beaks and we threw them some wholemeal toast. Jennifer seemed to have put the events of the previous evening to one side, although I noticed that when she cut the rind off her bacon she threw it to the ducks rather than to Boogie. He went for a walk along the towpath at this point.

After breakfast Jennifer pulled a box out of her bag and presented it to me. 'Many happy returns,' she said. I unwrapped the box carefully and folded the paper. It was a pair of binoculars and from that moment on the journey was never the same.

I focused on the ducks and immediately they took to the air and disappeared. I focused on a family of coots and they flapped and panicked and splashed into the safety of the reeds. I saw a rookery in the distance and the moment I focused on it the birds ducked down into their nests and became quiet. I saw a swan upstream but when it realized I had my lens trained on it it up-ended and showed me its tail. It was as if nature could tolerate only a certain amount of intrusion by man. Casual appreciation was encouraged, but binoculars were voyeurism and that wasn't allowed.

But I didn't tell Jennifer. I told her instead I was thrilled with my binoculars. I told her what a thoughtful, kind person she was, that she couldn't have given me a nicer present and that I was so glad she was here with me to see all this. She said there was nowhere she'd rather be, that she spent too much time in the city and not enough in the country, and that she needed to have people like me around her instead of the sycophants she worked with. She needed to change her priorities, redirect her energies in more spiritually rewarding areas, and she should begin by properly involving herself in this trip, and if the phone were to go now she wouldn't even answer it.

At that point the phone rang. Jennifer tensed then answered it. 'Jennifer Conway . . . Why . . . Of course . . . No . . . I don't care.'

She put the phone back in her bag. 'Sorry,' she said.

'It takes time to acclimatize, that's all,' I replied. 'It takes time to slow down into the rhythm of the river. You'll see. I've been wanting to say I think we should concentrate our efforts now on getting to the source. We should put all our petty differences behind us and remember we have a goal.'

She nodded and picked up her orange juice and stood up in the boat: 'To the source,' she toasted.

'To the source,' I replied, and we packed up and sculled away with the sun in our faces. A bark from the bank reminded me I'd forgotten Boogie.

At Buscot lock, Jennifer said to the lock-keeper: 'We're heading to the source of the river, any advice?'

'Yes, my advice is you'll kill yourself at the Castle Eaton Rapids. If you do get to though to Cricklade though, there's a pub you should call in at but I forget the name.'

'The Swan?' I said.

'No, there's no Swan in Cricklade.'

This was the first sign that Cricklade was a place beyond the limit of navigation. The lock-keeper said: 'It's different up there. Wild and, well . . . different.'

Then past the lock the spire of St Laurence's of Lechlade came into the view for the first time. I stopped sculling and ran to the bow, and stood on the end of the boat with my hands in the air: 'Lechlade. I can see Lechlade!' I said.

'What? Already?' said Jennifer.

'What do you mean, already? This is the beacon I've been heading for ever since I left London.'

'What's so special about Lechlade?'

I told her that Lechlade was the end of the navigable Thames; how from here on it was everyone for themselves; how the Thames Water Authority didn't advise any boats to venture further; how cruisers would run aground within a mile or two.

I tried to impress upon her the significance of the first sight of the spire of St Laurence, how the sight of it filled me with a spiritual warmth that only a traveller who has journeyed under his own steam could appreciate. I also tried to impress upon her how from here on the comforts of the downstream river would be denied us. Ahead lay the period of privation that must be endured in any search for the source of a great river, and that from now on things would get tough.

And she said: 'Great. Let's have lunch. Spaghetti with a Mexican sauce, I think.'

We moored under a willow. Jennifer dug out her hat. It was squashed and chewed and largely ruined. She sighed and said: 'That dog has slept on my hat. Look at it!'

'I'm sure it was an accident.'

'It's my new hat. He's squashed it.'

'Its green; it looks like grass. You're lucky he only slept on it.'

'I'm a tolerant person but there's . . .'

'You're not tolerant. You're intolerant. You're confusing the two.'

She screwed her face up which made her look painfully attractive, then she sat on the bank with Delia Smith in one hand and a clove of garlic in the other. A heron flew past and landed on a bough nearby. I picked up my binoculars and focused on it, and it flew away to hide in some trees.

As Jennifer cooked the chopped pepper and added the garlic she said: 'There are dog hairs in the olive oil.'

I said: 'I feel as though I've formed a special relationship with willows on this voyage.'

As she added the minced beef, red wine, chilli powder and parsley she said: 'There are dog hairs in the tomato puree.'

I said: 'Willows are such mournful trees. I feel their

arms reaching out to me. Weeping is the only way to describe willows.'

As she brought a pot of salted water to the boil and fed in the spaghetti, she said: 'There are dog hairs in the boiling water.'

And I said: 'I see faces in their bark; devilish faces.'

She started to grate some Parmesan cheese but then stopped and said through clenched teeth: 'There are even dog hairs wrapped around the cheese grater.'

'I'd like to be buried under a willow.'

'Did you hear me? There are dog hairs wrapped around the cheese grater.'

'Yes . . . they're mine.'

She held one up. 'Your hairs are not black and curly.'

'Ah, that could be one of Boogie's.'

'Of course it's one of Boogie's; they're all Boogie's. The dog is falling to bits.'

'Yes, it's a problem. Dog hairs in your bed, dog hairs in your bath, dog hairs in your soup. You'd be surprised how quickly you get used to it.'

'I don't want to get used to it. I don't feel as though I should have to get used to it. It needn't be like this, you know.'

'What do you mean?'

'Well . . . it's unkind to have a dog in the city.' She served out the spaghetti. It smelt strange. 'It's unkind to have him on the boat.'

I looked over at Boogie. He was looking very suspicious.

'We could find a nice home for him,' went on Jennifer

She put some Mexican sauce on my plate. It looked like mud.

'Have you ever thought about having him fostered?'

'Yes . . . No! He's my companion. He's my sidekick. How can you say such a thing? How can you be so cruel and thoughtless? That dog has come through thick and thin with me. He's . . . why has my Mexican spaghetti got hairs in it?'

In the afternoon we sculled towards Lechlade at speed. We had aggression to release again. At one point we overtook a cruiser called *Bridget's Legs* and Jennifer shouted at it to get out of the way. The driver shouted back: 'Look, it's *Three Men in a Boat*,' to which Jennifer stood up and retorted: 'I've three points to make here: 1) I am not a man 2) *Three Men in a Boat* is, in my opinion, a self-indulgent, blinkered book and nothing but English sentimentalism at its worst, not to mention being flagrantly sexist and I resent being in any way connected with it. And 3) I think your boat stinks.'

The driver of the *Bridget's Legs* reddened. I said to Jennifer: 'How could you say that?'

'His boat does stink.'

'About *Three Men in a Boat?*'

'Oh, not you as well!'

We passed through St John's lock, the highest on the river, where the statue of Father Thames reclines in front of the lock-keeper's house like a centrefold. Then at four o'clock in the afternoon, *Maegan* slipped under Lechlade's Halfpenny Bridge. A young girl waved and shouted. I waved and shouted back and she threw an empty milk carton into the boat, Jennifer caught it and threw it back and hit the girl on the nose.

We moored and I tied a double clover bowline with a reef on the second loop and a granny spring. 'We're here,' I said and put my arms out in a reconciliatory fashion.

Jennifer smirked and hugged me and said: 'Right, into town; we need provisions.'

'What for?'

'Your birthday party of course.'

Lechlade had pretensions of being a port. It took its role as the end of the recommended navigation seriously and modelled itself on a place of embarkation and arrival, rather like Zanzibar did. I imagined Lechlade would be a place where boats were bought and sold, where you could have a tattoo done if you felt like it, where watermen sitting in the corners of bars would tell stories of the river that would make you go out and check your knots. I imagined I'd meet the sort of people who'd give me first-hand advice on the stream ahead – on the perils of Hannington Bridge and the Sargasso Sea of Water Eaton, not the mention the route to the true source of the river.

But Lechlade isn't like that. It's a neat, well-swept, well-weeded, well-behaved town with a Lloyds Bank, a Barclays Bank, a Shell garage and a BP garage, and a Londis supermarket.

But the church in Lechlade is beautiful. It's weathered and worn and one's eyes climb slowly to its clock. Shelley, who rowed up to Lechlade from London in 1815, was inspired to pen 'Summer Evening in a Churchyard' here. The line 'Here could I hope, like some inquiring child sporting on graves, that death did hide from human sight sweet secrets' was printed on a plaque in the churchyard. Jennifer and I stood gazing at it. There was a chill in the air again. Jennifer said: ' "Or beside its breathless sleep that loveliest dreams perpetual watch did keep." '

'What's that?' I asked.

'The next line of the poem.'

'It's lovely.'

Old leaves were crackling in the wind, caught amongst the tombstones. The new graves had flowers, the old ones had stagnant water in their vases with insects floating on top. But there was a sense of celebration in the churchyard as well as one of peace. I put my arm through Jennifer's and we walked between the graves. Jennifer suddenly stopped and said: 'Quick, give me a pen and paper, I've had an idea.'

I tore a page off my notebook. She scribbled for a moment, crossed out a bit and then scribbled some more. She paused for a moment then looked to the church spire and with a flourish finished the poem. She said: 'I'm thinking of putting together a volume of poetry inspired by this trip. *Poems on a Journey up the Thames*, I think I'll call it. Listen to this: "Last night I slept neath a willow tree while the mist crept into my head, this river is sucking us into its mouth, it's a beast that must be fed." What do you reckon?'

'It's good, it's good.'

'I like the metaphor of the river being an animal and we're being drawn towards its mouth, helplessly, as if we were addicted.'

'That's what I said to you the other night.'

'When?'

'When you first arrived. I said the river is like a drug.'

'No you didn't.'

'I did.'

'Are you saying this is your idea as well?'

'I'm not exactly saying that, I'm saying that I've had that idea.'

'But I've just written it.'

'Yes, I know. I'm not disputing that, I'm just saying I had that idea as well. It was the first thing that occurred to me on the river – the river is like opium, I put.'

'Listen, from now on, don't tell me your ideas and I won't tell you mine.'

We went into the supermarket. We bought pork chops, onions and garlic. We bought celery, parsley and fennel seeds. We bought oil, cider and cream. There were six people in the queue at the checkout. Jennifer said to them: 'Could I possibly go in front of you? I wouldn't ask but

I've only got six months to live and I want to make best use of my time.'

Back in the boat Jennifer got out Delia Smith and said: 'We're going to have stuffed pork chop with fennel; a birthday treat,' and she set about softening the onion and garlic and mixing them with the celery, parsley, fennel seeds and bread crumbs. As she worked Boogie came and sat next to her and gave her a wink.

Next she cut out a hole in the pork chop and packed the stuffing in, then dusted it with flour and placed it into the hot oil. Boogie licked his lips.

Then she poured the cider over the chop and let it simmer for thirty minutes. Boogie grinned as the smells filled the boat.

Jennifer was just about to pour on the cream topping when the telephone rang. She breathed in deeply, picked up the receiver and said: 'Eeurgh . . . That's disgusting!'

'What is?'

'Look what the little bastard has done all over my Vodaphone.'

I looked at it. It certainly was disgusting. 'Yes,' I said. 'He does have bouts of being vile. It's amazing how quickly you get used to it though.'

She threw the Vodaphone to the floor and screamed: 'That's put me right off my food, that has,' and quick as a flash Boogie grabbed one of the pork chops and leapt out of the boat.

Jennifer screamed. Some coots paddling nearby ran for cover. She screamed again and the curtains were pulled back in *Maid Mind your own Business* across the water. She cried: 'I hate dogs. I really hate dogs. In fact . . .' and here she hesitated, 'I'm a cat person! I've never told you this but I'm a cat person! I like cats! I hate dogs! Understand. I hate dogs!'

There was a silence. The water slapped on the mahog-

any. An owl made a noise like a duck. I backed away from
Jennifer. Boogie stuck his head back inside the canvas and
looked at me with his 'did I just hear her right?' expression. There was an embarrassing silence, the first time
I've ever had an embarrassing silence with Jennifer in the
room.

Then she sniffed and said: 'Let's go and have lots to
drink.'

We left Boogie behind and went to the Crown, then to
the Red Lion, then to the New Inn and then to the Swan.
In the Swan we had a meal: cheese and herb crusted
cottage pie. It was delicious. I said to the barman: 'This
is delicious.'

'One of Delia Smith's,' he said. 'Comes from that *One
is Fun!* book. I just multiply the ingredients by sixty-five.'

We went back to the Crown, then back to the New
Inn, then back to the Red Lion, then back to the Swan.
By the end of the evening Jennifer had had two arguments
and swopped addresses with three people. We called in at
the Red Lion for a last one before closing time.

The bar was packed. A party of bright young things
wearing clothing from Next surrounded the bar. One of
them called out: 'Jennifer! Jennifer Conway?'

'Ray!' shrieked Jennifer and threw her arms around a
man with a square head and a shirt with a green banana
pattern. Then she pulled me over and said: 'Come and
meet Ray.'

Ray was horrible, so were Fliss, Michele, Clive and
Dominic. They were down for a wedding. 'There was a
marquee and we all got blotto,' said Clive, who had a
video camera.

Jennifer told them I'd rowed from London and Michele
said: 'We rode from London too, we rode in Dominic's
Cabriolet.' I suddenly wanted to be back on the river,
moored to a meadow miles from anywhere. I started to

miss the anonymity of the electricity pylons. Then Jennifer said: 'Let's all go back to the boat and have a party. It's Mark's birthday!'

They all insisted on singing happy birthday to me as we walked through the town. Clive filmed the occasion. I felt a real prat, Jennifer put her arm around me and I said: 'Who are these people?'

'They're a laugh, aren't they? I can't stand them. But I like lots of people I can't stand. They are a laugh though.' As she spoke I noticed Ray was walking down the street and changing round the notes in the milk bottles on the doorsteps.

When we reached *Maegan* they all said what a beautiful boat she was. Clive filmed her from three sides. Jennifer proudly swept back the canvas flap and said: 'C'mon in, folks; make yourself at home.'

We piled in and I lit the lamp and there at the back of the boat was Boogie with his legs wrapped round the hind quarters of one of Lechlade's least virtuous bitches. Michele screamed. Ray said: 'That's disgusting.' Clive said: 'What's he doing?' but didn't stop filming. And Dominic said: 'Whatever he's doing, he's doing it all over your sleeping bag.' Jennifer clambered up the boat, picked up her wok and belted Boogie over the head with it. It made a noise like a bell. Boogie and his girlfriend leapt out and brought down the tent. Jennifer stood alone in the stern covered in green canvas. She began to cry. 'He's spoiled my birthday party!' she sobbed.

'It was my birthday party!' I said.

'I don't care whose birthday party it is; he's spoiled it, like he spoils everything else. I've had enough. That's it! Either he goes or I go!' And she appeared from under the canvas in a rage. I wasn't so sure her short hair suited her now. She said: 'I'm going to make some telephone calls.

When I come back I expect you to have had him put down,' and she grapped her Vodaphone and strode off.

There was a silence amongst the rest of us. Clive, who didn't like silences, said they ought to go home but that he had the whole episode on film and we should all go round to his house one day and watch it. They left. I was suddenly on my own. Then from the back yard of the nearby tea room Boogie appeared. We went for a long walk along the towpath.

'The country is the place, you know, Boogie. The country is the place folks like you and I should live.'

Boogie licked something off a No Mooring sign.

'The trouble is I work in the city. But you? You could live anywhere. I mean, wouldn't you like to move out to a nice home in the country?' Boogie sat down and scratched his ear even more violently than before.

'Maybe it would be better if you were to stay in the country.' He stopped and gave me his 'typical! Well, just give me my can opener, mate. No need to worry about me' expression.

'Now c'mon. Be fair,' I said. 'What can I do? I know she appears unreasonable but I've got myself to think of. It's either you or her. It's an impossible situation. You'll be all right. You make friends easy.'

We walked a long way that night. When we got back to the boat Jennifer was in bed. I got in quietly beside her and touched her arm. She didn't turn to me; she just said: 'I feel desperate sometimes.'

I said: 'I know what you mean. I used to feel like that sometimes too. But since I've been on the river I've felt different. I feel the river flowing through me now like blood. All things change but the river keeps on rolling. Things are a lot clearer now. I can look at my life from a distance. I can feel the force of a natural flow in all that

I do. And there's an inevitability about everything. I see now that birth and death are irrevocably linked.'

She turned over and said: 'Why have you been talking such inane rubbish the last few days?'

'I don't know,' I said.

I had a vivid dream that night. I dreamt Delia Smith was in the back of the boat. She was wearing a black velvet evening dress and a sparkling tiara and she was cooking the most glorious meals for one then eating them all herself. She was angry with me. She offered me a glass of wine but it had a dead beetle floating upside down in it.

I woke with a start. In the moonlight I could see Boogie crawling out of *Maegan* and up on to the bank. A lump came to my throat. What a noble dog this was, and I was witnessing his finest hour. Like Captain Oates he was sacrificing himself so that the expedition to the source could continue. He could sense this was not a happy party. To end the conflict he knew there was only one course of action to take.

He walked off into the meadow. I called softly: 'Goodbye, Boogie. And thank you.' He stopped and turned. A car's headlights flashed in his eye, and in his mouth I saw a white object. At first I thought it was a bone but then I realized it was a Vodaphone.

He buried it, then trotted back to the boat, stuffed his nose under his tail and went back to sleep.

10. Meet Me at the Source
if You Like

In the history of exploration there is one man who towers above all others in the department of portage. He is Charles Sturt, an explorer with conviction if ever there was one, a man so sure that a country as vast as Australia could not possibly have such a poor water supply, that when he set out from Adelaide in 1844 in search of an inland sea, he took a boat with him.

I thought of Charles Sturt a lot over the next two days as I made my quest for Cricklade. He was an inspiration. He even managed to inspire me to take a jog the morning I left Lechlade, although after I'd run a hundred yards or so I felt silly and walked back to the boat. I felt drained from the previous forty-eight hours. But I also felt nervous and wanted to get moving. I knew from here on I would need to have my wits about me, from here on I would need to try to put aside all that had happened and concentrate my mind, from here on I was on my own again.

I doused my head with river water, and looked at my reflection. I had bags under my eyes. So did Boogie. He sat expressionless on the back seat. 'I understand,' I said and patted him. Presently the sun blasted through the mist and glinted off an ice-cream sign across the river. Lechlade tremored with church bells and I stripped down to my shorts and hat, and set off. Boogie, as if sensing the gravity of the moment, positioned himself on the stern, casting a cold, discerning eye upstream, seemingly alert to all the dangers ahead, actually alert to not a single one of them.

Our last contact with the civilized river was at the Inglesham Roundhouse where the abandoned Thames Severn Canal met the Thames. This link between London and Bristol was the first canal project to excite investors when news of Leonardo da Vinci's lock reached these shores at the beginning of the seventeenth century. So excited were they that a hundred and fifty years later they actually got round to building the thing. But it was beset with problems from the start, and as canals nationwide became more efficient, traders realized the Thames was a slow waterway and were reluctant to use it. The owners worked hard at bringing the navigation up to standard, finally turning it into an efficient route around about the same time that railways were invented. The rest is a predictable story of decline, and in 1933 all was abandoned.

The Inglesham Roundhouse – one of a series of buildings along the canal built as watch-houses for the lock-keeper – stood at the junction of the canal with the Thames and the river Coln. I'd seen many fine and beautiful houses on the river over the previous hundred miles, but this Roundhouse with its cottage hiding amongst a veil of willows was the most appealing of them all. It was all chimneys and vines and seemed a wonderful place to be born, grow up in and then come back to. It was more like a nest than a house. I looked hard but couldn't see a burglar alarm.

The house and the hamlet of Inglesham disappeared behind a bend and ahead of me was nothing but sky and field. Immediately the river narrowed and shallowed. For the first time I could see the bottom. No dredger had ever come up here, and without traffic the weeds and reeds

...ourished and soon grew out of control. It would have been possible just to force a passage, but I hated doing this, the coots built their nests on precarious platforms amongst the reeds and more than once when I pushed my way through I had ended up staring into the forlorn faces of five chicks whose home I had just bulldozed.

By now though I was useful with my sculls. I could turn *Maegan* on a lilypad and twist her through the narrowest inlet. The struggles I'd had coming under Maidenhead Bridge and through Hennerton Backwater now proved their worth as I picked and paddled a course through the obstacles.

I saw only a lone canoeist all day. He looked at me strangely and wouldn't have stopped had I not called out to him. I wanted encouragement more than anything, but he said: 'Cricklade? You'll be lucky, you're too heavy. You'll never make Castle Eaton Bridge,' and he wriggled his hips and swerved through the reeds like a water snake and was gone.

I kept going while the sun reached for the top of the sky. There was no shade here; this was wild country and for the first time on this trip I felt completely committed. At Hannington Bridge were the first shallows. I leapt out and felt the water fill my wellingtons, and I cringed as I dragged the boat over the river bed and the gravel scored *Maegan*'s belly.

But I had a different kind of energy that day. At one point when the sun was high, I remember I came to a mound of gravel that seemed like an unbreachable barrier, and the effort to haul *Maegan* over too much. But I closed my eyes and thought back over the previous three days, and I saw Jennifer standing there with her fists clenched, shrieking. I grunted and tugged and the boat rode over. Afterwards, I leant over the gunwales panting, and Boogie eyed me approvingly. He hadn't moved from the back seat since Lechlade. He'd won his battle and he wasn't going to give his position up for anyone.

I slipped past the mysterious village of Kempsford where the banks were high and vegetation thick and I could only see the church tower and some rooftops. I was beginning to feel what life on the river was like without other boats. I felt an isolation that was unnerving because it had a urgency to it, and the urgency mounted each bend I took – around the next corner there might be an obstruction that would end the journey there and then.

Now the river was only fifteen feet wide in places and the banks grew high and claustrophobic. I could no longer find the depth or width to use the sculls so I stood on the bow and paddled as the reeds grew more and more dense.

Then as the day cooled the water became clearer. Whenever I jumped in to haul *Maegan* I could see minnows gathered round my knees. And the shallows were so frequent now I was hauling more then paddling. It was as I was bent forward, heaving, with the rope over my shoulder, that I turned a corner and saw before me Castle Eaton Bridge.

It was an ugly metal structure, green, although the setting sun gave it a rusted effect. I paused and pulled my hat down. The river widened here and there was depth and room to manoeuvre, so I decided to take a run at the bridge. I climbed back in the boat, steadied myself and pulled away. Castle Eaton church flashed past. A very pleasant riverside pub called the Red Lion with a number of people in its garden flashed past. They called out to me but I kept going, I think I might even have given them a look of grim determination. I navigated the arch successfully but so fine had I cut it I had to pull my sculls in and I found myself leaning on my boat hook desperately trying to push my way past the rapids and into the safety of the pool I could see beyond. I pushed with mighty effort,

unged for another rock to support myself, missed, slipped
and tumbled out of the boat, and I was under the water
with an iciness in my ears.

I was only submerged for a second but it was long
enough to savour the experience; it was like a baptism. I
surfaced, clutching my binoculars, to find myself in three
foot of fast-moving water and I remember standing there
and thinking how, despite the effort, there had been a
strange peace over the river all day.

A cygnet came paddling towards me, screaming
pathetically, presumably searching for its mother. But no
adult was anywhere to be found. I smiled at the helpless-
ness of the thing, and couldn't believe how such a graceless
chick could ever turn into a swan. I looked at it through
my binoculars and it dived into some reeds, in tears. That
was when I noticed *Maegan* had vanished. I scratched my
hat.

'Hello,' said a voice from the bridge. I looked up to see
a woman with a napkin tucked into her front. She said:
'Is that your boat?'

'What boat?'

'That boat that just came under the bridge. It's yours,
isn't it?'

'Umm. Might be mine, did it have a dog onboard?'

'We were watching you from the pub garden. We were
having supper. Then your dog came running into the pub.
It was as if he was trying to tell us something. He probably
thought you were in mortal danger and he was trying to
save your life. We've given him something to eat, is that
all right?'

I waded out of the river and she offered me her hand
and helped me up the bank.

'You're wet,' she said.

'You've got pickle on your lip,' I replied.

'Did you fall in?'

'No, no. There's a cygnet down there I was studying. It's lost, I think. Did you know that swans keep the same mate for the whole of their lives?'

She led me to the other side of the bridge. 'There's your boat,' she said. *Maegan* was wedged in some willow stumps downstream.

'And there's your dog,' she added. Boogie was in the pub garden, not a drop of water on him. He was sat in front of the woman's husband being fed mouthfuls of quiche.

I joined them. Her husband said: 'Did you fall in?'

'He was looking at the baby swan,' said his wife.

'Wildlife expert are you?' said the husband.

'Well . . .'

'I knew someone like you, into animals. He wanted to study elks. He wanted to live with them. He wasn't odd or anything, he just liked elks. He tried everything to convince them he was one of them. He strapped antlers to his head. He ran around the forest on all fours. He moaned like an elk. No good at all. Then one day he got up really close to a grazing herd, and he started to eat leaves. And you know what?'

'What?'

'They all pissed off, ran a mile. He packed up after that. It wasn't worth the effort, he said. "I don't like elks that much," were his words. That's a nice boat. Travelling on your own?'

'No, well, my girlfriend had to go home. She had an accident.'

'Nothing serious I hope?'

'It's a long story.'

Actually it was a short story. I was woken that morning as the tent was ripped off and there stood Jennifer looking very worried. I'd never seen her so distraught. She was rummaging round the bowels of the boat, throwing luggage on to the bank, scrambling about in the bilges. I said: 'What is it?' And she looked up at me with mud on her face and a breathlessness: 'I can't find my Vodaphone. It's just disappeared. I always have it next to me where I sleep but it's gone.'

I lay there. 'Well don't help me find it, will you?' she said. She was losing her cool. I'd seen her angry before but her anger, though venomous, was always controlled. I looked round for Boogie. He was sniffing about on the quay, licking the petrol pump by the marina. For a moment I thought what I'd seen during the night had been a dream but now I remembered. Boogie had at last found Jennifer's soft underbelly and had gone right for it. I wanted to tell her but I couldn't. I just couldn't.

She cleared the boat in exasperation. Her eyes were wild, and she said: 'Right! There's nothing else for it.' And she composed herself and from her bag pulled out a black suit, a pair of black stockings and a pair of black patent leather shoes. She dressed there on the lawn in front of the tea shop, then she grabbed her handbag, took out her credit cards and threw the rest on the ground: 'I've got to go,' she said.

'Go where?'

'Back.'

'Back where?'

'To work!'

I said: 'Jennifer. Before you go, just tell me one thing. What exactly is it that you do?'

She shook her head, and strode off. I called out: 'Maybe I'll see you at the source.' But she didn't respond. She passed the petrol pump without looking at Boogie and that was the last I saw of her.

That evening I sat in the boat under the lamp glow as military aircraft hummed overhead. I prepared sautéed fennel with Parmesan followed by egg and anchovy salad

with herbs. Now Jennifer was gone it was just Delia and
me again.

There was no towpath to the river now so later I took
Boogie for a walk in the Castle Eaton churchyard. Con-
fetti lay on the ground. An owl squeaked and Boogie
licked something off a gravestone. 'I feel the trip is reaching a climax,' I said. 'I feel as though something is about
to happen. You know you've ruined my chances with
Jennifer for good now, don't you?'

We reached the river at the bottom of the churchyard.
It was hurrying, like a child learning to run, having to
keep going to stay upright. But it learned fast. You could
throw a rock in the water here and it would have an
immediate effect – a rapid would form and the current
would divert – but by the morning the river would have
compensated somewhere further downstream.

Back in *Maegan* I lay awake in my sleeping bag. I felt
as though I should have had a lot to think about but I
only wanted to occupy myself with the source. Boogie
lay in the back of the boat with his eyes on me. I briefly
wondered if his look was one of an animal with an uneasy
conscience. But I quickly dismissed that idea.

Outside the reeds rustled and inside I lay dreaming.
Delia Smith was sat in the back of the boat, cooking,
cooking, cooking, surrounding herself with stacks of pancakes, and growing fatter and fatter. She was adding
everything she could find to a stir-fry. All of Jennifer's
luggage: her shoes, her books, her plants. They all went
into the wok. Then she leaned over and tried to grab my
wellingtons. I woke panting and sweating. A Nimrod
enemy surveillance aircraft droned overhead.

The following day was just as hot. The heat shimmered
above the dry ploughed earth, and there was a taste of
dust in the air. The level of the river fluctuated from

ix foot to six inches without warning. At one point I remembered what Mark Edwards had said, and built a flash-lock out of rocks. And once, where it was possible to excavate the gravel, I dug a channel with Jennifer's wok. But these were mere interruptions. As I came to the area known as Water Eaton I met a far more serious obstacle, and found myself faced with something I'd always steered clear of on this trip – a showdown with the local swans.

I'd seen a number the previous day. But they'd retreated whenever I grew close. On this occasion there were only half a dozen birds to start with, but then from the reeds and the bushes and the air a whole squadron formed, about twenty-five birds. They blocked the passage, and this time it was clear they were going to stand their ground.

On the main river the swans were used to the boats and I could negotiate with them and slowly manoeuvre round them. But in these parts they were unused to interference and to being frightened. They were masters of the river and instinctively unafraid of all around them. So I stopped and squinted at them, waiting for a sign. But none came. They seemed nervous, paddling in between each other in a confused manner. I edged forward. They waited until I was within thirty feet of them, then suddenly took action. In pairs they rose up and came running along the water straight at me, wings drawn and thrashing, mouths open and hissing. Boogie dived under the seat. I picked up the wok ready to defend myself. But, just before they reached me, one by one with the greatest effort, they somehow managed to haul themselves into the air and clear the boat. I ducked as their shadows covered me and their undercarriages just cleared my head. They took off in waves like bomber aircraft. The sound was one of stretching muscle and physical stress. It was painful to watch.

For five minutes they kept coming, each following the example of the other, their wing tips touching, their necks straining forward. And then as soon as they were airborne they were caught on the stiff breeze and had no option but to bank and be blown downwind over the treetops.

Only one bird remained. It trod the water with one foot, the other lay embedded in its down. I waited for it to follow the others but it made no effort. To begin with I wondered if it was injured, but it was simply more inquisitive than the rest. I remember looking at it and thinking how it reminded me of Jennifer, elegant, aloof, assertive and with a long neck. For the first time I noticed a vulnerability in swans, and I realized I was coming to change my opinion of them. Having spent so long on the river I didn't find them as arrogant as before. It was dawning on me that all they'd ever done was treat me as an equal. I pulled a piece of bread from my loaf, broke it in pieces and proffered them on my hand. The swan lifted its head and turned a circle. I was drifting away from it but it followed me, and came closer until it could reach my palm. *Maegan* hit the bank and stopped and the swan leant forward and took the bread and I felt a thrill as its beak brushed my wrist. It swallowed the gift then leant forward for more, I reached for the packet and that's when Boogie stuck his head through my legs and the swan rose like a cobra. I shouted at Boogie who barked at the swan and the bird spat and hissed and tore off downstream. Boogie looked at me with his 'I've just saved your life; what have you got to say about that?' expression.

I pressed on. There was no channel now and *Maegan* had to carve a passage through the weed like an icebreaker; I pushed and pulled her for most of the day. At one point I decided progress was impossible and that I would have to stop where I was. It was unbearable to think that I should fail at this last hurdle; I'd already gone under Cricklade bypass and could see a housing estate. But I couldn't haul the boat over rocks. I needed a boost, and fittingly, it was Boogie who provided one. On this stretch he had spent most of the time in the river, partly because he'd taken to water now, but largely because I'd decided at the first shallows that I was damned if I was going to haul *Maegan* with him lying on the back seat, and so I'd thrown him out.

He was a little ahead of the boat knee-deep in water, when, suddenly, he disappeared under the surface. He came up coughing and covered in slime and I pulled him in to the bank and hugged him. He'd found a deep-water passage just when we needed it.

We continued as insects swarmed around the boat and creepers hung from the willows and coiled themselves around me. Then, from round a bend I heard voices, young voices with a heavy Wiltshire accent. I looked on in disbelief as two young boys appeared in a plastic dinghy.

'Hello,' they said.

'What are you doing here? You shouldn't be here!' I sounded incredulous.

'Why not?'

'Because this is an impossible stretch of river that most men fear.'

'We're paddling down to Lechlade.'

'From where?'

'Cricklade. We live on the estate. We're going to see our uncle. We often do it.'

And they were gone, gliding smoothly over the gravel with the current. They were about nine years old.

So! I thought. The local natives use this as a route to Lechlade. They've had to devise a special craft and they only send the young among them, but it is a viable passage.

Further encouragement came that afternoon when I saw a couple sitting in a field. I waved and shouted: 'How far to Cricklade?'

'A mile,' he said.

'More like three,' she said.

'It's a dump, anyway,' he said.

But I wasn't really bothered. I'd just seen the incentive I needed: the spire of Cricklade parish church poking up through the hedgerows like a finishing post, a mile away, no more.

I hauled the boat on past the back gardens and garages of Cricklade and into the town. In the distance I could see High Bridge with some kids sitting on top. I shouted to them and they were in the river with me helping me haul *Maegan* over the last fifty yards, singing and screaming as they pulled and pushed. Some members of the local cricket team took off their shoes, rolled up their whites and joined in. We manoeuvred *Maegan* to the bridge and I slumped over her exhausted. 'I've sculled this boat 130 miles uphill,' I said to one of the cricketers, and he replied: 'That's nothing, we lost by eight wickets this afternoon. Are you coming to the pub?'

'Yes,' I said. And when I got there I bought myself a Babycham.

It was an evening to remember. I told them of the trials I'd had coming under Hannington Bridge and of the wild swans of Water Eaton, and they told me of their slip fielder who had had twenty-four chances so far this season and dropped the lot. I told them of my ducking at Castle Eaton and how if it hadn't been for the wok I might not have made it, and they told me how their number eight batsman had once played for England, although not at cricket. Then I popped the all-important question: I told them of my quest for the source of the river and asked if anyone of them had any idea where it was? And they thought about this for a moment and then told me about their second change seamer who was the spitting image of the pope.

Later on though, I was sitting at a table with the wicket keeper when he said: 'I heard you talking about the source of the Thames earlier.'

'That's right.'

'Well, I know where it is.'

'Where?'

He looked at his empty glass, and grinned. I bought him another pint and he leant over the table and said quietly: 'It's near Kemble village at Trewsbury Mead, ten miles from here.'

I'd heard so many conflicting stories since London that it was tempting to treat him as just one more man in a corner of a pub, but he had a gleam of truth in his eye. I said: 'What evidence do you base this theory on?'

'I've seen it with my own eyes. I farm round there. I'd lost a calf one day. I was walking through the fields looking for it and suddenly I stumbles across a ring of stones. There was no water or nothing, just an ash tree inscribed with two initials, almost swallowed by the bark – the initials TH.'

'What does TH mean?'

'Thames Head.'

I gasped. It all slotted into place now.

'There was another clue there as well,' said the wicket keeper.

'What?'

'Right next to the tree there was a bloody great plaque that said: "This is the source of the Thames." '

After the pub shut I took Boogie a walk through the town. I felt satisfied. We stood on High Bridge and I looked downstream at the thin leg of water, and I smiled when I thought of the great expanse of river on which I'd started the journey.

The street light danced on the stream, and there in the trees I noticed a supermarket trolley. No one was looking so I clambered down on to the bank and pushed it in the water. The sensation was minimal. So I pulled it out and tried again – still nothing. I tried once more and derived no thrill or pleasurable feeling of any description. Despite all the talk, pushing supermarket trolleys into rivers is a pointless exercise.

Cricklade was unlike any other town I'd passed through. One reason was because it hadn't one familiar shop-front on the whole street, but it was also different because it was untouched by the river. I heard talk of a scheme to make the Thames navigable up from Lechlade, to install three more locks, and dredge it and so attract the pleasure craft, but talk was all it was, and the stream that was the Thames passed without interest through Cricklade. It wanted nothing to do with the town, and no one in the town had any use for it. If anything the river was a nuisance. The farmers laid gravel over it to create a cattle crossing.

This gave the town a different appeal because, unlike Marlow, Henley and Wallingford, it didn't need to flaunt its riparian status. It had wide streets and a wealthy past as a wool merchants' town and it could depend on its parochial qualities. If anything it reminded me more of a seaside town. The High Street climbed a hill at such an angle it looked as though you would find a cliff at the top.

I was up early the following morning and found a cafe. My plan for the day was simple enough but conditions would be different from here on. Now I was on foot rather than in the boat, and the river wouldn't dominate the countryside the way it had. Now it would sneak through fields; it could disappear into a patch of brambles and not come out again. The wicket keeper had told me that to get to the ash tree I must keep to the main channel no matter how small it became and no matter how many other streams tried to lead me away. There'd be times when the river was almost dry, he warned me, but I mustn't be deceived.

I had a fried breakfast and read a paper whilst all around me were conversations about the scout club and the rent rebates, the kind of conversations I'd not heard since London; conversations that didn't once mention the local regatta or the cost of overnight mooring or the journey time from Paddington. I was out of the commuter belt for the first time and it was like falling asleep on a train and waking up in a different country.

'Eggs, bacon and beans!'

'Thank you.'

I ate my plateful and wiped it up with some bread. It was time to get moving. Outside, Boogie was having his name taken by a local policeman.

I followed the river bank out of town. Fences had been put across the water by farmers to act as stock barriers, but there were fishermen's paths to follow.

I quickly came to the confluence with the River Churn, a sizeable piece of water but, like the Evenlode, the Coln and the Windrush before it, the Thames spat it out and continued.

Far more impressive was the stream I found just before Ashton Keynes. By this time the Thames was just a trickle and so I followed the larger body of water until I came to a bridge. A man with a shotgun leant over it.

'What sort of dog is that?' he said.

'Russian dalmatian.'

'Thought so.' He tried to change the subject, but he was having problems so I helped him. I said: 'Is that your car?' indicating the beautifully restored 1958 Morris Cowley by the roadside. It had been resprayed in its original light grey. The chrome had been dipped, the leather re-upholstered, the tyres painted. It was pristine.

'No,' he said.

There was another silence which we both felt comfortable with. This trip had taught me how to meet all sorts of interesting people and then not say anything to them. I felt a drop of rain. An aircraft flew low overhead. I trained my binoculars on it and spotted a pilot with black hair, a blue pullover and glasses.

Presently my friend said: 'You walking?'

'Yes. I'm following the river Thames.'

'No, you're not.'

'Yes, I am.'

'No, you're not. You're following the Swill Brook. That's the Thames back there.'

'But it's nothing but a ditch.'

'May look like a ditch but that's because the gravel pits drain it. You go into the village and you'll find ducks and everything swimming about. You can trust me, I'm a local character.'

So I retraced my steps and followed the ditch into Ashton Keynes and sure enough by the time the stream had passed the churchyard it had swelled to a size where I could have sculled on it again had I been with *Maegan*. I sent a postcard to my grandmother and continued through a blue haze of dragonflies.

By early afternoon the skies grew full of cold black cloud and my pace was quickening. Boogie seemed uneasy. In Somerford Keynes he had a fight with a rockery and the rockery came off better. He drank frequently from the river; it was as if he knew it was going to run dry soon.

It was crystal clear and sprinkled with white crowfoot, but it had degenerated to a dribble.

Another railway bridge and another main road and then the water was motionless, barely deep enough for a resident family of moorhens to splash about in. A hundred yards further and it disappeared into the ground. If I squeezed the earth water rose to the surface, but the river was gone and for the first time in almost three weeks there were no reflections around me, just a bright green dampness.

I followed a dry groove in the earth which was presumably flooded under wetter conditions. It led me past the distant spire of Kemble church, then under the Fosse Way and through a long meadow until ahead I could see a tree. I peered through my binoculars – a crow standing quite happily on a fence took off and vanished. I focused and recognized the distinctive leaves of an ash. And there beneath it was a ring of white stones. I strode on and reached the source of the River Thames at 3.30 in the afternoon of 28 May 1988.

It was an unimpressive setting really, just nettles, some dung and the dry cracked earth. There was supposed to be a spring beneath the stones, but they didn't look as though they'd seen water for years. I'd love to have found a coot's nest or a willow stump there, instead there was the plaque, proclaiming this spring in Trewsbury Mead as the true source of the great river. Boogie cocked his leg on it.

I stood there in reverence for a minute or two until I was disturbed by voices coming through the woods. A party of people climbed over a stile and walked through the field. As they came closer I could hear they were speaking German. They marched up to me and their spokesman said: 'We are looking for the source of the Thames.'

It started to rain. We were all standing in the middle of a field in Gloucestershire with our anoraks over our heads.

'Look no further,' I said.

'This is it?'

'Yep. And I was here first.'

They looked around. One voice said: 'Aber wo ist die Wasser?' And the spokesman said: 'But where is the water? We have come all the way from London and there is no water. I thought there would be a Little Chef or a Pay and Display at least but there is nothing. Are you sure this is the source?'

'Sure.'

'How did you get here?'

'I sculled.'

'You what?'

'I rowed.'

'Oh! You are *Three Men in a Boat* to say nothing of the dog. But where are the other two? My favourite bit is when Harris sings the song and can't remember the words. Why are you looking strangely? We have been travelling from London with nothing but Radio One for amusement. It took us two hours in a Toyota minibus. What a waste of time. My name is Felix.'

From somewhere Boogie appeared with a steak sandwich in his mouth.

'It is all right for the dog, isn't it?' said Felix.

11. I'll See You Sometime

I sculled back to Oxford in the rain. With the aid of the current it only took a few days. I just pulled my hat down and went as fast as I could.

One day the mist didn't lift at all. The river was cocooned in a cloud. Military aircraft on their low-level flying manoeuvres blasted overhead but I was blind to them. There were no other boats on the water, no people on the towpath. I travelled with my head down. *Maegan* knew the channel. All I remember noticing during those few days was that the dandelions were over, their white seeds scattered on the water. On this journey I'd seen them flourish, flower and die and now their ashes were strewn.

I got going each morning at first light when the river mist crept into the tent and dampened my covers. And I kept going until the daylight died and the crusts on my hands had dried on the sculls. I felt sedated. I stopped noticing the country I was passing through. But this had never been a scenically startling journey. The Thames was a steady river that dripped and flowed, hardly tripping up once on its way to the sea. Its influence was a subliminal one. I remember stopping one night in a pub called the Rose Revived. I sat at the bar and heard the barmaid talking to a customer about holidays, and how the destinations never lived up to expectations. She said: 'I went up the Nile the year before last. I didn't enjoy it. The pyramids just aren't worth the bother. The pictures on the postcards were wonderful but the real things are a disappointment.'

And the customer nodded and said: 'I know what you mean. The same thing happened to me with those fountains in Rome.'

The Thames conjures up castles and palaces and royal barges and regattas and a voyage through the history of England. And it is all of these things somewhere along the route, there's even a gorge or two, but it's essentially coots and willows and the plop of the chub and the knowledge that you're never far from a branch of Boots. On discovering the source to be a dry patch of ground in a field I wasn't surprised or disappointed. The idea of it spouting out of a lake over falls just wasn't suitable. The Thames is a civilized river and above such sensationalism. It inspires tranquillity and self-reflection rather than derring-do and getting up before eight for a swim.

Back in London I lay low for a while. I wanted to call Jennifer and tell her the task had been completed, but I felt uncomfortable about the whole thing. Not long after I'd been back my friend Sarah called round. She wanted me to look after her goldfish while she went away. I said to her: 'I thought you'd just been away, to South America?'

'I'm moving out there for a while. I've been offered the managership of the new branch of Sketchley's in Montevideo. It's promotion. So how was your trip?'

'It was good . . . It was good.'

'Did you find the source of the Thames?'

'Yes, indeed. I solved the mystery surrounding the source of that great river.'

'Well . . . ?'

'Well what?'

'Well where is it?'

'You'll laugh when I tell you.'

'Yes?'

'Well . . . the source of the Thames is in Trewsbury Mead, a field just over the A433 south of Cirencester.'

'Isn't that where most people thought it was?'

'Er . . . yes.'

' . . . '

'And . . . so . . . so the trip has been a resounding success, insomuch as I have proved most people are correct in their opinion as to where the Thames rises.'

'I see,' said Sarah. 'Listen, feeding instructions are on the packet,' and she handed me the fish bowl.

Most people were similarly impressed, and yet I couldn't help but feel it was a hollow success. The problem was I could see little of worth had come out of the journey. At one point I hoped it might have been of scientific value as research into the use of dogs on long river expeditions, but reading through my notes the only conclusion they reach is that dogs are of no use at all – they inspire people to say boring things to you from the bank.

But the rewards of a journey aren't always immediate and aren't always manifest. The point is should we count milestones or miles? And the truth is I learned a lot from my time on the river – learned a lot, that is, about myself.

This may not sound so special. After all, most journeys offer travellers an insight into their own personality. But the difference between this trip and any other I've been on is that although I know I did learn a lot about myself, now I'm back I can't for the life of me remember what it was. As soon as I left the river its spirit drained away from me. The morning I woke up in bed again I no longer felt that insouciance the river inspired. I suddenly felt responsible again. It was as if I'd been addicted to something then suddenly forgot what the addiction was.

And that's rather how I feel about Jennifer now. I think her problem was she was fighting the river all the time rather than trying to harness its energy. Even Boogie could sense this, and he knew it was a weakness. She was rigid. I remember when she said: 'Coots are fun to watch but they aren't very efficient animals. They could be far more productive. Ergonomically, they're a disaster. I'd never employ one,' it was clear she wasn't ever going to be a waterwoman.

But I should have realized this beforehand. And while I can blame all sorts of people and animals for what happened, I know I'm liable as well. It didn't dawn on me in time that Jennifer isn't impressed by men who try to impress her. I imagined someone so inaccessible could be reached somehow. There had to be a key to her, a secret channel no one had ever taken before, a backwater through which her defences could be breached. But treating her like a river was my downfall, and I know now that even if we had reached the source together there would have been nowhere else for us to go but back downstream. Boogie may have realized this. His actions, though vulgar to an unacceptable degree, may have been with the best intentions. He may have seen the lack of communication between Jennifer and me. He may have noted the lack of negotiation, the lack of genuine affection, the lack of trust between us. He may have noticed my infatuation and decided he had to take the initiative. He may have decided Jennifer was coming between him and me. He may have seen the link between man and dog threatened and the expedition put in jeopardy as a consequence. In the end honour may have forced him to act. I'd like to think so. But he probably behaved the way he did because he can't stand pseuds.

I haven't seen or even spoken to Jennifer since. I called

her office and her PA answered and said: 'May I ask who's calling?'

'Mark Wallington.'

'What company?'

'Personal call.'

'I'm sorry, Ms Conway is on the other line at the moment, can I ask what it's about?'

'Yes. I'd like to know her opinion on where our relationship stands at the moment and what, if any, effect she feels the time we had together on the river had on our future. I feel that I spent too long competing for her rather than against her which was patronizing on my behalf I know, but I feel that if she analyses her own behaviour she will come to see that she was lacking in the essential skills needed to be a travelling companion. Before we went on this trip I would have travelled to the ends of the earth with her. I still would but now I think I'd be tempted to leave her there. Maybe she'd like to meet for a drink sometime and talk it over. I've got plans to climb a mountain. I've also got her handbag and her wok. Tell her to call me when she gets time.'

'I told you it would all end in . . .'

'Yes, yes, I know you told me.'

But she hasn't called yet. Not many people do call when you're writing a book. They think you don't want to be interrupted. And then whenever the phone does go and I say I'm writing about a rowing trip up the Thames, everyone says 'Oh, you mean *Three Men in a Boat*.' At first I gave my rehearsed response, about how my book and *Three Men in a Boat* have nothing in common, that the river has changed beyond recognition in a hundred years, and it's stupid to imagine I could re-create such a trip. But I don't bother now. I chuckle and say: 'Well, yes I suppose so.' I think people prefer it that way. I've even tried to convince myself. I say to myself: 'It doesn't matter about the motorboats and the housing estates and the branches of Waitrose and Pizzaland, these changes to the Thames are all peripheral. The river itself is as languid and as oblivious as it ever was, as timeless as Jerome's book.' I'm not sure about this though.

I have, however, discovered one similarity between Jerome's book and mine, and that is they were both written in the summer time, in a room at the top of the house, looking out over London. And I think I feel closer to him because of this than anything to do with the Thames. I imagine him sitting in a room above the rooftops with pigeons pattering over his tiles just as they do over mine. I look at them with my binoculars sometimes and they fly off and hide, so I turn my attention to the street. It's full of puddles, has been for most of the summer, and as the daylight fails the gas showroom is reflected in the pavement and I'm immediately taken back to the wonderful reflections of Cliveden Deep and of Pangbourne, of Mapledurham House and of Tadpole Bridge, and of the willows. It's at times like these that I know the only reason I can live in this city is that only occasionally does it remind me of the country.

This tenuous connection with Jerome was the excuse I sought and I no longer felt the need to distance myself from the man. In the autumn I even went back to the river to visit Ewelme in Oxfordshire where he's buried. I drove down there on a frosty Sunday morning. The village looked delightful and the church of St Mary's was frozen into place under the blue sky. A bonfire smoked over a wall, and the rooks' nests were clearly visible in the bare trees. I found Jerome's family plot not far away from the church door, his wife and daughter lying by his side. I'd read a biography of him during the summer and hadn't been surprised to find him hint at an ambivalence to his success. He wrote: 'I have written books that have appeared to me more clever, books that have appeared to me more humorous. But it is as the author of *Three Men in a Boat (to say nothing of the Dog)* that the public persists in remembering me.' I stood there for a couple of minutes breathing a cloud. I just wanted to have a look.

After visiting the churchyard I walked Boogie down to the river at Benson. Six months on and the ducklings were having formation flying lessons. The immature coots sat in the middle of the channel developing their bald patches. The grebes were learning karate, and the cygnets were no longer squat grey squirts. They'd lost their fluff and grown their necks and turned into beautiful graceful creatures with a natural vanity. Boogie looked confused at first but then we walked along the towpath and slowly he identified his surroundings. At one point a heron landed near us and we stopped and watched it feed. And as the bird's head dived into the water and emerged each time with a fish in its beak, Boogie wagged his tail and grinned and I was sure he was recalling our trip.

When we got home that night he stuck his face in the fish bowl and ate Sarah's goldfish.